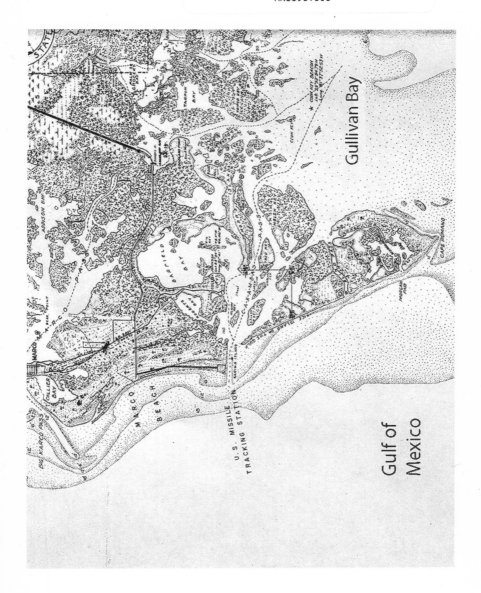

Journey to the Edge of Eden

Journey to the Edge of Eden

Gary W. Schmelz

Hardback ISBN: 978-1-300-19862-8
Paperback ISBN: 978-1-300-19863-5

Contents

Acknowledgements

I would like to thank Dr. Terry Trimble for reading and suggesting revisions to an earlier version of this book. I would also like to extend my appreciation to the management of Collier Enterprises and Barron Collier Company for letting me print sections of D. Graham Copeland's map of Marco Island and the Ten Thousand Islands. Finally, a special note of thanks is extended to my wife Bernice for her valuable suggestions and help in editing. Without her support this book would never have become a reality.

Prologue

No one makes life's journey alone. It is those we share the journey with who make it extraordinary.

The idea for this memoir began as I was looking out over the lagoon at Tigertail Beach on Marco Island, Florida. The brilliant blue, early morning April sky was devoid of clouds and the lagoon was teeming with life. An osprey hovered overhead looking for fish, shorebirds scurried across wet sand searching for tiny worms and crustaceans, and a hissing carpet of fiddler crabs created a kaleidoscopic wave of life near the water's edge.

Tigertail was one of the first places I visited when I came to Southwest Florida in 1970. It was also one of the first places in Florida my father and I went fishing. Besides fishing, the two of us spent many years together studying the plant and animal life in its lagoon. It was an activity that ultimately helped us unravel some of the mysteries of this shallow coastal water habitat. In later years I would share many discoveries we made with groups of school children and newly established residents. And like us, they fell in love with this magical place that has since been preserved for future generations to enjoy.

Tigertail and other wilderness areas in Southwest Florida are light years away from the urban environment where Dad and I were born and grew up. In the cities where we were raised, it was hard to imagine that such unique places existed. When I was a teenager my family occasionally escaped into the countryside on the weekends and we took short vacations to Cape Cod, but none of these environments were comparable to the southwest portion of the Florida peninsula that merges into the emerald green waters of the Florida Keys. The rich diversity of life that thrives in this wilderness region is hard to imagine. There are not enough words to describe the beauty of the neighboring subtropical swamps of the Fakahatchee Strand and the Big Cypress Preserve. The orchids and air plants that thrive in these swamps create a breathtaking mosaic of life that rivals the world's most beautiful tropical gardens.

Life is full of memorable moments. Some are breathtaking adventures, others laughable mishaps that make us smile. This book recounts some of the memorable moments Dad and I experienced as we journeyed to the edge of Florida's Eden. It begins in the noisy apartment-lined streets of the metropolitan areas surrounding New York City. We shared most of this journey thanks to my work and Dad's retirement. During our adventures, the bond of love and friendship between us grew, and we developed a better understanding of our natural environment and why it is important to preserve it for future generations. Today, Dad's ashes are part of the tannin-stained waters of Florida's Ten Thousand Islands—a place he dearly loved and a place I still explore and fish. In the not too distant future we will share these waters again, and it is here the final chapter of our journey will come to its conclusion.

Hard Times

My dad, Henry Schmelz, believed he was born in New York City around October 17, 1908, although he never had an official birth certificate that added credence to the day he entered this world. When I was a young boy he often talked about seeing Halley's comet as a child and how frightened people were when they saw it in the night sky. If his recollections were correct, then my guess is he was born a little earlier than 1908 since the comet did not appear until April 1910 at which time he would have only been one and a half years old. Not too many of us remember things that happened to us that early in life, so I assume he was born around 1906 or 1907.

Dad's parents immigrated to this country in the late nineteenth century. His brothers said that their father came from a wealthy Jewish family who lived in Germany. While his father was attending the University of Milan studying linguistics, he fell in love with an Italian girl and, despite the objections of both families, the young lovers married and fled to the United States where they had high hopes of starting an exciting new life. Like many newly arrived immigrants, however, they found life in the new world much more difficult than they anticipated. Work was hard to find and their shiny image of paradise was quickly tarnished.

About fifteen years after his folks arrived in the United States, Dad's mom found herself dealing with four willful boys. Fred was the oldest of the group, followed by Bill, Walter, and Dad. As the two younger boys approached school age a tragic series of events quickly shattered his parents' tenuous existence. While climbing a stepladder, Dad's mother fell and severely injured her leg. There was no money to pay a doctor so the family tried to treat the injury themselves. Unlike today, antibiotics did not exist, and the injured leg soon became gangrenous. Dad only vaguely remembered his mother's painful demise but he did recall visiting her bedside at a local hospital just a few hours before she passed away. Clutching her bed as tears rolled down his face, he pleaded with her not to die and then his father led him from the room.

With the death of his wife, Dad's distraught father was left with the four boys and no one to look after them while he was at work. Some of his neighbors graciously agreed to help out by taking care of Walter and my dad and making sure Fred and Bill went to school. However, the boys proved to be an unruly bunch, and whenever their father was away they quickly got embroiled in all kinds of mischief. Dad recalled one incident when he and his older brother Walter were given the task of mopping up their neighbor's floor. Neither of them, of course, was seriously interested in doing that, so the two of them doused the floor with soapy water and slid across it on their bare bottoms. When the neighbor came back to check up on them she was shocked at the mess and gave Dad's father an earful about their unorthodox behavior.

Truant from school, getting in fistfights, and vandalizing property quickly tried the patience of the local residents who eventually reported the boys' shenanigans to the authorities. Warned by the court to find some way to provide better supervision for his children or have them placed in foster homes, Dad's father faced a serious dilemma. He needed to work in order to take care of his children, but if he worked there were no relatives he could ask to take care of them. Still grieving over the loss of his wife and unable to manage the boys, he fell into a state of deep depression and started drinking. One day while the boys were staying with a neighbor he went into his bedroom and committed suicide.

Dad did not remember his father's funeral. He said he didn't think he had one. His oldest brother, Fred, said their father was buried in a pauper's grave. Shortly after their father's death, the boys were sent to an institution for the homeless, but Fred promised to get the family back together. His plan was to run away, lie about his age, and join the military where he could earn some money. As soon as he got out of the service Fred promised his brothers he'd find a place where he and the rest of the boys could live together.

Unfortunately, his plans never materialized. While serving as a cook in France during World War I, he was killed attempting to bring food to the soldiers on the front line. According to Dad, everyone had read about their brother's heroics in the local newspapers, but the boys weren't told about his death until they were gathered together by the head of the institution. The older boys remembered crying when the letter from the Army was read aloud. They weren't impressed with the fact that their brother had died a hero. Nor did they care that he had received the Distinguished Service Cross. They had lost their last opportunity to get back together as a family and their future looked grimmer than ever.

Shortly after the death of their brother, the boys were split up and sent to foster homes. Having foster parents can sometimes be a good experience, but in Dad's case it turned out to be a nightmare. The first foster parents that took in my father needed someone to help them with their farm. Subsequently, Dad wound up being treated more like a slave than a foster son. At nine years old he was forced to work twelve-hours days seven days a week and not allowed to go to school. He was also severely punished whenever he failed to finish his chores. Many times the punishments were in the form of beatings. Life on the farm ended when the farmer found Dad fooling around with matches in the barn. When he saw what Dad was doing he strung him up in the barn, tore his shirt off, and struck him repeatedly with a whip. After the farmer finished whipping my father, he left him strung to the rafters and went out into the fields to work.

Dad said he passed out after the beating, and when he regained consciousness he began screaming for help. Attracted by my father's pleas, one of the farmer's neighbors came to his rescue. The neighbor was horrified by what he saw. My father was covered with blood and there was very little skin left on his back. Dad remembered the man cutting him down and carrying him to his wagon. My father said the trip to the hospital over bumpy roads was excruciatingly painful and he thought he fainted once more before they reached their destination. Ultimately, Dad was placed in a new foster home with a family that he grew to love and admire. The farmer that beat him was never arrested, and as long as Dad lived he had to be careful about removing his shirt and exposing his scarred back to the sun.

Life with Dad's new foster parents was good. They fed and treated him well and made him feel like part of their family. But school proved to be a challenge. He was now twelve years old and had spent less than a year inside a classroom. For some reason the educational system decided to place him in the fourth grade. Dad didn't like the idea of attending classes with much younger children, but his new foster parents insisted he follow through with his schooling. By the time he reached the eighth grade he had learned how to read and write and do basic math. He was also sixteen years old and sick of attending school with younger students. So when his eighth-grade teacher, Miss Canary, sent him to the second grade for a day for fooling around in class, he decided he had had enough "learning."

By this point in time his older brothers, Bill and Walter, had left their foster homes and were making a bundle of money bootlegging liquor, so Dad decided to join them. The brothers had also accumulated enough money to run a speakeasy in Jersey City, so when Dad showed up at their door they hired him to clean up the place during the day, serve as a lookout at night, and help smuggle booze across the state border. Life was good; Dad had money for the first time in his life and he used some of it to buy a Model "T" Ford. However, his "easy" life didn't come without risks, and throughout prohibition the boys were always trying to stay one step ahead of the "fuzz." Dad recalled that on several occasions the cops nearly caught him and his brothers when they were smuggling liquor across the state line.

When prohibition ended in 1933 the two older brothers decided to open up their own saloon. Bill and Walter hired my father to work for them during the years of the Great Depression but their business didn't generate enough money to pay Dad a decent wage. Dad often recalled how hard times were during the Depression. He said he would take any job he could get to earn extra money: hauling ice up five flights of stairs in apartment buildings, shoveling coal, copper-plating baby shoes, and working on highway construction projects. Still he couldn't earn enough to make ends meet and there were many times he went to bed hungry.

I remember sitting with him one day in New York City's Central Park, feeding pigeons, when he began to reminisce about his life during those times. "Food was hard to come by back then," he reflected as we tossed a handful of seed in the birds' direction. "Once I was so hungry I decided to try to capture a pigeon. I thought it would be easy. But I guess a lot of other people must have had the same idea because those birds were so scared of people that whenever I got within six feet of them they would take off and land on the ledge of an apartment building. I finally built myself a pigeon trap and baited it with birdseed. I tied a string to the door of the trap and hid behind a fence and waited for the bird to walk inside. I figured it would be no time at all before I had my dinner, but those birds were smarter than I anticipated and I sat behind that fence for nearly two hours before I was able to capture one. Once he was inside I remember swooping up that trap and letting out a holler you could hear all the way down the street. Then it occurred to me that I had never killed a bird before. I remember looking inside that trap and watching that frightened bird and thinking maybe I should let him go. But then my stomach began to growl and I knew I couldn't do that. So I finally got up enough nerve to wring the bird's neck and pluck out its feathers. There wasn't much left to that creature when I finished, but I was so famished I couldn't wait to eat it. After looking around to make sure that no one had seen what I'd done, I took the bird into an abandoned lot, built a fire and roasted him until he was crispy brown. There couldn't have been more than two bites left on him when I was finished, but that was a heck of a lot better than nothing. I remember chomping down on his plump little body and feeling like I had just sunk my teeth into a rubber ball. That bird was the toughest piece of meat I ever sunk my teeth into. It took me forever to swallow it. After that day I never thought about eating another pigeon, no matter how hungry I got."

One of Dad's jobs during the Depression was stock clerk at the Great Atlantic and Pacific Tea Company (A&P). He said that working in an A&P back then was a lot harder than working at a food market today. "There was no self-service. We had to weigh out coffee, sugar, and butter. Eggs were counted and placed in a bag, and milk had to be dipped out of a container with a ladle and measured."

It was at the A&P that Dad met my mother, Katie. Dad claimed he was smitten with her the first time he saw her. Her wavy chestnut hair, attractive smile, and seductive demeanor were too much to resist. Whenever she came into the store he said he would ask how she was and try to help her find the things she was looking for. It appears Mom was not too anxious to get involved with Dad and gave him the brush off whenever he tried to strike up a conversation. But Dad's persistence finally won out and she ultimately agreed to go out on a date.

"He was skinny and losing his hair," my mother once observed, "and I didn't like the sloppy clothes he wore. I couldn't believe what a pest he was. I don't know how many times he asked me out. Finally, I agreed to go out with him hoping that after one date he would stop bothering me. However, our first date didn't turn out to be anything like I thought it would. He was a lot nicer than I expected so I decided to give him a second look."

Dad had heard some rumors about Mom before they dated. His friends told him she was self-centered and not very interested in men. Dad, however, was determined to find out what she was like for himself. One of the first things he discovered was that both my mother and her sister Francie distrusted men. The reason for this distrust didn't reveal itself until after they'd dated for several months. It turned out that my mother's father had had an incestuous relationship with her and her sister. When Dad asked Mom if her mother knew what was going on, she said she thought she did but never did anything about it. In order to escape their wretched home life both, girls married as soon as they were old enough. Francie married an older man. Mom said she didn't love him, that she was only interested in his money. Mom married a butcher. He was also a lot older than she was. Mom said she married him because he had a good job and she couldn't imagine anything worse than staying at home with her lecherous father.

Francie's husband Pete died while she was still fairly young. I remember being in Francie's home when her husband was ill and it surprised me how little time she spent with him during his final days. After Pete passed away she told my parents he'd left her well enough off so she'd never have to work again. Francie added she had had it with men and that she never wanted to remarry. Unfortunately, Francie's life didn't quite work out the way she thought it would, and when her money ran out she started dating again. Dad said there were several nice gentlemen who were interested in marrying her, but she told my father that she was waiting for someone with enough money to let her lead the comfortable lifestyle she thought she deserved.

"When the right one shows up," she informed my parents, "I'll let him feel me up just enough to get him excited and then I'll cut him off. I don't have any intentions of giving him anything more than that until he puts the wedding ring on my finger."

Mom's first marriage didn't last very long either. After giving birth to my sister Charlotte, my mother divorced her husband. She claimed he was jealous of her and locked her in their bedroom. When she tried to escape he confronted her with a butcher knife and threatened to kill her. Mom said she was terrified about what might happen to her and her daughter, so when the opportunity presented itself she ran away. It was several years before the divorce was finalized and, like her sister Francie, she vowed she would never marry again.

On one of their first dates, Dad discovered Mom had a strong aversion to hairy men. She told Dad she thought men with lots of hair were disgusting. So whenever they went out she kept trying to find out how much hair Dad had on his body. Dad said her probing became embarrassing at times, but apparently he passed the test. I was never quite sure how my mother accomplished this, but I'm certain she didn't do it by taking him to the beach since Dad was wary about exposing his scarred back to the sun.

Dad proposed to Mom on several occasions but she steadfastly refused to marry him. She told him that she was never going to let any man have control over her life. Eventually my parents reached an agreement. She informed Dad that he could live with her but only if they pretended to be married. According to Dad, she didn't want her mother and daughter believing they were living together without having "tied the knot." Dad obviously loved Mom enough to go along with the deception and it was one that apparently fooled a lot of people, including my sister and me. Neither Charlotte nor I learned about this ruse until Mom passed away. I still remember the day it happened. My wife and I were going through some of my parents' personal papers after Mom died when we found a box with a yellowed piece of paper under the trailer floor. According to the marriage certificate they were wed in Snow Hill, Maryland, in 1964. Dad was furious with himself for letting us find the marriage license. He had promised

Mom he would destroy it after she died. I could see the anguish in his face when he saw that we'd uncovered the truth. Later that day when I tried to discuss it with him he just shook his head, walked into the bedroom, and shut the door.

When I was growing up Mom always made a big thing about telling me how she and Dad got married by the justice of the peace and how, after the ceremony, they went to the Jersey shore for their honeymoon. She made the story even more believable by complaining that she had to share her honeymoon with Dad's fishing poles. She said she woke up the morning after they got "married" and discovered my father had disappeared. "There was no note—nothing. I couldn't imagine what happened to your father. Then I saw that his fishing poles were gone. After desperately looking for him for nearly an hour, I found him fishing along the shoreline next to the hotel. I should have known right then and there what kind of marriage I was getting into and left him on the spot."

I have only fragmentary information about what happened with Mom and Dad during the early years of their live-in arrangement. I know those years were times of great economic hardship. Initially, they lived in a small apartment above a shoemaker and Mom worked at a handkerchief factory in Jersey City. During those years Mom was very concerned that people at the plant would discover she and Dad were living together as husband and wife. She told Dad that if her boss found out about their living arrangement she was certain he would fire her. Dad said that during those days the factory wouldn't keep "married" women on the work force because they were concerned they would get pregnant.

Although the pall of the Great Depression still weighed heavily upon my parents, they eventually managed to borrow enough money to open a stationery store in Jersey City. Later, Aunt Francie lent them enough money to establish a store at a better location in Union City. Mom once insinuated that the loan was given to her in the form of a bribe. According to Dad, when Mom's father passed away, her mother insisted on living with Francie. But Francie apparently couldn't stomach her mother because she never made any effort to stop her father from raping her. So when Mom approached Francie for money to open the store, Francie agreed to help her out providing Mom agreed to let their mother move in with her.

Mom's mother stayed with our family for a number of years before she died of a heart attack. I was born on July 24, 1939, just prior to my parents moving into their new store in Union City. Dad told me that my birth was a momentous occasion. He said Mom had always wanted a boy and now that she had one she intended to make sure I was raised properly and got the best education possible. I never thought too much about my birth date but my mom proudly announced one day that I was born on the same day as Amelia Earhart. In later life I did look up what auspicious things happened in 1939 and the only two events that attracted my attention were the conviction of Scopes for teaching evolution in Tennessee and an announcement that the Carolina parakeet had been officially declared extinct.

The fact that Mom and Dad didn't get married until much later in life had some serious repercussions. When the United States entered World War II in 1941, there was a massive build up of military personnel. As a married man with two children Dad would have been exempt from the draft, but since he and Mom were not legally married his draft board declared him eligible for active duty. According to my mother, when she heard that Dad was going to be drafted she went down to the draft board and pleaded with them not to take him. None of her efforts prevented the inevitable. Shortly after Dad received his draft notice, he was inducted into the Navy and shipped to San Diego for basic training. After basic, he returned home on leave and informed Mom that he thought he was about to be shipped out to the South Pacific. Family friends and relatives described things as being pretty glum in our household when Dad reported back to the base. My distant cousin Lottie said Mom cried a lot and complained bitterly about how she wasn't going to be able to manage the store and take care of two children by herself.

Weeks passed without any letters from Dad and then my mother got some surprising news. Dad was being discharged. It was a miracle! What had happened to turn things around? It turned out Dad had another physical when he got back to San Diego, and the doctors found out he had a heart condition and declared him unfit for duty.

Everyone was elated with Dad's return home. What wasn't so welcome by Mom was the tattoo Dad had engraved on his upper arm. It was the bust of an Indian maiden. Dad proudly announced he'd had it done when he and his buddies had gone out drinking to celebrate his discharge from the military. In a fit of jealously, Mom demanded that he remove it, but Dad refused, claiming he really liked it. From that day on, whenever anyone referred to Dad's tattoo Mom would shake her head and refer to it as Dad's "Jewish Indian Princess." I had no idea what a Jewish Indian Princess looked like, so one day when I was several years older I asked Mom how she knew Dad's tattoo looked like a Jewish Princess. "No Indian has a big nose like the one in Dad's tattoo," she grumbled while shaking her head. "Only Jewish girls have noses like that. That tattoo probably looks like one of the girls he picked up when he was on liberty." I never told Mom, but I kind of liked Dad's Jewish Indian Princess, especially when he flexed his muscle and made her nose wiggle. I thought she was kind of cute.

My friends always thought that I was rich because my parents owned a stationery store, but the truth was we were just as poor as everyone else in the neighborhood, perhaps even poorer. Mom and Dad worked long hours. Dad would get up at five a.m. every day, open the shop at six and return home at one a.m. the next day. After Mom saw me off to school she would join Dad in the shop. From one to three p.m., Dad would take a nap in our apartment and then return to work for the afternoon rush hour. In the early years they worked in the store seven days a week. For the last twenty years they ran the business six days a week and took off on Sunday. Life in the store consumed them and for the first thirteen years of my life they never took a vacation.

Nearly all children endure family arguments. My parents' arguments focused on their lack of money and the best way to make the business more profitable. Dad had a creative flare and was always looking for ways to attract more customers. Mom didn't like most of his ideas and never wanted to spend money on them. I remember one time when Dad wanted to create a display to attract customers to some toys they'd purchased. Mom said, "Not while she was part of the business," but Dad went out and did it anyway. The tremors from that fight were probably felt across the Hudson River in New York City. To make things worse, Dad's idea worked and Mom never liked admitting it. I can still see Dad boasting to one of the customers about the display, while Mom grouched to me about Dad's "dumb luck."

Salesmen were another issue. Mom did not like Dad talking to them. She claimed that the salesmen would wait to come into the shop when she wasn't there because they knew Dad would be more inclined to buy their merchandise. Dad said that most of the time he agreed with Mom about the type of merchandise they should purchase, but there were several occasions when he felt Mom refused to see the value in some of the things they were offering. One day when I returned from school I found them shouting at each other in the back of the store. Dad had purchased some item that she didn't like and Mom wanted Dad to call up the salesman and tell him to take it back. When Dad refused, Mom gathered up everything Dad had bought and took it back to the salesman herself. Dad became furious; he felt she'd made him lose credibility with the salesman and that they'd lost a good opportunity to make some extra money. For days afterwards my parents hardly spoke to one another, and from that day on Dad would make his own deals on the sly whenever he thought he could get away with it.

Looking back upon these confrontations I feel that most of these fights arose from my Mom's lack of trust in men, which made her want to be in control. It wasn't just a lack of trust in the decisions that Dad made; it was a lack of trust in any action taken by a man. She would often say to me, "Men can't be trusted to do anything right." As I grew older and thought more about my Mom's relationship with my father, I often wondered why they stayed together. There is, of course, no easy answer to this question. Relationships between people are often convoluted. Dad's gentle demeanor and loving and tolerant nature provided a comfortable environment for Mom. In addition, my father's willingness to maintain a live-in relationship allowed her the freedom to walk out on Dad whenever she felt things weren't going exactly her way. Conversely, Dad benefited from Mom's savvy and intelligence. Certainly working as a store proprietor was a much more meaningful job than he could have gotten elsewhere. I also believe, that despite Mom's domineering personality, Dad loved her very much.

One incident that nearly led to my parents separating took place several years before they planned to retire. In 1969, Dad read a newspaper article that said that the price of silver was going to increase dramatically in future years. After reading the article, Dad told Mom he thought they might make some extra money if they saved silver dollars and other silver coins that people spent in the store. He said that they could hold on to them until their market value increased and then sell them at a 100-200 percent profit. Mom didn't buy this idea and told Dad that their money would be better off in the bank. So without telling Mom what he was doing, Dad started saving all the silver dollars people spent in the store. After about six years he'd squirreled away about $1,000 in coins which he intended to sell for two or three times their face value.

When the price of silver increased significantly, Dad decided to make his move. He had found someone who had agreed to buy the silver coins at their increased value and all he needed to do was carry out the transaction. The morning of the sale he had someone watch the store while he went over to pick up the coins. Entering the garage where he'd horded them, he breathed a sign of relief as he unlocked the storage cabinet and spotted the chests he'd been storing them in. It wasn't until he lifted the first wooden box and went to put it into his car that he knew something was wrong. He had expected the chest to be heavy, but instead it hardly weighed anything. Panic set in. Frantically lifting up the lid of the chest, he peered into the empty box and groaned. Someone had stolen all his coins. The question was who? He was the only one who had the key to the cabinet and as far as he could tell no one had broken into it. Then it dawned on him. It had to be Mom. She had uncovered his plan. Could he get to her before she got to the bank? Racing back to the apartment, he confronted Mom about the missing coins and asked her what she had done with them. Smugly, she told him that she had gotten someone to help her take them to the bank where a very appreciative teller had exchanged them for dollar bills. His vision of a 200 percent profit had been shattered and his nest egg for retirement had evaporated. In 1980, when the price of silver reached $16.00 an ounce Dad bemoaned the loss of those coins to me while we were hiking the Fakahatchee. There was nothing I could say to make him feel any better. What was past was past. So I just squeezed his shoulder and suggested that there might be other opportunities in the future for him to make some money. Unfortunately, there never were.

By the time I entered high school in 1952 my parents' financial status had improved considerably. They stopped working seven days a week, Dad bought a new car, and we starting going on vacations. Being a kid, I assumed that our new "affluent" lifestyle had come about through my parents' financial success with the store. This assumption proved to be way off target. Mom and Dad's new affluence, as it turned out, had arisen from their involvement in the numbers lottery. The lottery was an illegal gambling enterprise in which a gambler would select three single digit numbers from the "mutual" numbers listed in the newspaper. Bets were placed at a "betting parlor," which generally was a saloon but in some instances a stationery store like the one my parents owned. If you "hit" the numbers, the payoff could range from 600 to 800 percent. Not a shabby return on a bet whose return was entirely tax-free. For taking bets the "betting parlor" received a percentage of the money they took in and sometimes a generous winner would give the parlor's owners a tip. In addition to running a betting parlor, Mom also convinced Dad that she should become a "runner." No one would suspect a woman of collecting bets and delivering them to the bookie Mom told Dad, and they could earn an additional 10 percent on the bets.

Dad later admitted to me that letting Mom become a runner was a bad idea. A local gang found out what Mom was up to and cornered her in an alleyway one night. When she refused to turn over the money they beat her up pretty badly. Dad said he wasn't aware of what happened to her until a neighbor found her lying in the street.

As far as I know the local police never bothered my parents, but somehow the IRS got wind of the fact that they were running a betting parlor and began to put pressure on them for unpaid taxes. For years they investigated my parents' business practices, and although no criminal charges were leveled against them, the IRS found enough irregularities in their back taxes to level a hefty fine.

Dog and Cotton Tales

When I was about eight years old Dad bought me a dog. Like most young boys I had pleaded with him to get me one. "Yes," I said, "I'll feed him." And of course I absolutely promised I would take the dog for a walk twice a day.

Ultimately, Dad relented and purchased a beautiful black, male cocker spaniel puppy with sad eyes and large floppy ears. The entire family loved him the minute we set eyes on him and we decided to call him Mr. Chips, a name that was later changed to Chipper. Unfortunately, Chipper was part of a stolen litter that had been sold to the local pet shop and his rightful owner soon showed up at our store looking for him. By this time, however, Chipper had developed distemper and was barely clinging to life. Not wanting to be burdened with a sick animal, the former owner left the dog with us certain it wouldn't live more than a couple of days. Everyone prepared for the worst. But miracle of miracles, Chipper survived! His recovery was mostly due to Dad's hard work. He took him to the vet, force-fed him, and made sure that Chipper took his daily dose of medicine.

During the time Chipper was sick he was never allowed to go outside. This meant that Dad had to train him not to lift his leg when he peed. Although getting Chipper to pee like a female helped him survive, it presented problems later in life. When Chipper went for his daily walk, male dogs would often run over and check him out. As soon as they discovered Chipper wasn't a female they would begin to growl and bark at him. On the other hand, some of the male dogs didn't seem to mind that Chipper wasn't a member of the opposite sex. And as soon as an opportunity arose they would jump on top of poor Chipper and try to mate with him. This inevitably led to a dogfight in which Chipper suffered serious humiliation.

After Dad saved Chipper's life, the dog bonded with my father and followed him wherever he went. On special occasions Dad and I would take Chipper for a walk behind some apartment buildings on the outskirts of town. This was one of the few places that had any trees and bushes and the dog loved running through the underbrush chasing everything that moved. One day he cornered a rabbit. Snarling and barking ferociously, he charged headlong at the rabbit and tried to grab hold of the frightened creature. However, his barks soon turned to yelps. The next thing we saw was Chipper running out from behind the bush with the rabbit clinging to one of his floppy ears. The dog had discovered the only rabbit living in Union City and it turned out to be one savvy, floppy-eared beast. From that day on Chipper never chased another animal. In fact, whenever another dog looked at him and growled he would take off in the opposite direction with his tail between his legs.

A couple of years after we acquired Chipper, Mom and Dad decided to obtain a "store" cat. My parents said they needed to get rid of the mice that were nibbling at the candy bars on the display shelves and the traps they were using didn't seem to be doing the job. Dad told Mom he knew some people whose cat recently had a litter of kittens and he would contact them to see if they'd be willing to give us one. These folks turned out to be more than happy to get rid of one of their kittens and within a week we were the proud new owners of a "store" cat.

Dad named the cat Cotton. Cotton was no ordinary beast. Besides being a good mouse catcher, he was smart and ornery and for some reason decided to become Chipper's best friend. Whenever Dad finished taking Chipper for his walk, the dog would race into the store looking for his buddy. As soon as the cat heard Chipper coming he would climb up onto one of the store shelves and leap onto the dog's back. Chipper would then yelp with surprise while the cat tumbled to the floor and ran off in the opposite direction. Now the chase was on. The dog would run after the cat while the customers danced out of the way in order to avoid being toppled. Round and round the two of them would go until Dad finally got hold of Chipper and made him stop.

Cotton and Chipper quickly learned to work as a team. They became masters at stealing food as well as fending off dogs that intruded upon their territory. If the entire family had to leave the dinner table to wait on customers, the two of them would spring into action. It was Chipper's job to climb up onto the table and push the food onto the floor. Once the deed was done, the two of them would divvy up the spoils. In no way was Chipper allowed to eat any of the food when he was on the table. If he did that, Cotton would hiss at him and give him a painful swat across the nose.

On several occasions large dogs would follow their owners into the store and race after Chipper. Terrified by the dog's snarling outbursts Chipper would start yelping and initiate a hasty retreat to the back room. Alerted to his buddy's dire circumstance, Cotton would leap to his rescue. Cotton's mode of attack was to jump on the dog's head and use his sharp claws to scratch at the dog's eyes. Once Cotton had the dog under control, Chipper would heroically return to the fray and begin to chew on the dog's leg. I don't think the two of them ever lost a fight when they were in the store. Outside the store, however, it was an entirely different matter. And some of the neighborhood dogs had long memories. Consequently, Chipper was never too anxious to step outside to do his daily walk unless Dad checked everything out to make sure the coast was clear.

Both Cotton and Mom were strong willed individuals and Mom was determined to show who ruled the roost when it came to the store. When she caught the cat and dog stealing food from the table she made sure the two of them paid for their dastardly deed. Out would come the broom. Seeing what was about to happen, Cotton would snarl at her and take off for the nearest hiding place. Poor Chipper had no place to run to so he would cower in the corner waiting for the broom to land on his backside. Swish would go the broom followed by the dog's sorrowful yelps. Then it was the cat's turn. Out the cat would dash to its next hiding place as mom started to hunt him down. Storage boxes would be thrown asunder and eventually the broom would land squarely on the cat's rear end. Snarling and attacking the broom in frustration, the cat would ultimately retreat to a place where it could lick its wounds and plot its revenge. "That will teach you never to eat my food again," Mom would shout as Cotton glared down at her from an unreachable perch and swished his tail.

But the battle was not over, and the cat knew it. Patience is its own reward and Cotton lived by that motto. Mom also knew that the confrontation wasn't over and just how the cat intended to get its revenge. Casting aside the broom, she immediately headed for the telephone booths at the back of the store and made sure all the doors were shut. A sign was then hastily put on each door that read, "Please shut doors when finished." No matter. The cat knew people seldom paid attention to signs, so he watched and waited for the right moment. Usually the careless customer was a teenager. Once the telephone booth door was left ajar Cotton would initiate his plan. Scurrying into the booth while my parents were busy with customers, the cat would defecate right at the entrance where he knew the next patron would step on it. Climbing to safety atop the display cases, Cotton would then wait to see the outcome of his infamous deed. It didn't take long. Within minutes an unsuspecting customer would enter the booth and step on the "present" left by the cat. Shrieks of anguish would ensue, followed by threats from the customer to report my parents to the Board of Health for operating a filthy store. After a profusion of apologies and time spent cleaning up the mess, the hunt for the cat would begin all over again. Ultimately, Dad would climb up the ladder and try to dislodge the cat from its perch in the stockroom while Mom waited for him with the broom. But most of the time the cat was too adept at avoiding them, and whenever my parents got within swatting distance, the cat would leap to another unreachable location. More curses and frustrated shouts would follow while Cotton quietly stared down at them with a smug Cheshire grin.

It didn't take too long for my parents to reach the conclusion that the cat was more trouble than it was worth but they didn't have the heart to take him to the pound. The culminating event that led to the cat's demise was my parents' decision to take a vacation on Cape Cod. This would be our very first vacation and they were determined that nothing was going to ruin it. Chipper was to be cared for by one of the boys in the neighborhood. Cotton, however, was another matter. My parents didn't trust leaving the cat alone in the store. The only answer was to find another house where he could stay. But nobody wanted him. Finally, the Rafts, who owned a bakery shop across the street, agreed to house Cotton in their basement. Now the question was how to get the cat across the street into the Rafts' basement. The solution was left to Dad. Either he found a way to do it or there would be no vacation. My father knew he would only have one chance to succeed, consequently his plans to capture Cotton had to be meticulously orchestrated. After thinking it over for several days he arrived at an idea he thought would work. He would lure Cotton into the store's bathroom with his favorite treat then scoop him up with his fishing net and dump him in a burlap bag.

When the fateful day arrived I hid behind a partition and waited to see if Dad would succeed. Cotton saw the treats in the bathroom, but he made no move to eat them. To his mind things looked awfully suspicious. Pacing back and forth in front of the bathroom door, his tail twitching from side to side, Cotton waited for Dad to leave the room before he made his move. Finally, some customers showed up and Dad left to wait on them. Now the odds were in the cat's favor. With Dad gone, the cat was about to get a bellyful of treats before my father came back. But Dad had prepared for this eventuality, and as soon as he was out of sight he had Mom take care of the customers while he went into hiding. In dashed Cotton to devour the treats and out came Dad from his hiding place. There was a heavy thud as the bathroom door slammed shut. Loud snarls and hisses erupted from inside the room. Dad began to curse. More snarls and hisses followed by lots of thumps and banging. Finally, everything went quiet. Had the cat defeated my father? I held my breath and waited to see. Moments later Dad stepped out of the bathroom triumphantly holding up the burlap bag with the snarling cat inside. It had not been an easy conquest. Dad's arms and face were covered with scratches, but he'd saved the day. Now we could go on vacation.

Shortly after capturing Cotton, Dad deposited him in the Rafts' basement. The cat took no fancy to his new environment and quickly disappeared into their coal bin. Thinking everything would eventually turn out all right we hopped into Dad's Desoto and took off for Cape Cod. We should have known better. On the third day of our trip we got a call from the Rafts informing us that Mr. Raft had injured himself while trying to feed the cat. Apparently, after we left, Cotton refused to leave the coal bin and wouldn't eat a morsel. Concerned that the cat would die of starvation, Mr. Raft entered the coal bin and tried to encourage the cat to eat. This move turned out to be a disaster.

The minute he stepped into the bin the cat jumped on his head with talons extended. Jolted backwards by the ferocity of the attack, Mr. Raft fell over a shovel and broke his arm. Out went the coal bin light as the shovel handle flew up and smashed into the bulb leaving Mr. Raft to escape the cat's onslaught in the dark. Now, no one in the Raft household wanted to enter the basement and feed the cat. From now on they informed us they were leaving food and water on the top step of the basement and that was as far as they were willing to go to take care of Cotton. In fact, the sooner we came back to take the cat off their hands the better.

Dad and Mom weren't about to come home early to retrieve the cat, so they apologized to the Rafts and told them they fully supported leaving the cat's food and water at top of the basement steps. When we arrived back in the city a week-and-a-half later we discovered that the cat had eaten very little and was still hiding in the coal bin. Dad was once again called upon to do the impossible. If we were ever going to get Cotton back, he was the one who had to go into the coal bin and retrieve him. Dressed in heavy winter clothes and a hat with earmuffs and carrying a flashlight and fishing net, Dad entered the cat's lair anticipating the worst. The light had not been replaced in the bin since Mr. Raft had hurt himself and the wooden enclosure was inky black. Shining his light back and forth, Dad finally caught the glint of two eyes staring at him from the top of the coal pile. Snarls and hisses greeted him as the cat prepared to attack. But it only took one swipe of the net to capture Cotton who was so emaciated he was unable to put up an adequate defense. Carted unceremoniously back to the store in a burlap bag, Cotton was so weak he didn't even resist getting a bath.

Life was not the same for Cotton after this experience. His spirited nature had been sapped and he no longer played games with Chipper. Bounding into the store one morning to look for his friend, Chipper found Cotton dead in the storage room. For days afterwards Chipper returned to the place where he had found the body of his friend and lay there for hours with his head between his legs. It is hard to appreciate the level at which animals bond with one another, but in some ways I felt that Chipper held Dad responsible for Cotton's demise, and from that day forward the relationship between Chipper and my father was never quite the same.

City Life

We adapt to the environment we live in; that doesn't mean we like where we live. I know I didn't. I hated living in the city and Dad didn't like living in the city any more than I did. Sometimes when we were sitting around the dinner table at the back of the store Dad would talk about moving to the Jersey shore. He dreamed about running a marina and renting boats to fishermen. I thought his plan sounded great, but Mom didn't let him get too far with the idea. She said she had no intentions of becoming a fisherman's maid, cleaning out smelly boats while Dad stood around shooting the breeze with their customers.

I first learned that there was something different from cement sidewalks and eight-story apartment buildings when I went to school. It's difficult to remember how old I was, but I think I was in the second grade. Some of my classmates would come back from summer break and start talking about how they went to visit their relatives in the country or played on the beach at Cape May. The stories they told sounded really neat so I started asking my parents if we could go to places like that. "Don't I have an aunt that lives in the country?" I asked.

"Sure," Dad said, "but we don't have time to visit her. We're busy seven days a week and there's no time to take a bus out to her farm."

Books were my next approach. I was a pretty precocious youngster and I started to read at a very early age, so I began to study everything I could about nature. To my amazement there were all kinds of unusual plants and animals that lived in New Jersey. And even more astounding were the creatures that lived in the ocean. By the time I was nine I was continually pestering my parents about going to the zoo or the Museum of Natural History in New York. It took months before they finally agreed and the things I saw that day were absolutely incredible. Some of the animals in the zoo were huge, but they weren't half as big as the replica of the blue whale or the skeletons of the dinosaurs I saw in the museum.

After seeing all the amazing animals in the zoo and looking at all the displays in the museum it became absolutely essential that I learn more about them, so it was back to the books. "Did dinosaurs live in New Jersey?" I asked my father. And what about great white sharks? Had anyone seen them in the Hudson River? The more I read the more I wanted to know. But reading about plants and animals in books wasn't enough. I wanted to see the things I'd read about and the city didn't provide too many opportunities.

It wasn't until I was ten that Dad took me on my first trip out of the city. Mom was going to cover the store while Dad took me fishing for striped bass. I don't think I slept at all the night before our outing. Now I was going to see what other places were like. Dad got a friend of his to drive us to the fishing spot. It was situated along the west bank of the Hudson River at the base of the Palisades. As the car left the city, I became enthralled with the wooded areas that lay just north of us and wondered what it would be like to wander around in them. When we reached the fishing spot, Dad's friend parked the car and we walked to a rock wall along the bank of the Hudson. After taking a few moments to enjoy the view across the river, we set up our poles and baited our lines. Then Dad gave me some instructions on how to cast. Now all the fish had to do was cooperate. Minutes passed but nothing happened. "Do you think anything is going to bite?" I anxiously inquired.

"I don't know," Dad sighed. "They usually bite real well on an outgoing tide. Fishermen need to have patience. Let's give it a little while longer."

For another hour I stood watching the poles hoping to see something strike, but nothing took our bait. Now I was getting real antsy, so I asked Dad if I could go over and check out a rocky stretch of shore along the river. I'd read that lots of interesting creatures lived under rocks and I was anxious to see if I could find some. Dad gave me the okay but told me to be back in an hour. He said if the fish didn't start to bite we'd pack up and head home.

At last I was going to get the chance to discover something. Racing over to the shoreline, I scrambled down into the rocks and began turning them over. Nothing I uncovered looked anything like what was in the books. The rocks were oily and covered with tar and the only things I found were worms. There were lots of them. But where were the other creatures that lived in places like this? More rocks were turned over until finally I found something that was really neat. It was long, white, and slippery. Maybe it was a jellyfish. But it was unlike any jellyfish I'd ever seen in books. Certain that Dad would know what it was, I slid it onto a piece of wood and took it back to him.

"Look what I found," I proudly announced. "I think it's some kind of jellyfish."

Looking down at the sack-like blob, my father shook his head in disgust and ordered me to throw the creature into the river.

"Do you think it's still alive?" I asked.

"Just throw it in the river," he insisted.

Flipping the creature into the murky water, I watched it slowly disappear beneath the surface as creamy stuff oozed from its body. "I think it's hurt," I lamented. It wasn't until many years later that Dad told me the creature I'd discovered was a sperm-filled condom.

Months passed before I made another trip out of the city. We didn't go far. Mom asked Dad to borrow my uncle's car to pick up some smoked shad from a fisherman that lived in a dilapidated barge moored along the bank of the Hudson River. When we arrived at the fisherman's shack there were long lengths of net draped over poles near the water's edge. I had never seen nets like this before so I asked Dad what they were. "They're gill nets. The fishermen set them in the river to catch shad. Each end is tied to a buoy. They usually set them out at night and the fish swim into them and get their gills caught."

"Are there a lot of shad in the river?" I asked.

"Only in the spring. They migrate up river to lay their eggs."

The fisherman who came to greet us was tall and skinny and had a scruffy beard. Most of his front teeth were missing and I was totally mesmerized by the huge wad of tobacco he was chewing. "Can I help you?" he asked as we maneuvered ourselves across a narrow plank to the barge.

"We'd like to buy some smoked shad," my father said.

"You're lucky," the fisherman replied, "we had a good haul yesterday. The fish aren't coming up the river like they used to. The river is so polluted the fish are dying off before they spawn."

"Who's polluting the river?" I asked.

"We all are," the fisherman responded as he shifted the wad of tobacco in his mouth and spit some brown juice into the murky water. "Just look at some of the fish we caught last night." Reaching into a fly covered barrel, he pulled out a large silver fish covered with red sores. "You see those lumps on the body. That's cancer. The poison in the river is causing that. Soon there won't be any shad for us to eat."

Cancer. I knew what that was. My best friend's mom had cancer and Dad said it was killing her. "You mean if I swim in the river I could get cancer like those fish?" I asked.

"It wouldn't surprise me," the fisherman replied as he spat more tobacco juice into the river.

Looking over at my father to see what he thought about all this, Dad grimaced and shook his head. "You shouldn't tell the boy things like that. You'll frighten him."

"Both of you should be frightened," the fisherman warned as he weighed two fish and wrapped them in newspaper. "That'll be a $1.25."

"Is it true that the river is polluted?" I asked Dad as we drove back home.

"From what I've read in the newspaper it seems that way," Dad replied. "When I was young a lot of people swam in it, but now nobody does."

"Do you think the fish we bought were sick?" I asked.

"I don't think so. I checked the fish we bought and there were no sores on them."

"What kind of pollution causes sores like that?" I asked while unwrapping one of the fish to make sure it was all right.

"I don't know. But people dump a lot of garbage and chemicals into the river. Some people say that the river washes all that stuff out to sea and there's no reason to be alarmed. But I'm not so sure they're right."

The rest of the way home I kept looking towards the river and wondering if the polluted water was the reason we didn't catch any striped bass the day we went fishing. I also wondered if it was the reason I didn't find anything but worms underneath the oil-coated rocks.

There was a small vacant lot behind the apartment building where my parents had their stationery store and it was great place to collect earthworms. The worms in that lot grew to an enormous size, mostly because people threw their garbage into it when their dumbwaiters stopped working. Besides worms, the lot harbored a huge population of rats. At night you could hear them scurrying around as they rummaged through the garbage. Dad claimed that the rats that lived in that lot were the biggest he'd ever seen. Once when he was out there he said he saw one that was over a foot long and must have weighed close to a pound.

My parents told me a hundred times they didn't want me playing around in the lot, but I was interested in digging up worms. "I need to get some so we can use them for bait when we go fishing," I told Dad. Dad said there wasn't any need for me to go digging around in the garbage. He said he'd buy bait when we needed it. He warned me that the garbage was full of all kinds of nasty germs and I could get really sick digging through the stuff. "Okay," I said, pretending to be listening, then off I went, at the first opportunity, to shovel up the biggest worms I could find.

"What are you going to do with all those worms?" Dad asked me one day when I proudly held up a bagful.

"Keep them in an aquarium filled with dirt. Then we won't have to pay for bait when we go fishing."

"You don't seem to listen very well about not digging around in that garbage, and besides, we don't have an aquarium," Dad grumbled.

"We do now," I said excitedly. "I found one in the lot." Lifting up a busted aquarium I grinned from ear to ear as I showed it to my parents.

"Those worms aren't staying in my house," Mom announced while shaking her head.

"But there must be some place we can keep them." I pleaded. "Maybe we can put them outside on the fire escape."

After further discussion and endless pleading, my parents agreed to let me keep the worms on the fire escape but only if I took care of them. So out I went to dig up some dirt and set up my terrarium.

Worms, of course, are not the most exciting creatures to care for, but when I was bored I'd climb onto the fire escape and watch them crawl through the dirt. Over time the worm population in the terrarium dwindled to almost nothing. Birds would eat some and some would escape and later be discovered draped over the ledges next to our neighbor's apartment. Whenever this happened I headed down to the lot and dug up some more.

Once when I was digging for worms an old lady by the name of Mrs. O'Hallaran stuck her head out of her apartment window and offered me some cookies. "You'll have to come up to the apartment and wash your hands if you want some," she shouted as I hastily wiped my hands against my shirt.

Mrs. O'Hallaran lived by herself some of my buddies told me. They said her husband had died in World War I, and she had no children as far as anyone knew. Smiling at me as she opened the door, Mrs. O'Hallaran pointed to the sink and suggested I give my hands a good scrubbing before I sat down at the table. "I've been watching you for some time," she said as I seated myself and began to gobble down the cookies. "Just what do you do with all the worms you dig up?"

"I'm saving them to go fishing," I said. "Would you like some of the fish my Dad and I catch?"

"Sure," she replied, "my cats and I love fish."

"Good. I'll make sure to bring you some when we go out."

There must have been a least a dozen cats living in Mrs. O'Hallaran's apartment—grey and white striped ones, tan ones with short hair, and a large white one with fluffy hair and blue eyes. "They keep me company," she mused as she stroked one of them over the head and watched me gobble down the last of her cookies. "I don't think I'd be able to live without them."

That afternoon when I went home I told my mother about Mrs. O'Hallaran and the cookies she gave me. "You should write her a thank you note and give it to her the next time you see her," she suggested.

I wrote the note over the weekend and several days later knocked on Mrs. O'Hallaran's door. When no one answered I decided to dig up some more worms and come back later. It was late afternoon before I knocked on her door a second time. When no one answered I slipped the note under the door and was about to leave when I detected a peculiar odor in the hallway. Maybe one of her cats died when she was away I thought to myself as I was leaving the building. The next day they found Mrs. O'Hallaran dead in the kitchen surrounded by her cats. One of the policemen who had entered her apartment found my note and gave it to my mother. He said Mrs. O'Hallaran had died of a heart attack. For a long time I thought about Mrs. O'Hallaran dying alone in her apartment and how terrible that must have been. I also thought about her cats and wondered who was going taking care of them. When I asked Dad if someone had adopted them he shook his head and said one of the policeman gathered them up and took them to the pound.

I never did use the worms I'd collected to catch fish. We wound up using squid, clams, and small bait fish that Dad purchased at the marina. Eventually, I took the worms back to the lot and let them go. On the day that I did it, I looked up at the apartment once occupied by Mrs. O'Hallaran, and a boy and girl were watching and waving to me from her window. When I saw them I waved back and thought about what it must be like to live in an apartment where someone had died.

During the summer there was not a lot to do in the city. Most of the time it was hot and humid and the sidewalks reflected the heat and magnified the putrid odors left behind by animal waste and rotting garbage. To this day I can still remember the stench that arose from some sections of the city and the yellow haze that enveloped us.

When school was out I spent a lot of time listening to baseball games on the radio, playing stickball in the streets and going to the movies. My folks were avid New York Giants fans so whenever I could I'd listen to the baseball games on the radio while I waited on customers. Willie Mays was my hero. In my mind he was the greatest hitter and centerfielder in the game. Most of my friends rooted for the Yankees and would insist that Mickey Mantle was twice as good as Mays. But there was no way I believed that. Long arguments often ensued whenever they tried to convince me, some of which ended in fisticuffs, and as you might expect neither one of us was ever able to convince the other who was the greatest player.

On rare occasions my folks would get someone to cover the store and we would head over to the Polo grounds to watch my hero play. We'd hop a bus into New York City then take a double deck bus up to the Polo Grounds. Sunday was the best time to watch them play and if we were lucky we got to see a double header. We always tried to get there early to watch batting practice and sometimes talk to the players while they were on the field. My greatest hope was to sit in the bleachers and snag a home run hit by Willie. A couple of times I came close, but it always bounced in the other direction and someone else got the ball.

When I wasn't listening to a baseball game some of my friends and I would put together a team and play stickball in the streets. Stickball was a city kid's alternative to baseball. We played with a broomstick handle and a Spalding gas ball. Since there were not a lot of vacant lots, the game was played on streets that didn't have a lot of traffic. We used chalk to mark out the bases and the ball was bounced towards the batter at home plate. A good pitcher could twist the ball and make it hop in different directions or fling it with a lot of "mustard" so it raced past the batter before he or she could swing at it. Most of the teams were made up of boys, but sometimes girls would fill in if we couldn't find enough guys to play. Some of the guys I knew were pretty good at the game and could slap a gas ball a city block, but my prowess at striking an inside fast ball was pretty weak and most of time I struck out.

The biggest problem we had playing stickball was having enough gas balls to last nine-innings. On occasions the batter would strike the ball over our heads and it would bounce into one of the sewers before we could reach it. This meant that before each game we would have to round up four or five new balls. Since a new ball cost fifteen cents, this became an expensive recreational activity. Dad usually gave us one new ball from the store, but the rest had to come from someplace else. Once in a while one of the other guys brought a new ball, but most of the time we had to figure out other ways to get them. Sometimes we traded baseball picture cards to get the balls and sometimes we would let girls play on our team if they brought a ball with them.

One day when we were sitting on the curb outside my parents' store discussing how we could get some more balls to play a game, my father overheard us and suggested that we get them out of the sewers. "But how?" one of my friends asked. "I know there are lots of them down there but I've never figured a way to get them." Retreating to the back of the store my Dad came back five minutes later with a long stick and a wire coat hanger. After straightening out the hanger, he wound one end around the stick and created a loop at the other end whose diameter was just a little less than the diameter of a gas ball. "Follow me," he said as he walked across the street and peered into the sewer in front of Raft's bakery. "Do you see any balls?" he asked. Scrunching up our noses, we bent over and spotted two slime covered balls floating on a viscous layer of black ooze. "Watch," he said as he lowered the stick into the sewer and retrieved the first ball and dumped it onto the sidewalk.

"God, it stinks," one of my friends complained as he scrunched up his face in disgust. "It smells like shit."

"You're right," Dad chuckled, "but when you clean it up it'll be just as good as any ball you buy in the store. Besides, can you tell me a better way to collect balls?"

We had to admit we couldn't think of another alternative. So after that day the guys and I always spent a couple of days before each game plucking balls from the sewers. When I came home Mom could always smell what I'd been up to and made me scrub up at the sink before I came to the dinner table. She also never forgave Dad for teaching us how to retrieve gas balls from the sewers.

Saturday afternoon during the summer was movie time in the city. There were several movie houses I used to go to, one was on Summit Avenue and the rest were situated along Bergenline. In the early 1950s, it cost twenty-five cents to go to a show if you were under twelve and fifty cents if you were older. Most of the time my parents didn't have the money to send me to a show so I had to find my own. Again, it was Dad who showed me how to do it. One Saturday afternoon while Mom was working in the store, Dad walked me along Bergenline Avenue and pointed out a bunch of grated areas next to the apartment buildings. When we got to the first one he asked me to look down through the grating and tell me what I saw. At first I didn't see anything except some bits of broken glass and assorted bottle caps. When I told him what I saw he told me to look a little closer. This time I scanned the area underneath the grate a lot more carefully and I spotted some coins. There must have been nearly thirty cents in pennies, nickels, and dimes. "I think you'll find all the money you need to go to the movies underneath these grates."

"But how am I going to get the money out? The grate is locked into the cement."

"That's easy," Dad responded and lifted up a slender stick he'd been carrying and attached a wad of bubble gum to it. Down went the stick between the holes in the grate and up came the money attached to the bubble gum. Dad was a genius! I was going to be rich and now I could get all the money I needed to go to the movies. Of course things didn't quite work out that way. Another lesson I learned in the city was that your competitors were always watching. When other kids saw what I was up to, my source of revenue quickly dried up, and I had to expand my territory and do some of my hunting at night when others couldn't see what I was up to.

One thing that really turned me off about life in the city was how much we shared other people's lives. Buildings were built so close together and the walls in some apartments were so thin you heard what everybody was saying. If your friend's father came home drunk, you could hear the family arguments through the walls. When your best friend's father beat his wife it was hard to block out her screams. One day after playing stickball with one of my friends, we went back to his apartment to find it surrounded by a crowd of curious people. When we asked what had happened one of the neighbors said a man had just shot himself. It turned out it was my friend's father. He had lost his job and blown his head off with a shotgun. I still have nightmares about my friend's screams as he ran past the police trying to get into the apartment. Nothing was private. We shared all the bad moments in other people's lives, and shortly after my friend's father killed himself I was determined to run away and find a better place to live.

Fortunately for me, Dad intervened. The next afternoon when he found me trying to sneak out of the apartment he grabbed my shoulder and asked where I was going.

"To visit my aunt," I grumbled. "I'm sick of living in the city."

"Does your aunt know you're coming?" he inquired.

"No. But I'm sure she'll let me stay with her. Anything is better than living in this crummy place."

"And what about school?" he asked.

"I can go to school where she lives."

"Maybe. Don't you think we should talk more about it before you take off," Dad insisted. "Mom is going to be pretty upset."

Somehow Dad managed to convince me to stay. He told me there were better ways to escape. "Stay in school and tough it out," he said. "A man with a good education can choose the kind of life he wants to lead. He can also live wherever he wants."

Dad's suggestion was a good one. When I entered high school several years later I seriously began thinking about going to college and finding a job that would satisfy my interest in animals and the environment.

The Dream Machine

When the money started seeping into the family coffers from the numbers lottery, Dad set out to achieve one of his life-long ambitions—owning a new car. As a young man he had owned a used Model T Ford for a short while, but it was nothing compared to the new cars being produced when World War II was over. After scouting the car lots for several weeks he came home one day and announced he'd made his selection. Mom, of course, was not going to allow Dad to choose a car without her input, so after Dad made his announcement she demanded he take her to the car lot so she could take a look at his "dream machine." The car he'd selected was scrutinized with the utmost care. Color and safety were my mother's paramount concerns. After numerous family discussions and a trial ride, Mom finally agreed the blue Desoto with whitewall tires that my father had picked out was just right for us. It was roomy enough to take people out on Sunday drives, it had lots of storage space for luggage, and it was built like a tank. It didn't matter whether or not the car got good gas mileage. Gas was only twenty-five cents a gallon and every gas station in the United States was offering special bonuses such as dinnerware and wine glasses to encourage you to buy their gas.

As you might expect, getting a car came with a whole lot of responsibilities. First and foremost you had to get car insurance. Then you had to find a place to keep your car. This was no easy feat in the city. Dad looked everywhere for a garage where he could house the automobile but none was immediately available. He needed to get on a waiting list. "And how soon will a place be available?" Dad asked. "Three years," was the standard reply. This meant parking his car on the street.

The thought of parking his dream machine outside and subjecting it to all kinds of foul weather sent waves of anxiety running through Dad's body. What if the neighborhood kids decided to play on the car, or worse yet, what if another car ran into it while it was parked on the street? There was only one solution. During the day he would park the car in front of the store. That way he could closely monitor what was happening to it. And at night he would try to park it next to the apartment building where we lived so he could check on the car from his bedroom window.

The day Dad brought his new Desoto home he was beaming with pride as he parked it next to the store. Its shiny blue exterior glistened in the afternoon sun as a host of neighborhood kids came around to appraise Dad's new dream machine.

"What do you think?" I asked my friends as they stood back and evaluated it.

"My dad said the only car worth buying is a Cadillac," one friend announced as he ran his hand over the car's glistening fender.

"I don't know," another responded. "I like cars that go fast. How fast does this one go?"

"I have no idea," I admitted, "but I'll l find out this weekend. Dad said we're going to take it for a drive."

"Where do you plan to go?" one of my other buddies asked.

"Somewhere out in the country. Maybe we'll go to my aunt's farm."

The most vivid memories I have of Dad's car were these Sunday drives into the country. We always began preparing for them on Saturday. That was the day Dad would wash and wax his dream machine. I asked him once why we had to clean the car before heading out onto the highway and he gave me a puzzled look.

"It helps keep the car in good shape," was his immediate reply, "and besides no one wants to see us driving around in a dirty car."

I, for one, didn't care if we drove around in a dirty car and I was certain that none of my friends did either. But my vote didn't count for much. Walking out the front door of the store with a wash bucket and container of wax in his hands, Dad often enlisted my help to wash the car, while I listened to the shouts of my friends playing stickball down the street.

I had to admit, however, that the dream machine did get dirty sitting out on the street. Throughout the year soot, produced by the city's grimy incinerators, rained a thin layer of black "gunk" down on everything. People, dogs, cats, and cars were covered with the stuff. This residue from incinerated garbage, I now realize, had all kinds of carcinogens mixed with it. But back then no one was aware that this "black gook" could be harmful to one's health. In fact, so much of this stuff rained down from the sky that piles of it would accumulate on the roofs of tenement buildings. One day an article appeared in our local newspaper, *The Hudson Dispatch*, in which one enterprising individual claimed he had discovered traces of gold in the gunk and suggested it might be worth mining. Before Dad found a garage for his vehicle I'm sure we washed a ton of "valuable" gold-filled soot off of his dream machine. Gold or no gold, this was not, as you can probably imagine, a labor of love on my part and even today, no matter how dirty my car looks, I refuse to wash and wax it.

My parents loved Sunday drives. Despite the fact that I was anxious to get out of the city, I learned to hate them. Most of the time we didn't leave the car to explore the countryside, and when we did stop, it was only to eat before we headed back into the city.

Our drives always began at eight a.m. Cousin Lottie, her husband Al, my parents, and I would pile into the car and without any idea of where we were going head off into the hinterlands of New Jersey. Dad always drove, which proved to be quite a feat since he was only five feet foot four inches tall and his head barely reached above the steering wheel. No one else in the car could drive, but that didn't stop them from giving Dad advice on how to operate the car and where they wanted him to take us. Mom would frequently complain that Dad was driving too fast and that he needed to watch where he was going. I had to admit the latter comment was true. Dad couldn't quite see where he was going. As a result we would all grab on to the edge of our seats whenever he turned onto narrow roads that were barely visible from the driver's seat. Wheels would screech, Mom would close her eyes, and the rest of us would cringe expecting the car to turn over at any moment. Fortunately, we all survived these traumatic experiences, even though I probably became the only fourteen-year-old to develop high blood pressure.

Endless arguments would erupt during our drives. Most of them focused on where we should eat or when to give the ladies a "pit stop." I still vividly recall the times Mom would yell at Dad to pull over at an approaching restaurant. Zooming past the lunch spot, Dad would shrug his shoulders and tell Mom she needed to let him know sooner if she wanted him to pull over. Mom would then grumble that she didn't even know what road she was on no less where the next restaurant was.

"Why can't we turn around?" she inevitably would ask as our growling stomachs complained at another lost opportunity.

"That place was closed," Dad would grumble as he continued down the highway. "I promise to stop at the next place we see."

Thirty minutes and two restaurants later we still wouldn't have stopped to eat. By that time we would be famished and Mom and Lottie would start to complain that if we didn't stop soon they were going to pee in their pants. I don't think that ever happened, but it always seemed a good way to get Dad to pull off the road at the next place we came to.

Getting lost was sometimes the whole purpose of a Sunday drive. Dad would randomly select out-of-the-way roads that would take us to places we had never heard of. This was all very exciting, but then we had to find our way back. After we got to our "unknown" destination and had our lunch we would unfold our road map and try to figure out where we were. If Dad did an especially good job of getting us lost, a lot of apprehensive moments would ensue as we tried to ponder which route would take us back to the main highway. None of us, of course, could ever agree which road would do that. Dad would always tell us not to worry. All we needed to do was retrace the route he had taken to get lost. But getting back never proved to be quite that simple.

After making a few incorrect turns we inevitably got to a point where we were totally confused. Dad would say straight ahead, Mom would say left, Al would vote for right and Lottie would say nothing at all. More often than not we would find ourselves driving around in circles with everyone but Lottie shouting at each other that they knew we should have gone in the opposite direction. If we were lucky we made it home in time to listen to the end of a Dodger-Giant baseball game. If we weren't, we staggered into the apartment building after dark with Dad promising Mom he would purchase a better set of road maps before we set out on our next Sunday "adventure."

Perhaps the worst thing about Sunday drives was having to breathe smoked-filled air. Both Dad and Al were addicted to cigarettes. On cold days during the spring and autumn my parents would close the car windows and a dense cloud of smoke would envelop us. As soon as the windows were shut my eyes would begin to water and I would start to develop a severe headache. All I could think about was getting out of the car and finding some place where I could breathe. Pleading with my parents to stop the car and let me out did no good, and the longer I remained in the car the sicker I got. I couldn't wait for the drive to be over. If we were going to a friend's house, I would often ask to lie down on one of their beds with an ice pack on my head in order to get rid of my headache. Mom complained that I was just pretending to be sick because she wouldn't let me stay home. After months of agonizing headaches and several instances when I staggered out of the car and vomited my breakfast over somebody's lawn, my mother took me to a doctor. "He has these terrible headaches," I remember my mother complaining to our family physician as we sat down in front of him. "I think it's all psychological," she added. "I think he's only trying to get back at us because he doesn't want to go on Sunday drives."

After the doctor finished listening to my mother's concerns, he tactfully asked her to step out of the office while he examined me. "Tell me about these Sunday drives," he asked me as he ran his hand through his thinning head of black hair.

"I can't stand them," I grumbled as he examined my eyes and listened to my heart with his stethoscope.

After hearing my tale of woe he invited my mother back into the office and explained that I was allergic to cigarette smoke. "If you care for your boy's health," the doctor said, "your husband will have to give up smoking."

Finally someone agreed with me, but asking Dad to give up smoking? That was well beyond the realm of possibility. In the early 1950s nearly everybody smoked, including our doctor. No one thought about how harmful smoking could be to your health. There were no nicotine patches or other products people could use to break their habit. If Dad was going to quit smoking, it meant that he had to go "cold turkey"—no medical solutions. To my utter amazement Dad did just that. It wasn't easy. Several times he stopped and just as quickly started back up again. On his fourth try he finally succeeded. He was in his mid-forties when he achieved this feat, and until the day he died, Dad never smoked again.

As far as our Sunday drives were concerned, my parents never stopped going on them. Al, of course, was told he could no longer smoke in the car which meant we had to make a lot of pit stops for smoke breaks. It wasn't until I entered my third year in college that my parents gave up insisting that I join them on Sunday drives in Dad's dream machine.

Bounty Hunters

Having a car, together with the extra money my parents earned from the numbers lottery, meant that we could take a two-week vacation. Some people we knew went to Florida for winter vacations. We didn't have enough money to go to Florida and winter was a busy time at the store, so we went to Cape Cod in the summer. Months were spent preparing for these trips. We had to determine which part of the Cape we were going stay on and how close it would be to the best fishing and crabbing spots. The latter was extremely important since these trips were more than vacations—they were food-gathering expeditions.

Once we had decided where we were going to stay, our gear had to be checked out. The outboard motor, which Dad had partial ownership in, had to be serviced and run to make sure it was operating properly. Fishing tackle had to be replenished, reels oiled, crab nets restrung, and clam rakes sharpened. Nothing was left to chance. The list of supplies was checked and rechecked to make sure we were fully prepared for our assault on Cape Cod's marine resources.

Cousin Lottie and her husband Al were always invited along on our "vacations." Lottie was Mom's best friend. The thing I most remember most about her was her shy demeanor and smiling face. Whenever there were major tasks to do Lottie always pitched in and helped Mom out. I don't I believe I ever heard Lottie complain about anything during the entire time I knew her. Al, on the other hand, was a tall, sinewy man with a grumpy disposition who loved to drink beer and smoke cigarettes. Al made a good living loading and unloading trucks and never reported any of his income to the IRS. He was a proud member of the Teamsters Union, and during their strikes he would spend a good part of his time sitting at home drinking beer and worrying about whether or not the union would negotiate a new wage and benefit package. According to Dad some of the Union's demands were absurd, like the year they demanded that all of the Teamsters get off on their grandmother's birthday.

As soon as we got on the Cape, the first thing Dad, Al, and I did was check out the nearest marina. "How are the fish biting?" Dad would ask the owner. If the answer was positive, a whole litany of additional questions was rattled off. "What are they biting on? Are there any new fishing regulations we should know about? Where are the best mussel beds? And, where are the best places to clam and catch blue crabs?"

Armed with all the appropriate information we returned to the cottage to plan our assault. Catching fish was our first priority. Mom liked summer flounder, locally known as fluke, so we spent the first day gearing up to catch them. Leaders were prepared and extra sinkers and hooks placed in our tackle box. Our scoop net was checked one more time to make sure there weren't any holes in it and a gaff was added to our gear just in case we caught a whopper.

By six a.m. Dad, Al and I were headed out the door to the marina. By seven, Dad had rented the sturdiest fishing boat he could find, hooked up the outboard, and had the three of us motoring down the channel. Visions of monster flounder danced through our heads as we sputtered along to the "secret" fishing hole everyone on the Cape knew about. Would this be the year we would have a bonanza catch? Dad was always convinced it would be. Killifish was the best bait for catching summer flounder. Local residents called them mummichogs, a name derived from the fishes' ability to survive the winter in a "mummified," semi-frozen state along the marsh banks. Live killifish were hooked to the end of our lines and the boat allowed to drift over sandy banks where the summer flounder were known to collect. If the fishing was good, we would catch a dozen or more that weighed between a pound-and-a-half and three pounds.

As soon as we landed a flounder we put it on a stringer that was hung off the back of the boat. This kept the fish fresh and saved us the expense of having to bring along a cooler full of ice. Around midday we usually stopped fishing and brought the flounder back to the cottage to fillet. Each fish was cut up into four strips (two each from the top and bottom), and Mom and Lottie would package the fish into meals that could be frozen. The packages of fish were then taken to a freezer locker until we were ready to return home.

Blue crabs were another of Mom's favorites so we always made at least two crabbing trips. Al wasn't too interested in crabbing so he usually stayed at the cottage downing a half dozen beers while Dad and I crabbed the creeks in Orleans using chicken parts or pieces of menhaden for bait. The bait was hooked to a weighted wire that was connected to a long length of line. Eight lines were tossed into shallow water up against the marsh bank. Since crabbing was a somewhat boring activity, Dad and I would often entertain ourselves by fishing for snappers while we waited for the crabs to bite. Every few minutes we would check the crab lines to see if they were taut. It they were, we knew a crab had grabbed hold of our bait and we slowly retrieved the line until it was close enough to scoop up the crab. In good years we'd catch a bushel of crabs by midday, but most years we only caught a half to three quarters of a bushel after a full day's outing.

If the crabs weren't biting, Dad would anchor the boat along the shore and we'd walk the grass flats looking for soft crabs. Soft-shell crabs were one of my favorites. I liked to eat them in sandwiches topped with lettuce and tomatoes or have them lightly fried in beer batter and served for dinner.

In order for blue crabs to grow they need to shed their external skeleton. The new skeleton grows underneath the old one, and when its growth is complete the crab hides in sea grass beds where it backs out of its old "shell." When shedding is finished water flows into the crab's soft body causing it to blow up like a balloon. Newly shed blue crabs look and feel like a handful of Jell-O and are very susceptible to predation. It was these newly shed crabs that Dad and I hoped to find but it was an activity that always required a great deal of patience. The best indicator that a soft crab was nearby was its shed. Whenever we found one we would methodically search through the sea grass until we discovered where the vulnerable crab was hiding.

We kept soft crabs in a bucket of moist seaweed. Hard crabs were placed in a wooden bushel basket with a moist cloth over the top to protect them from the sun. We learned early on that if wanted to keep the crabs alive and fresh never place them in a bucket of water. If we did, the crabs would quickly use up all the oxygen in the water and suffocate.

After we returned to the cottage, Dad would clean the soft crabs by removing their gills and internal organs and then cut away their mouth parts and eyes. Mom and I would then wrap the crabs individually in wax paper and freeze them. The hard crabs were boiled in freshwater that had salt, bay leaves and vinegar added to it. When the crabs turned red they were removed from the pot and cleaned. Cleaning involved lifting away the crab's carapace and removing its gills and internal organs. This was a tedious, time-consuming process that required everyone's help. Once the crabs were cleaned, Mom bundled the crab claws and bodies into separate bags and froze them.

Mussels and clams were the easiest for us to harvest. In Orleans, the tidal waters were free of pollution and there were places where huge beds of blue mussels grew along the bank. Harvesting them merely involved steering the boat up onto the mussel beds, tearing the mussels off of the rocks, and tossing them into wooden bushel baskets. Clam rakes with long sharp prongs were used to extract hard clams from the mudflats and shovels were used to dig up soft clams from exposed sandbars. Dad, Al, and I hosed down and scrubbed the mussels and clams before we steamed them. Soft clams were placed into a bucket of seawater to which cornstarch had been added. We did this in order to get rid of the sand in their digestive tracts. After the mussels and clams were steamed, we packaged up the meat and Mom and Lottie stored the broth in separate containers so they could use it in sauces and soups.

In good years we harvested several coolers of seafood. The challenge was keeping the food frozen during our trip home. Dad solved that by making arrangements to pick up packets of dry ice from an ice cream plant in Rhode Island. Most of the time this worked. However, once when we got to Rhode Island the ice cream plant was closed. As you might expect, it happened during one of those years we'd harvested a lot of seafood. Dad said there was no way he was going to have all that food go to waste so we stopped at a general store and started calling every business in Rhode Island that might sell dry ice. Just before noon we found one. Jumping into the car, Dad floored the gas petal and managed to reach the icehouse just as it was about to close. Everyone gave a big sigh of relief when they let us in. Another vacation was saved and we were once again insured a good supply of seafood throughout the winter.

Our success at harvesting seafood varied from one year to the next. Some years there was an abundance of crabs and a good supply of fish. At other times we had to put a lot of work into catching what we wanted. Weather had the greatest influence on our success and the weather on the Cape was very fickle. Some days it would be clear, calm, and sunny while the next day, cold wind from the north would howl across the open water. A long stretch of bad weather meant no food gathering and lots of sullen looks and grumbling from my parents.

One year a hurricane arrived on the Cape about the same time we did. No one in our family had paid any attention to the weather forecasts for the Cape when we left home. We just assumed that the weather would be the same as always. Maybe we would have a few days of rain and wind but nothing so extraordinary that it would make us want to cancel our vacation. The first clue that something was amiss happened as we drove onto the Cape. Everyone was driving in the opposite direction. Mom commented to Dad that she thought this was rather strange but neither of them seemed too panicked. It wasn't until we got close to our cottage and a policeman pulled us over that we knew we were in trouble. "What's the problem?" my father asked after he rolled downed the car window.

"The problem is the eye of a goddamn hurricane is going to pass right through this area in a couple of hours and if you don't find some shelter real soon, I'll be notifying your next of kin."

"Can we get off the Cape?" my mother asked as leaned over and anxiously looked at the policeman.

"Lady, they closed the only bridge off the Cape an hour ago. I suggest you head to wherever you're going and pray that the building doesn't blow away."

I don't think I'll ever forget the look on my parents' faces as they pulled up to our cottage and made a mad dash to get inside. By then the wind must have been blowing sixty miles an hour and bits and pieces of tree branches were flying past us. "Stay away from the windows," Dad yelled as we all hunkered down in the corner of the cottage. Soon the whole building began to shake and all of us were certain it was going to blow away.

"We're going to die," my mother screamed as a large tree limb smashed into the porch.

"No, we're not," Dad insisted as one of the trees in the back yard flew past the window.

The sustained winds of Hurricane Edna were reported to be a 120 miles-per-hour, but I'm certain the wind speeds around us gusted to a least 135 to 150. After the storm passed we drove through the fields of debris and were shocked to find entire homes ripped from their foundations. Boats were sitting on the highway, windows were smashed, electric and telephone lines were down, and many people in town were walking around in a state of shock. One woman we met was sitting on a bench crying. Her home had been destroyed and her husband was missing. Dad invited her to stay with us, but she declined. She said that some friends were stopping by to pick her up. For a week after the storm we had no electricity and the only thing we had to eat was canned food.

Because of Hurricane Edna, we lost over a week of food gathering, and with only a few days of vacation left, Dad was desperate to make sure we returned home with something. In an effort to turn things around he drove up to one of the marinas in Orleans and checked to see if they were still operating. It turned out they were, and they were only too happy to find someone crazy enough to rent one of their boats.

The next day Dad, Al, and I piled into the car and headed to Orleans to go fishing. The day was clear and sunny and there wasn't too much of a breeze when we got in the boat and headed towards the channel. Mussels were gathered from along the creek bank and a dozen or so fluke were hauled in from the mouth of the inlet. Everyone's spirits were up and we were certain that we were going to come home with a good haul. It was then that Dad suggested we head outside the inlet to catch mackerel. He'd seen a flock of birds feeding near the surface and he was certain we could fill the boat with them. Al and I weren't too keen on his idea, however, because it meant we had to plow into some large waves at the mouth of the channel to get to where the fish were.

"Don't worry about the waves," Dad said as he started up the engine, "I can make it through with no trouble." Turning the bow of the boat towards the mouth of the channel, he put the engine into full throttle and off we went. I had to admit there were moments when I thought we'd never make it to the mackerel feed. After plowing into the crest of one wave, we would jettison down its backside into the crest of another. Four times we took the plunge and each time I closed my eyes and prayed that we would survive. My heart was still pounding when we reached our fishing spot.

"You can open your eyes now," Dad laughed.

I didn't think it was so funny, but my fear quickly subsided when the mackerel started biting on nearly everything we threw at them. We had landed over twenty fish before I noticed that the wind had begun to pick up. The roar of the waves pounding against the beach had also grown louder and more white caps had started to form along the crests of the swells. Anxiously looking over at Dad I suggested that we might want to head back. After looking across the horizon, he agreed and started up the engine. I knew Dad was just as apprehensive as I was because he seldom agreed with me when it came to operating the boat.

As we got closer to the channel it was apparent that the trip back was going to be a lot worse than the one coming out. This was not any amusement park ride; this was the real deal and I was scared out my wits. Edging up the backside of a large wave, Dad waited for just the right moment and then turned the engine's throttle forward. The foam from breaking waves quickly engulfed us as we raced towards the entrance of the channel at mind-boggling speed. Maybe we'd make it after all, I thought to myself. I could see the channel markers looming in front of us. Only a hundred feet more and we'd be safe. *Whap* came the hammer-like thrust of a second wave as it hit us broadside. The next thing I remember was being catapulted through the air into the icy water. I'll never forget plunging into that freezing abyss and frantically trying to reach the surface. Just as my head bobbed above the water another wave crashed on top of me and sucked me under. Struggling to reach the surface, I had visions of crabs chewing on my hide while seagulls fought over what was left. Then, with a resounding thump, I was unceremoniously thrown up onto the beach.

I don't remember how I managed to crawl away from the waves that sucked at my body, but I do remember the panic that set in when I began to think about what had happened to my father and Al. My legs felt like rubber as I tried to stand up and look for them. At that point I realized I couldn't force myself to go any further so I started to yell. That proved to be a waste of time. The pounding surf was so loud it blotted out my desperate shouts. My God, I thought to myself, what if Dad and Al were dead. Then I saw them. They were just a little further down the beach. Dad was wading around in the water trying to recover the boat while Al was sitting near the edge of a sand dune holding his head between his hands. What a wonderful sight. I couldn't believe they were both alive.

To this day, I find it incredible that we made it back to the marina in one piece. With help from Al and me, Dad was able to rescue the boat and get the engine started. Nearly all of the fish we caught were gone but we did manage to retrieve some of our fishing gear plus one oar and the gas can.

Our trip back to the dock was bone chilling. Between our wet clothing and the icy wind, nearly all of the heat had been sucked out of our bodies. I was certain that none of us would ever stop shivering. As we pulled up to the marina and started to trudge past the owner, there was a huge grin on his face. Squeezing the bottom of chin, he asked, "Rough day?" as his eyes chuckled. What an understatement that was I thought to myself. I couldn't wait to get back into the car and warm up.

After piling what was left of our fishing equipment into the car Dad suggested we drive behind a bush and throw our wet clothes in the trunk. "We'll feel a lot warmer when we get rid of these wet things and I turn on the heater." That sounded logical, so off came the clothes and on went the heater. We were just beginning to feel normal when, halfway to the cottage, we heard this horn honking at us. When I turned around to see who was blowing the horn I spotted a Greyhound bus barreling down the highway heading in our direction.

"What's he honking about?" Dad asked.

"I don't know," I responded as I turned around to look, "I think he wants to pass."

Sure enough the bus pulled into the outside lane, but instead of passing he started honking his horn and waving at us. It must of have been great sport for the driver to find two naked men and a boy in a car. You could see him laughing and giving us the thumbs up sign as he pulled slightly ahead so all of his passengers could get a good look. Dad floored the gas pedal but to no avail. The bus pulled up alongside of us again and honked its horn as the passengers pressed their faces against the bus window. Soon we could hear all this hollering and laughing as the bus stayed glued to the outside lane. For over two miles that bus stayed with us. Thank God no one seemed to have a camera, otherwise we might have wound up as front-page news.

When we got back to the cottage Dad told us he was going to drive up next to the front door where we could make a mad dash into the house. That would have worked if Mom had been home, but she wasn't. Just as we pulled up to the cottage the proprietor spotted us and started racing in our direction waving her arms to get our attention. Before we could cover our private parts she started banging on the car window, urging Dad to roll it down. I don't think I'll ever forget the expression on her face when she realized that we had no clothes on. To her credit, after stammering a bit and turning red in the face, she regained her composure and told us, in the most dignified manner she could, that Mom called and wanted us to know that she and Cousin Lottie would not be back home until later. We never heard another word from the proprietor about the encounter, but she did have a big grin on her face when Dad checked out and returned the cottage key.

Hook and Liners

Dad would have loved to earn his living as a fisherman. Nothing made him happier than being out on the water hoping for the next big fish to come along and swallow his bait. I have no idea why Dad became such an avid fisherman. He just was. Mom thought he got interested in fishing while he was living with his foster parents but she wasn't sure. Like our vacations, Dad's fishing expeditions were carefully orchestrated. In the spring we would fish for porgies and weakfish. During the summer we would go for fluke, and in the fall we would pursue bluefish, tautogs, and winter flounder.

Working six days a week didn't leave Dad much time for fishing. So in order to fish, he sometimes had to find someone to help Mom out in the store. Usually he would hire one of the neighborhood boys, but if it was Saturday and they weren't available, I got assigned the job. Dad liked Saturday because he could rest up on Sunday before going back to work. But most of the guys who had partial ownership in the outboard motor we powered the rental boat with preferred to go on Sunday. Mom also preferred Sunday because it meant she didn't have to take care of the store when Dad was away. That was also fortunate for me because when I got older I was able to go on a lot of his fishing trips.

A great many of our fishing spots were a good distance from where we lived so we had to get up very early. Two in the morning was our usual departure time and I could never sleep the night before. I would spend the night rolling over in the bed thinking about the big fish I was going to catch. When the alarm finally rang I would jump up and start to look for my clothes. Grubby socks and pants were grabbed out of the dresser, and if it was cold outside, gloves and a winter cap and coat were pulled from the closet.

Mom would always get up with us and make sure that we had something to eat before we left. She would also lecture me about behaving myself and tell me to make sure Dad didn't get into any trouble. "Sure, sure," I would reply while I hastily gulped my food and raced downstairs to the car. The city streets were eerily quiet at that hour in the morning and the only things we ever saw moving about were stray dogs or large rats scavenging for food in the garbage bins. In the spring and fall, the night air was crisp and cool and when I huddled with the guys to talk about our impending fishing trip we were frequently enveloped in a cloud of magical fish vapor. As we stood around flapping our arms to keep warm someone would inevitably begin by announcing how good the fishing had been the week before.

"Was there any size to them?" someone would ask.

"Yeah, I heard they were real whoppers," another would reply. When all the hype was over, I had inflated visions of myself standing in front of the store with two trophy size fish. Flashbulbs from a newsman's camera would go off and the next day there would be a picture of me in the sports section of the newspaper.

Most of our fishing expeditions were to Greenport, Long Island. This involved several hours driving before we got to the marina. If it was Sunday, it also meant that we had to stop at St. Patrick's Cathedral in New York City. Most of the guys were Catholic and they promised their wives that they'd attend mass. Before we pulled up to the church the guys would start betting on how long it would take for the priest to say mass. There was one priest they claimed could do the mass in fifteen minutes and we always hoped he was the one on duty. Dad was the one who took the bets and kept track of the time since he wasn't a churchgoer. If I remember correctly, the record time for the guys getting through mass was an unbelievable fifteen minutes and twenty-two seconds.

On cold mornings the guys would bring several thermoses of coffee to drink while we headed east on the Long Island Expressway. This ultimately meant that somewhere along the way Dad would have to stop so the guys could relieve themselves. Usually this pit stop went without incident, but there was one morning when it got us into big trouble.

As soon as Dad pulled off the road all of us hopped out of the car and headed for the bushes. No one thought to close the car doors since we weren't going to be gone that long. Unbeknownst to us, however, there was a creature lurking in the darkness and as soon as he saw us lumbering in his direction he made a beeline for the back seat of Dad's car.

With the pit stop over, everyone jumped into the car and gave a big sigh of relief. We were all in high spirits talking about the upcoming fishing trip as we drove down the highway when one of the guys in the back seat reached down and felt something warm and fuzzy sitting next to him. All of a sudden his conversation came to an abrupt halt. "What's the matter?" the guy next to him asked.

"I think something has crawled into the car with us," the guy whispered.

"What do you think it is?" Dad asked.

"I don't know. But it's pretty big."

"Maybe it's an opossum," someone suggested.

For a few seconds no one moved. Then Dad told me to get the flashlight out of the glove compartment. "Shine it on the back seat and see if you can find out what it is."

On went the light and up popped the head of a rabbit. "Grab him," someone shouted.

Terrified by four pairs of clutching hands the rabbit panicked and started hopping all over the car. First he was in the front seat then in the back. None of us could get hold of him. Finally, Dad pulled off the highway and everyone scrambled out of the vehicle.

"Where's the rabbit?" Dad asked.

"I think he's still in the car," one of the guys shouted.

Sure enough there he was scrunched under the back seat his heart probably pounding away at two hundred beats per minute. One of the guys thought we should leave the car doors open and wait for the rabbit to leave. That sounded like a good idea, so we all stood around the car flapping our arms to keep warm while we waited for the rabbit to make its move. Nothing happened. After ten minutes the rabbit was still tucked underneath the back seat wiggling its nose staring back at us.

"Why don't we grab it and toss him out of the car?" someone else suggested.

"But what if he has rabies?" Dad sighed and scratched his head. At his point the rabbit had wedged itself even further under the seat and we weren't sure if we'd ever get rid of him.

"There has to be some solution," one of the guys grumbled.

"Why don't we use one of the fishing poles to pry him out?" Dad suggested.

"That might work, but I wish we'd hurry up. I'm freezing to death," someone else complained.

Up went the trunk and out came one of Dad's fishing poles. "Bring the light over here so I can see," Dad shouted.

Numerous thrusts were made with the pole followed by several frustrated groans. Finally, someone yelled, "There he goes."

"Quick, shut the doors," someone yelled.

Slam—click, slam—click. All the car doors were shut. Success had been achieved, definitive proof that we were up to the challenge. Everybody gave a triumphant roar and then turned around to see if they could find the rabbit.

"He's probably peeing in the bushes," one of the guys chuckled as we proceeded to get in the car.

"Could someone unlock my side of the car when they get in," Dad asked as he pulled on the door handle.

"I can't get in either," someone else complained.

Looking down at the front seat of the car, Dad spotted his car keys and realized we were in big trouble. In our haste to get rid of the rabbit we had locked ourselves out of the car. As for the rabbit, he was standing in the front seat of the vehicle with his nose pressed up against the window.

Needless to say there were no cell phones in the 50s to call for help so Dad had to hitch a ride to the nearest gas station, which turned out to be ten miles from where we were. "When does the owner open up?" my Dad asked the kindly old gentleman who'd picked him up.

"In about an hour," he replied. "But I wouldn't count on that. He tends to sleep late on the weekends."

Two and half hours later Dad showed up with the garage mechanic. By then we all envied the rabbit sitting in the car while we huddled together to keep warm. I'll also never forget the grin on the mechanic's face as he approached the side door and saw that rabbit looking out at him.

Aside from the fact that it took us until ten a.m. to get out on the water the day of the rabbit incident, fishing was always good around Greenport. Massive numbers of porgies would move into shallow water during the month of May. The larger ones fed over hard bottom and we would use a two-hook rig with squid for bait. One hook was attached near the sinker and the other was placed about a foot from the end of the line. For a kid like me, who loved to fish, porgy fishing provided the best action you could imagine. The minute the sinker hit the bottom and I took up the slack, the porgies would bite. Most of the time I would get two fish on at the same time. The majority were between one and two pounds and they always put up one heck of a fight. In a single day's outing we would easily catch a potato sack full in a couple of hours. Dad never kept that many because he said they were too boney and Mom didn't like to eat them. But most of the other guys would bring home two or three burlap bags full. The majority of these fish would go to their friends and relatives but when they wouldn't take them they would send me over to the convent to give them to the nuns.

May was also the month that northern puffers would breed in the waters around Greenport. Our family loved to eat puffers, so after we finished catching all the porgies we wanted, Dad and I would head over to a site where we could find large concentrations of puffers. A lot of people were afraid of eating them because some species possess a poison in their liver and reproductive organs, but the northern puffers that Dad and I caught off Greenport had very little toxin in their internal organs and no one we knew ever died from eating one.

We initially baited our lines with a small piece of squid, but the puffers were very adept at nibbling it off. This frustrated the heck out of Dad. Then one day he noticed that if we put a large piece of squid on the line and retrieved it before it was all gone, several fish would follow it to the surface. This observation led to an "aha moment."

"Why bother to try and catch them," he said, "when we can scoop them up with the net after they follow our bait to the surface."

That idea sounded great to me so on went a big piece of squid and down went the line. Within minutes there were dozens of tugs from hungry puffers and when we lifted the bait to the surface there must have been a half dozen fish still chomping away at our squid. With one quick scoop Dad landed four of them and from that day on we employed the same technique to capture puffers. Mom was especially pleased with the results of our new technique and teasingly declared Dad to be the best puffer fisherman in Union City, not the greatest honor to have bestowed upon you, but one that Dad always acknowledged with a graceful bow.

Cleaning puffers was relatively easy. All we needed to do was flip the fish on its back, place the knife behind the pectoral fins, and cut through the animal's body until we reached the skin on the opposite side. At this point we took the head and skin that was still attached to the fish and pulled them back towards the tail. What was left looked like a meaty drumstick. Cooking them was equally simple. Mom sautéed them in a fry pan after dipping them in garlic salt and butter. Today, of course, you can do it even quicker in a microwave. As far as I'm concerned puffers are one of the best tasting fish in the ocean. Their flesh is white and firm and has a shrimp-like flavor.

Fishing with Dad was always an adventure. I'm sure Mom sometimes wondered whether or not we'd make it back home from our expeditions. On several occasions, I wondered the same thing. I distinctly remember one foggy day when we were fishing offshore near a shipping channel. The fish weren't biting too well so Dad suggested we move into the middle of the channel. He said he'd often observed that the fish moved into deeper water during an outgoing tide. This day Dad's observation turned out to be right. As soon as we lowered our lines the fish began attacking our bait. Then we heard a loud *baaronk* from a freighter's foghorn. Staring into the dense fog, neither one of us could see anything, but I started to get apprehensive.

"Don't you think we better head towards shore?" I asked Dad as I stared into the dense, wispy shroud that surrounded us.

"Nah. That ship's still pretty far away," Dad insisted.

I wasn't too convinced of that. The fog was so thick that I couldn't see the hand in front of my face. *Baaronk*. The sound from the ship's foghorn now pounded against my eardrums and when I looked up there was the bow of this massive ship bearing down on us. Up came our fishing lines and yank went the motor cord. *BAARONK*. Three more pulls on the cord and still the engine didn't start. Now the ship was so close I could see the rust on its bow. Another pull on the cord and the engine coughed to life. Seconds away from disaster, Dad gunned the motor as we slipped past the ship's bow. Thank God, I thought. But then I looked up and spotted this enormous wake bearing down on us. Once again I found myself holding on to the sides of our boat as a series of huge waves catapulted us towards shore. Somehow we managed to survive another catastrophe. Happily, it was also the last time Dad ever fished in a shipping channel.

On rare occasions, Dad would insist on taking Mom fishing. It was beyond me why he wanted to do this since Mom hated fishing. The two instances when I went on one of these "family outings" turned out to be disasters. The first time I remember him doing it was in Cape Cod. That year the summer flounder were biting so well Dad told Mom she would really enjoy fishing for them. In order to make sure things went well my father played the role of the ultimate gentleman. He helped Mom into the boat, placed a dry cushion on the seat for her to sit on, and made sure that no water splashed up on her as we headed out to the fishing grounds. When Mom caught her first fish he quickly removed it from her line and placed new bait on her hook, and when Mom got her line tangled he gave her a new pole to fish with while he fixed her gear. All of this attention didn't impress Mom. After an hour of fishing, she began to complain that the boat stank and the smell was making her sick. When she got into this kind of mood, Dad should have known that it was time to take her home but the fish were biting so well he just couldn't quit. Mom then complained about the boat leaking and getting her shoes wet. Still Dad refused to take her back and pointed out what a beautiful day it was and how wonderful it was to be out on the water. Mom was not about to have any of this nice day stuff, so the next time she yanked on her pole she "accidentally" dropped Dad's favorite fishing pole overboard. That got his attention.

"I guess we'll have to go back now," Mom said with a smug look on her face, "it seems I don't have a pole to fish with anymore."

"I guess we will," Dad snapped and swore under his breath about losing his best pole.

Needless to say the trip to the marina was not pleasant, and when I got on shore I made sure I got as far away from the two of them as possible.

Several years after that ill-fated outing, Dad tried taking Mom fishing again. I knew Dad could be stubborn, but trying to get Mom to like fishing was like trying to get Dad to enjoy socializing with Mom's girlfriends at a Sunday morning breakfast. This time we tried fishing from the shore on Staten Island. Mom didn't have to go out in a boat and Dad had brought along a comfortable chair for her. After finding Mom a good fishing spot, he rigged up her line and cast it out into the channel. Unbelievably, as soon as Mom's bait hit the water a fish swallowed it and Dad helped her bring it in. This good fortune went on for nearly an hour. By then there were ten flounder in the cooler. With this kind of luck Dad was certain Mom would want to continue fishing, but that didn't turn out to be the case. Before Dad got a chance to throw his line out, she announced that she'd had enough fishing, folded up her chair, and demanded Dad take her home. Staring at her in disbelief Dad mumbled something about not being given a chance to catch any fish, but no amount of persuasion on his part got her to change her mind so off we went without Dad ever getting his line wet.

Fishing trips with my cousin Bright were inevitably adventurous. Usually he would call up the night before we planned to go fishing and ask if he and one of his girlfriends could go along. Bright did this whenever a relationship was getting serious. It was his way of checking to see if the girl was worth marrying. If she handled the outing well, he'd continue to date her, and if she didn't, he'd drop her and look for someone else. None of the girls he took on fishing trips ever passed the test. Inevitably, Bright and the girl would fight over something during our outing and that would be the end of their affair. I vividly remember one gal by the name of Nestor. Bright told Dad that she was the love of his life. He had never met anyone like her before and he was certain that she was the one he was going to marry. When Bright showed up with Nestor that morning I had to admit she was a knockout—the type of woman men would begin ogling the minute she stepped into a room. She had thick shoulder length hair that glistened under the lamplight and an hourglass figure that was accentuated by a provocative smile.

As you might imagine Nestor wasn't into fishing, but when Bright asked her to go out she reluctantly agreed. Throughout the trip Bright fawned over her. He baited her hook and gently removed the fish whenever she caught one. Everything was going extremely well until Nestor whispered into Bright's ear that she needed to use the restroom. At that point Bright motioned to Dad and suggested we quit fishing so Nester could "walk on the beach." At first Dad thought Bright was nuts. We were right in the middle of a major feed and we were hauling in one fish after another. However, when Bright pressed the issue a second time, Dad got the message and we headed for the nearest island. Shortly after we pulled up on the beach Nestor turned towards Dad and asked him where the nearest ladies room was. Somewhat surprised by Nestor's request, Dad explained to her that there were no restrooms, that it was a deserted island. He told her that he often stopped here whenever one of the guys needed to take a potty break.

"What about snakes and wild animals?" Nestor purred.

Dad tried to convince her that nothing would harm her, but Nestor refused to believe him. Finally, Bright intervened and said he would find a safe place for Nestor, and promised to stand guard. Nestor wasn't thrilled about the idea, but she finally agreed to go with Bright. Twenty minutes later the two of them came walking down the beach hand-in-hand. Nestor was adoringly looking over at Bright and the two of them were laughing and kissing.

About a week after our fishing trip I met Bright at his father's saloon and asked how things were going with him and Nestor. "Not too good," was his sullen reply as he shook his head. "She ditched me."

"Why? What happened?" It turned out that Bright was just as much a neophyte in the woods as Nestor and the place he chose for her "restroom break" turned out to be a patch of poison ivy. Her doctor said he had never seen such a severe case and estimated it was going to take Nestor over a month to fully recover.

The Best Way to Go

It was time to make a decision. There was no doubt in my parents' minds that I was going to college. The dilemma was choosing the best path to get there. I was thirteen and about to enter high school, so it was now time to decide which school I was going to attend.

"I don't like the idea of him going to Emerson," Dad sighed. "It's a public school and close by but that's about the only good thing I can say about it."

Mom nodded. "As far as I can tell there haven't been a lot of students that have gone on to college from that school in the last several years. What about the Catholic high school, St. Michael's?"

"It's a good school," Dad admitted, "and quite a few of their students go on to college. The trouble is it'll cost us money to send him there and we're not Catholic."

"I know. But some of the students that go there aren't Catholic and maybe he can get a scholarship to pay for his tuition," Mom suggested.

"It's worth a try," Dad said as he looked over at me. "Do you think you can pass the entrance exam?"

I had no idea whether I could pass the entrance exam, but I told him I'd try. I had to agree with what my parents were saying. My chances of getting into college from Emerson were a lot less than they would be from St. Michael's. When our class from Hudson Grammar School was given a tour of the school, not a lot of education was taking place. Several fistfights broke out while we were visiting classes and one individual was hauled off to the principal's office for trying to rape a girl in the clothes closet.

Thankfully, the entrance exam to St. Michael's wasn't too difficult and by some miracle my parents were able to get me a partial scholarship. It is hard to describe the relief I felt at getting a chance to go to a school where my opportunity to get into college was a lot better. It was going to be my ticket out of the city, and I was determined to make sure I made the most of it.

There were new school guidelines that I had to follow. The first rule was that all male students had to wear a jacket and tie to class. Successful people wear jackets and ties we were told the first day I entered school and this was our initial step towards demonstrating that we were refined, educated people. I had to admit I wasn't too keen on this rule, but it seemed a small price to pay to get a good education.

The rest of the rules were fairly straightforward. Students were not allowed to talk back to teachers. If they did, they were either given detention or expelled. Failure to show up for school on time resulted in detention. Repeated tardiness resulted in being thrown out of school. Failure to hand in homework was unacceptable and often resulted in detention. Smoking in school was absolutely forbidden, and if you failed to achieve a satisfactory grade point average, your career at St. Michael's was terminated. For me, and a lot of the other kids, being kicked out of school was frightening. It meant disappearing into that nebulous black hole called Emerson.

My Latin class was the one I feared the most. I can still remember our redheaded Latin teacher, Mr. O'Neal, standing on top of his desk slapping his yardstick against the blackboard and staring down at us through his glasses. The silence that followed was one of pure fear. We all knew what was going to happen next. Mr. O'Neal's yardstick would swoosh through the air and then rapidly level itself towards one of us. "Please stand up and read last night's assignment," Mr. O'Neal would insist from his lofty perch. Coming to attention beside our desk, trembling hands would seek out the appropriate pages after which one of us would falteringly begin reading our translation. God forbid if Mr. O'Neal's chosen victim had not done their homework. Cries of outrage would reverberate throughout the classroom as the condemned student was forced to slink back into his or her seat in a state of absolute disgrace. Quite frankly I'm not sure how I made it through Latin I & II, and I'm pretty sure Mr. O'Neal never figured it out either.

I did well in all my other classes except typing. "If you're going to go to college, you need to learn type," someone advised me, so I reluctantly signed up for the course. I can still see that mechanical monster resting on the table in front of me during my first day of class. "Don't look so glum," an attractive blond seated next to me said. "You'll get the hang of it real fast. I know did."

Who was she kidding, I thought to myself as I tried to imagine how my stubby fingers would ever scamper across the keyboard to create a formal letter. Class after class I pecked my way through one disastrous typing test after another. The ultimate dismal results left no doubt in my mind that I would be a complete failure as a secretary. Fortunately for me, my sympathetic typing instructor took pity on me and gave me a grade of C-. When I opened that report card, I expelled a large sigh of relief as I stared at that grade next to my As in Biology and English.

My high school years went by quickly and before I knew it I was making plans to go to college. During my last year of school I applied and was accepted to Wagner, Bloomfield State, and Fairleigh Dickinson University. All of them could give me the training I needed in the biological sciences but I couldn't afford to go to any of them. My parents had put aside some money to send me to college but the amount they'd saved was just enough to pay for one year. The question was where was I going to get enough money to pay for the remaining three years. In 1956, there was no student loan program that I was aware of, competition for scholarships was fierce, and I had no wealthy relatives. Once again it was time to sit down with my folks and see if we could come up with a solution.

Mom and Dad wanted me to go to Wagner. It was a nice school and it would have been my first choice, but there were problems. It was the most expensive of the three that I'd been accepted to and I would have to travel a good distance each day to get to my classes since I couldn't afford to live on campus. "You can work summers to pay for your tuition," Dad suggested as the three of us sat around the kitchen table mulling over my options.

I agreed with Dad, but in order to make enough money to pay for my tuition at any of the schools, I'd have to work during the school year as well as during the summer. During my last year at high school I had started to work part-time at the post office where I delivered mail and bagged postal packages at night. The job paid well and I wanted to keep it, but in order to do so I would have to select a school where I could work nights and weekends. This negated any chance of going to Wagner and Bloomfield State since both involved too much travel time. As a result, Fairleigh Dickinson seemed to be the logical choice. It was closer and easier to get to than the other two schools and I felt I could arrange my class schedule so I could get more hours at work. My parents understood my logic but were disappointed that I wouldn't be going to Wagner.

At the time I went to Fairleigh Dickenson the locals called it "Fairly Ridiculous." It acquired this name because nearly everybody who applied was accepted. I remember that the entrance exam was extremely easy—I don't think I answered one question incorrectly.

On the first day of school on the Teaneck campus over six hundred students gathered in the university's auditorium for an orientation. On that day we were told to take a good look at the students to the right and left of us because by the time we graduated they would no longer be with us. I have to admit that announcement got my attention and made me wonder if I was going to make the grade. It was also during this meeting that we were given the ground rules that we would have to abide by for the next four years. All male students would have to wear a jacket and tie to class. That rule didn't come as a shock since I was already doing this at St. Michaels, but the others were a bit of a surprise. No one was allowed to belong to a fraternity or a sorority. If you became a member of one of these organizations, you would be expelled from the university. In order to graduate you had to pass English Composition I & II with a grade of C or better. All tests and compositions submitted in any course had to be done using proper grammar and spelling. If a professor felt that a test or composition exhibited poor use of grammar and or spelling, the paper was given to a departmental committee for evaluation. If the paper didn't meet the standards for proper English, you were asked to take a test at the end of the year, and if you didn't pass the test, you were asked to repeat English Composition I & II. More than a few of my classmates wound up repeating English Composition I & II and some never did graduate.

The rule that was the biggest shock to me regarded work. No student was allowed to have even a part-time job while they were attending the university full-time. Work, they announced, interfered with your studies; subsequently any full-time student with a mandatory sixteen-hour credit load discovered working would be expelled from school. This really shook me up since there was no way I could pay for my education without working part-time.

After orientation I sat down with Dad to talk over things. "I don't know what to say," Dad said after I described the school's rule regarding work. "If they expel you from the university, you'll be drafted into the military before you get into another college. My advice is to keep your mouth shut and don't let anyone know what you're up to."

I followed through on Dad's advice but there were lots of dicey moments where I nearly got caught. One involved a weekend Genetics Lab. Without the help of my lab partner I would never have passed that course without someone finding out that I had a job.

My studies were also a lot more rigorous than I anticipated. Organic Chemistry during my sophomore year was described as a "weeder course." I had no idea what a "weeder course" was but it didn't take too long to find out. It was a course that separated those who were going to make the grade at the university from those who weren't. About sixty students enrolled in Organic Chemistry the year I took it and about fifteen of us got a passing grade. If I remember correctly, there was one A, three Bs and the rest of the passing grades were Cs. With a lot of sweat and sleepless nights I got a grade of B+.

The course that frightened me the most was English Composition I; it was a nightmare. I could feel my stomach churn every time I sat down in that classroom. Our instructor was an Irishman by the name of Kevin O'Sullivan who was convinced that none of us were capable of writing a decent essay. Every week we were given a writing assignment and every week we waited to find out which one of us would be identified as the most illiterate student. At the beginning of class papers were frequently tossed into the air as professor O'Sullivan stomped across the room shouting obscenities about our incompetence. Then, reaching into his briefcase, he would pull out the three worst compositions of the week and ask those students to go to the blackboard and write out a portion of their paper. "Who taught you to write?" he would ultimately snarl as our knees shook in anticipation of further scathing criticism. "Perhaps one of your classmates can improve upon your grammar."

None of us wanted to do that, but there was no place we could hide. Looking down at the floor, we cringed as we waited for one of our names to be called. "Perhaps you, David, can correct this insult to the English language." At this point David was told to come to the front of the room and correct the student's mistakes. "Tell us what is wrong with this paragraph," O'Sullivan would hiss. "Your classmates and I need to be enlightened." The silence that usually followed was unbearable. Trembling with the fear, the student who was selected seldom had the courage to speak out, at which point professor O'Sullivan would slam his hand against the desk and ask that the student speak out so we could all hear him. God forbid if the person selected couldn't correct the mistakes that confronted him or her. A scathing litany of derogatory abuse would be dumped upon them as professor O'Sullivan's banished them to their seat.

The crowning point of abuse came during a session in which Professor O'Sullivan declared that we were nothing more than a group of "babbling imbeciles." That day the highest grade anyone had received on a paper was D and that person, O'Sullivan declared, had received the grade out of the goodness of his heart. "All of you are a disgrace to this institution," he announced with a flurry of frustrated hand waving, "subsequently, your next assignment is to diagram the Gettysburg Address." Was he kidding? Everyone in the class looked at one another in disbelief. I still have nightmares about that assignment and the two weeks of torture we went through as each of us trudged to the blackboard and diagrammed a segment. It was the most humbling and humiliating activity I ever undertook.

Somehow I survived Professor O'Sullivan's course. But most of my classmates did not. No one got an A. Among thirty students there was one B, two Cs and the rest failed. I couldn't believe it, but when I looked at my grades for that semester I had received a C-.

I have to admit work did take its toll on my grade point average, but I did manage to graduate in four years. Of the six hundred plus students who started as freshmen on the Teaneck campus, fewer than one hundred made it to graduation. Eighty-three percent of my classmates had dropped out or were expelled from the university. I've often thought that perhaps another reason they called the school "Fairly Ridiculous" was because it was so ridiculously hard to graduate.

Deals and Wheels

In 1961, I finished my undergraduate studies at Fairleigh Dickenson University and decided I wanted to attend graduate school to study marine biology. I'd scored fairly well on my Graduate Record Exams but in order go to graduate school I needed to get financial assistance. When I wrote to the schools, most of them were interested in my application but none offered me a fellowship or teaching assistantship. They said before they could offer me monetary assistance I would have to complete courses in physics and a foreign language. This came as a surprise since my college advisor had never told me I needed to take these courses. To correct these deficiencies, I decided to attend night school, but it also meant that I would have to stay at home an extra year and work during the day. The plan involved some risk. The schools made no guarantee that I would receive financial support the following year, and if I didn't get financial assistance, I would be in the same situation I was in when I graduated college. Nevertheless, I thought it was a risk worth taking.

The biggest challenge I faced was getting my parents to agree that this was the right thing to do. I decided to approach this formidable task one evening just after dinner. As we sat down in the store I outlined my plan and waited to hear what Mom and Dad thought about my idea. At first neither one of them said anything, then Mom pursed her lips and shook her head. "What happened with that job the pharmaceutical company offered you?" she asked.

I explained that I didn't go four years to college to become a salesman—that I wanted to do something that was more meaningful and interesting.

"But it was a good paying job," she countered with a scowl. I told her that I knew that it was, but it wasn't very exciting. I anxiously watched as she gave a deep sigh, and looked over at

Dad. "I knew this would happen," she said angrily, "you're going to turn out to be a bum like every other man I've known."

I grimaced at that statement and wondered how Dad felt when she expressed her discontent. I responded by promising her things wouldn't be that way. If, after a year, I didn't get a scholarship, I would find a good job and move out.

"His idea seems alright to me," Dad said. "Why don't we give him a chance? If things don't work out, he's offered to find a good job." Mom shook her head in disgust and said she knew Dad would agree with me. She remained steadfastly convinced that no one was going to pay me to go to school and that my entire plan was doomed from the start. After several more hours of heated discussion in which Dad was very supportive, Mom finally relented and agreed to give me the year I requested.

One thing I didn't plan on when I decided to go to graduate school was the United States Military. My father had pointed this problem out when I suggested I continue my college education. Like every young man that reached eighteen years of age in the 50s and 60s I had to register with the draft board and be prepared to go on active duty. Theoretically, no one avoided the draft. Once you were eighteen you had a number of options: get drafted after high school and serve two years in the military, enlist, go to college and receive a deferment for as long as you were in school full-time and then serve your two years, or leave the country.

Since I had already gone to college for four years and graduated, it was time for me to step up and do my patriotic duty. However, it was my hope that I could complete my coursework and get into graduate school before they served my draft notice. Nice thought, but it didn't work. Several months after I started night school Dad handed me a letter from the draft board. It was not the most auspicious day in my life. It informed me that in a week I was to report for my induction physical into the armed forces.

President Kennedy had made a campaign pledge to increase the number of men serving in the armed forces, and our local draft board was hard pressed to meet its quota. At the time I was growing up in the city many of the draft-age men came from families who had immigrated to the city from the island of Puerto Rico. A large number of these young people could not speak English and many had serious health problems. Subsequently, when I boarded the bus to get my induction physical in Newark I found myself surrounded by dozens of frightened young men filling out papers in a language they didn't understand. On the day I reported, dozens of buses were parked outside the armory with hundreds of young people from different parts of the state. All of us were herded into a huge gym where we were examined by a bevy of doctors to see if we were fit to serve. A good number of the young men from Puerto Rico were rejected immediately because of health issues. Another portion was rejected because they could not read, write, or understand English. By the time I was ordered into a second room to take the intelligence test, I would estimate that only fifty percent of us remained. After the written exam, that number was reduced to approximately thirty percent.

When I got back home that afternoon I told Dad I'd passed my physical and was expecting to be called up in about two weeks. He asked me if I had told the military I was still going to school. "I did," I replied, but they informed me since I had passed my physical and was not attending school full-time my only option was to serve two years. Shaking his head, Dad suggested I think about signing up with another branch of the military. "Sometimes you can cut a deal with one of them and they'll let you finish school before you go on active duty."

Dad's suggestion seemed the best solution so I immediately began talking to recruiters. Fourteen days remained on the clock. If I didn't resolve the problem within that period, I would spend the next two years of my life as an Army "grunt." First I tried the Air Force. Rejected. My eyesight was too poor and I had some color vision problems. Next I tried the Coast Guard. Rejected. They dismissed me for the same reasons as the Air Force.

"How about the Navy?" Dad asked. So I went to their recruiting office and discussed my situation.

"Let's see," they said. "Poor vision and color recognition problems; there's not much we can offer you. However, we do have a security division in Jersey City you can sign up with. It's a reserve outfit and you'd be able to finish graduate school before going on active duty."

What luck, I thought. With two days to spare before I was about to become an Army "grunt," I signed up with the Navy and became a "swabby." That winter and spring I passed my night courses in physics and French and during the summer I was shipped off to boot camp at Great Lakes in Chicago. Dad drove me to the airport and wished me well. His parting words were to keep my mouth shut and do whatever they told me. "You'll be fine," he added, "just don't step out of line."

I have to admit boot camp was a real eye opener. I had no problems enduring the rigorous training they put me through, but living with some of my future shipmates was entirely a different matter. My third day in camp I met two seamen who were lapping up the contents of two large tubes of toothpaste. At first I thought it was some kind of punishment they'd been assigned by their drill instructor, but one of them told me that they loved to eat the toothpaste because it tasted great. "We have nothing like it where we come from," they announced. When I left they were squeezing the last drop of paste from their tube while making plans to get back to the ship's store before it closed.

Then there was Ralph. He said he had a girlfriend back home and couldn't stop thinking about her. Whenever Ralph jumped into his rack at night he placed a condom over his penis and masturbated. Ralph's pumping and grunting seemed to go on for an eternity. Finally, the drill instructor put him on the midnight watch so we didn't have to listen to him anymore.

Perhaps the weirdest person I encountered was in the mess hall. I remember sitting across from him and starting up a conversation when all of a sudden he started stabbing himself with the cutting edge of a knife. I couldn't imagine what this guy was thinking. But when I attempted to stop him he grinned at me and shoved my hand away. "I enjoy feeling pain," he said. When I mentioned his behavior to the drill instructor he told me not to get too excited. "He's only trying to get a medical discharge. I see that kind of stuff all the time."

When I got home from boot camp Dad handed me a letter from the University of Delaware informing me that I'd been accepted into graduate school and that I had received a teaching assistantship and summer fellowship to pay for my education. That Sunday my parents held a big party in my honor and invited all of their friends over to share in the good news. I suppose the thing I was most grateful about was that I wouldn't be sharing the mess hall with a knife stabber or listening to Ralph pump and grunt in the upper bunk. Unfortunately, I was a bit too hasty with those assumptions.

Now that I had gotten into graduate school I needed to buy a car so I could travel from the University's main campus in Newark to its marine labs in Lewes. Young people today can't wait to pass their driver's test and own a car. When I was growing up I seldom thought about owning my own car. First of all, I never had enough money to buy a car, and even if I did I wasn't going to be able to afford the insurance. On a few occasions I did drive Dad's car to and from school but busses were my main mode of transportation. As far as I was concerned it was a real nuisance to own a car in the city. Finding a "safe" place to park it on the street was never easy. If you parked it a couple of blocks from where you lived, you might come back the next day and find your tires gone and the windows smashed.

Winter snow and ice storms were also a problem. A heavy snowstorm of six to ten inches meant you had to clear the snow from around your car so you could drive to work. Often after you did, the city would plow the streets and push all the snow back into the spot you'd just cleared. Then there was the daily fluctuation in temperature. During the day the air temperature would often rise causing the ice and snow on your car to melt. Then at night the temperature would plummet and the melted snow would refreeze. This meant that every morning you had to scrape away a new layer of ice on your windows so you could see where you were going. In addition you had to solve the problem of the car lock. If the water froze in the lock, you needed to find some way to unfreeze it. Sometimes people would use their bodies to block the wind while they used a cigarette lighter to melt the ice. Dad used to boil water, put it into a closed container, and then hike down two flights of stairs to pour the hot water over the outside of the frozen mechanism.

Snow chains were a must for driving on icy roadways. If you didn't have them, there was good chance you'd get stuck or lose control of the car and bounce off some other vehicle. Of course you didn't want to drive with chains on until after it snowed which meant that you had to install them after the winter storm had passed. Needless to say that was a miserable process. The chains were heavy, the wind would frequently whip up the snow so you couldn't see, your hands became numb, and the mucus pouring out of your nose would form icicles.

After you cleared away the snow and put your snow chains on the next challenge was to drive to work. On went the car heater to keep warm. Next the windshield wipers were put into motion so you could see through the wind driven snow. Now the adrenalin kicked in causing your heart rate and blood pressure to rise as you slithered precariously towards your destination. If you were lucky, you didn't encounter too many accidents, and if you weren't, your car became a pinball that bounced from one stalled vehicle to the next. Ultimately, a drive that normally would take ten minutes might wind up taking an hour.

In Dad's case, when we lived across town from where the store was located, it meant he had to get up early so he could look for a cleared parking spot close to the store. This was no easy feat because it meant "stealing" an open space from someone who had just cleared it and gone to work. In the city, people often guarded these spots with bulldog tenacity. Children were sent out to watch over them and make sure that no one would "steal" them while their father was gone, and if you tried to drive into one, his wife and children would sometimes step into the cleared space and dare you to run over them. Even when you found a spot you could steal, your worries weren't over. The former occupants would frequently become outraged with your thievery and wreak vengeance upon your car. Aerials were broken, keys were used to scratch the paint, and sometimes people would go so far as to poke holes in your tires.

I suppose you can say that in some ways, besides the fact that I couldn't afford car insurance, it was because of all the negative experiences Dad had with his car that I didn't want to own one. Now I had no choice. The day of reckoning had arrived and I needed to take the plunge.

While I was working and going to school at night I managed to save $700. This, as it turned out, was close to the amount I needed to purchase a second-hand car in 1961. Dad said he would help me pick one out, so off we went to see what was available. We spent several days with car salesmen talking about cars and negotiating prices. Everyone said they had just the right car for me. I wanted to buy an automatic because it was the type of car that I had learned to drive, but none of the dealers had one for $700. Ultimately, I bought a Fiat. "It's a great car," the salesman declared. "It has four new tires, and I'll make sure it's in tip-top shape before it leaves the dealership." What he didn't tell me was that the person that sold it to him never wanted to see the car again.

The plan was to have me learn how to drive a stick shift before I took off for Delaware. Days went by but we never heard a word from the dealership about the car. Calls were made and excuses given, but still no car. Finally, the day before I had to leave, the dealership called and said my car was ready to be picked up. Dad was not too happy with the whole scenario and said he would go to Delaware with me and teach me how to drive the car on the way down—not exactly the type of driving lesson I was hoping to get, but at this point I didn't have a choice.

After a sleepless night I wedged my body into the front seat of my "new" Fiat and placed my sweaty hands on the steering wheel. Dad pointed out where the clutch, brake, and gas pedal were and informed me that I would need to press on the clutch whenever I shifted gears. This car had five forward gears and that meant that I had to press it four times before I got to cruising speed. The suppressed moan I elicited after Dad finished his initial instructions did not go unnoticed by my father who patted me on the shoulder and told me I'd do fine. On went the ignition and down went the clutch as I shifted into first gear.

"Now gradually release the clutch and press on the gas pedal," Dad said as the car catapulted out of the parking spot. Further words of encouragement followed as the gears ground into one another and I lurched along Bergenline Avenue. About halfway through the city I realized that this experience was just as bad for Dad as it was for me. Beads of sweat had formed on his forehead and several times he cringed as we approached oncoming traffic.

Once out on the highway things went a lot better; that was until we reached Wilmington, Delaware. It was there that I encountered my most formidable obstacle—a hill. With an automatic car all I had to do when I got to a red light at the top of a hill was put my foot on the brake. With this car I had to slow the car with the brake, down shift with the clutch, and keep my position on the hill by maintaining equal amounts of foot pressure on the clutch and gas pedal. Without thinking, when I got to the top of the hill I hit the break and the car lurched forward and stalled. Now what was I going to do? "Put the car into neutral and turn on the ignition," Dad said as he wiped his brow, "then shift into first gear and press on the gas."

Was he kidding, I thought to myself? After starting the car and shifting into first gear, I tentatively pressed on the gas peddle. Thump went the car and off went the ignition. Now the car started to roll back down the hill. Quickly looking down the hill to see what traffic was approaching, Dad shouted, "Try it again, only this time give it more gas."

Again I tried to follow Dad's instructions and again the car stalled. Soon we were surrounded by all kinds of traffic coming up the hill. Horns honked, cars swerved, and my foot remained permanently glued to the brake. All I could do was cringe and close my eyes hoping no one would hit us.

I don't know if all Dads would have handled the car situation the way mine did, but I was forever thankful for the way he took charge. Reaching across the front seat, he placed his hand firmly on my shoulder and said in a calm voice, "I know you're scared, but neither one of us are going to make it off this hill unless you gas this car after you shift it into gear." Then, step-by-step, he slowly repeated the procedures I needed to follow in order to get that car over the hill. It was a lesson well learned, and after that I never had another problem with hills.

One thing I could always depend upon while I was living in Delaware was that my Fiat would break down. Once while driving back from Wilmington the fly bolt holding my carburetor together snapped in two causing my car to sputter to a halt. After looking under the hood I quickly identified the problem and felt sure I could fix it without too much difficulty. All I needed to do was purchase another fly bolt and screw it on the carburetor. So off I hiked to the nearest gas station where I told the mechanic what I needed. "I'm sorry," he replied, "we don't sell parts for foreign cars. You'll have to call up the dealer that sold you your vehicle and see if they have the part you're looking for."

Knowing that I wasn't about to get the car fixed that evening, I hiked back to the Fiat, locked it up, and left a note on the windshield explaining what had happened. The next day I called up the car dealership and asked if they could send me the part.

"No," they responded, "we don't have the part you're looking for. You'll have to pick one up from a Fiat dealer."

"And where was the nearest Fiat dealership?" I asked.

"I think there's one in Newark."

"Delaware?"

"No, New Jersey, but I'd call first to find out if they're still in business."

Great I thought. Picking up the phone I called the number they gave me and asked the company if they had the part. "Sure," the supply parts person responded "do you want me to mail it to you?"

"How long will that take?" I asked.

"Maybe a week."

A week!! Was he kidding? They'd tow my car away before it arrived. Next I called Dad up and asked if he could help me out. He said he'd pick up the fly bolt and give it to a friend who was headed my way. A couple of days passed before it arrived and I couldn't thank the person enough for delivering it. Then I asked if he'd mind driving me out to my car. Fortunately, the car was still where I left it, but the police had placed a friendly note on it saying they planned to tow it in a few days if I didn't pick it up soon.

Most of the problems I had with the Fiat dealt with its electrical system. For no apparent reason the car would simply stop running while I was driving down the highway. None of the mechanics in Delaware seemed to know how to fix it so I had to drive it back to the dealership in New Jersey. Every time I picked it up they told me that they'd solved the problem and that the car was as good as new. Who were they kidding? As soon as I got the car back to Delaware it would break down again. Ultimately, more frustrated calls were made to New Jersey, and during exam week I had to have Dad pick up the car in Lewes and drive it back home after it stalled on the road for the tenth time. As far as I was concerned I never wanted to see the car again. Another two months passed while the dealership worked on it. This time they swore that the car would be as good a new. There was no way I believed that, so I told Dad to sell the car to anyone who would give him $500.00. After checking around, Dad found a college student who needed a car and was willing to pay my price. I must admit I felt guilty about selling it to him, but overjoyed with the fact that I'd no longer have to deal with this pile of junk.

Strange Encounters

While I was going to graduate school, life for my parents began changing for the worse. They continued to work long hours but the amount of profit they made steadily declined. Dad blamed their problems on the large outlet malls that were springing up along the highways. He said people weren't hanging around the city on the weekends making purchases from local businesses. He said the outlet stores could buy large quantities of merchandise and sell it a lot cheaper than he and Mom could.

It was the money my parents made from the numbers racket that kept them in business. Besides the decline in store sales, Dad said other changes were taking place. Drugs had begun to make their way into the city and there was a lot more violence on the streets. He was particularly concerned about Mom, who refused to give up work as a bag lady, saying if she gave it up they wouldn't be able to make ends meet. Dad offered to get a second job, but Mom said no; she didn't think she could handle the store by herself anymore.

Meanwhile, I was glad to be out of the city. I really enjoyed graduate school even though the course work was rigorous. For the first time I was able to do research, which turned out to be something I really loved. What I didn't like was living off campus in the same house with Rainey. Rainey was a graduate student in the history department at the university working on his master's degree. He was also a self-proclaimed Nazi.

The day I dropped Dad off at the train station and drove back to my new residence in Newark, Rainey greeted me at the front door. "Heil Hitler," he announced as he peered at me through thick glasses, clicked his heels together, and raised his right hand. "I understand I'll be living with a f___ing Jew" Was this guy for real I thought to myself as I stared back at this slender unshaven creature with my mouth agape? Just what I needed—I'd graduated from a person who enjoyed self-mutilation to a person who pictured himself as a member of the master race. I probably should have smacked Rainey in the face when we first met but I decided against it. It just wasn't the way I wanted to begin graduate school.

After I gave Rainey an earful about my low opinion of the master race he reluctantly allowed me to contaminate "his" domicile. Later in the week when I called home I told Dad about Rainey. He suggested I stay as far away from him as possible. It was interesting advice but I knew I wasn't going to accomplish this since we both lived in the same house. Fortunately, Rainey's and my schedules didn't coincide so we mostly saw one another when we were entering and leaving the house. However, our landlady, Mrs. Tasker, had to put up with him on a daily basis. According to Rainey, she was a wimpy, inferior human being whose sole purpose in life was to serve people like him.

I don't know why Mrs. Tasker tolerated Rainey; there was definitely something weird going on between the two of them. One day when I came back to the house I heard Mrs. Tasker crying out for help. Her shouts were coming from the kitchen so I raced to the back of the house to see if I could be of assistance. When I got there I found her tied to a kitchen chair. My first thought was that she had been robbed, so I ran over and asked her if she was all right.

"I'm fine," she sobbed as tears rolled down her chubby face.

"Who did this to you?"

"Rainey."

"Why?" I stammered.

"I forgot to clean his clothes," she grimaced as she struggled to free her hands.

"I'm going to call the police," I said as I untied her and started towards the phone.

"No. Don't do that," she begged. "It'll only make things worse."

No matter what I did I couldn't convince her that she would be better off if she would let me contact the police. At one point she even got down on her knees and pleaded with me not to do it. I finally relented, but I told her I was going to talk to Rainey about what he'd done. When Rainey got back to the house I pulled him aside and asked what the hell he thought he was doing tying up an old woman because she didn't clean his clothes. He informed me it was none of my business. "She needed to be taught a lesson. I told her I needed freshly pressed clothes because I was teaching today and she didn't do it." I couldn't believe what he was saying to me. I told him that if it happened again I was going to call the police. My threat appeared to work, but several days later Mrs. Tasker pulled me aside at the bottom of the stairs and told me I shouldn't have said anything to him because it made Rainey very mad.

Rainey got his master's degree at Delaware and went on to teach. I don't know who hired him, but I often wonder what thoughts he planted into the minds of the young people he came in contact with.

Another issue I had to deal with while I was going to graduate school was the Navy. When I moved to Delaware the reserve division in Jersey City told me that I would be reassigned to an outfit in Wilmington. Unfortunately, the papers from Jersey City never arrived in Delaware. When the Wilmington division informed me of this I called Dad and asked him if he could find out what was going on. After contacting the reserve unit in Jersey City he discovered that my papers had been sent to Wilmington, North Carolina, not Wilmington, Delaware. As a result, when I didn't show up in North Carolina the Navy officially listed me as AWOL and sent out the Shore Patrol to find me. Fortunately, the mix up with my papers was straightened out before I spent my first week of graduate school in the brig.

It was while I was doing my reserve duty in Wilmington that the Navy passed along another piece of "good" news. There was no security division in Delaware. This meant that instead of taking a test to become a Petty Officer Third Class, I was demoted to Seaman Apprentice and placed in the deck division. By the time I left Delaware with my master's degree I had regained the rate of Seaman in the deck division, but I had no hope of becoming a Petty Officer, in part because there was no rate in oceanography and in part because of problems I had with my eyesight.

Initially, I expected to go on active duty after I graduated, but to my surprise I was told I wasn't going to report for duty until September. This put me in a bit of a bind. What exactly was I going to do between June and September? I hated the idea of moving back to the city and I didn't want to burden my parents by moving in with them. Fortunately, my graduate school advisor came to the rescue and offered me a job at the university marine lab during the intervening period.

When I finally reported in September, I knew there was a good chance that I would be shipped out to the Pacific because of the Vietnam War. I remember arriving at the receiving station in Philadelphia wondering what kind of ship I would be assigned to. After the usual rounds of physicals and paper work I reported to a huge transit area where I was told I would be given my assignment. There must have been a hundred guys sitting in that room waiting to receive their orders. Squeaky fans pushed stale, humid air, and a lot of anxious conversations filled the room. Everyone wanted to know where they were going and what ship they would be serving on. These murmurs came to an abrupt halt when a smartly dressed Chief Gunner's Mate with mirror-polished black shoes stepped to the front of the room with a clipboard. In a gruff voice dozens of names were called out in alphabetical order; the last twenty were assigned to an aircraft carrier headed for a shakedown cruise at Guantanamo Bay, Cuba. My name was next on the list. Sweat formed on my brow as I waited for it to be called. "Schmelz, G. W." That was me. I felt sick to my stomach as I stood up and anxiously walked towards the tiny cubicle where my orders were waiting.

"Survey ship, Philadelphia," a clerk with thick glasses announced as I stood outside his narrow cubicle.

Philadelphia? My homeport was going to be in Philadelphia? I couldn't believe it.

"Are you alright, son?" the clerk asked as he looked over at me. I guess he thought I was about to faint.

"Sure. I'm fine," I stammered. "Where's she located?"

"Not too far from here. She's at the main dock. Her name's the *San Pablo*. I'd hurry on down there if I were you. She's scheduled to leave shortly for Puerto Rico."

The *San Pablo* was an old seaplane tender that had been converted into a "research" vessel, but her primary mission was to survey the ocean bottom and determine where cables could be laid to detect Russian nuclear submarines. Besides having a large complement of military personnel, the ship also carried a small contingent of civilians from Suitland, Maryland, and corporations like Texas Instrument. My job, as it turned out, was to help these people with their survey work and to make sure that all of the equipment they needed was safely on board before we left port.

I enjoyed the work, but it was labor intensive. In port, last minute changes in our plans often made it difficult to get the equipment we needed and a lot of juggling had to be undertaken before we left on a mission. At sea, when we were running transducers off the ship's fantail to generate images of the ocean bottom, we often spent days without getting much sleep. I'm not sure how I survived these ordeals. After forty-eight hours with no sleep it was hard to concentrate. I can remember a number of occasions when I stumbled up and down ladders barely conscious of what I was doing. And when I couldn't bear it anymore I hid in the ship's dirty laundry bags to take a catnap.

A shipmate came up to me one day and said that he thought he would rather be in prison than serve on the *San Pablo*. And there were times when I thought he might be right. Our entire division was bunked above the ship's refrigerators near the fantail. In the Navy they're called reefers. All of the perishable food we brought on board was stored in these compartments and it was the job of the mess cooks to keep them clean. However, the cooks never seemed to do an adequate job, especially when we were at sea. Food would often collect beneath the metal grates and, after several weeks, the spillage would begin to rot. It was like sleeping above a garbage dump. The odor was so rank it would have made a seagull vomit. Even though everyone complained about the smell we had no choice but to live with it until we reached port and the cooks scrubbed the compartments down. By then the odor from the reefers had seeped into everything. Even our hair stank of rotting food. Some guys went AWOL after spending their first tour of duty aboard our ship, but I wasn't about to do anything that stupid. When liberty was announced and we were in a foreign port, I hit the streets and checked into the nearest hotel. You can't believe what a luxury that hotel's shower was. For the first half hour I just stood underneath that stream of hot water rubbing my skin raw.

Cockroaches were also a problem. At night they would crawl out of the ship's insulation and scamper across your body while you were sleeping. Those of us who occupied the upper bunks tried to sleep with our mouths shut otherwise the obnoxious creatures would topple from the overhead pipes into our mouths. You can take it from someone who knows—these pests were not the tastiest morsels to sink your teeth into. To this day I still have nightmares about swallowing one of them.

Perhaps the most dehumanizing aspect of life aboard the *San Pablo* was the "head." For those who've never served aboard a ship, the "head" is what you would commonly call the restroom. If I could, I would get up thirty minutes before *reveille* to beat everyone else to the head. Sometimes, because of the watch schedule, this wasn't possible. Whenever this happened, I was forced to share the head with twenty other guys all of whom anxiously waited in line to relieve themselves. As quickly as possible, I'd search for an open stall, plop my butt on a not so sterile doughnut hole, and pretend not to listen to the grunts of my constipated fellow sailors. Common courtesy called for us to immediately flush the toilet after we did our "job," and if we didn't, a barrage of raunchy expletives was directed at us about the foul odor. Whenever I had to go through this ordeal I kept thinking about that wonderful hotel I was going to visit during my next liberty and how much I was going to enjoy its amenities and privacy.

Besides having to endure the ship's daily routine, we had to coexist with some very bizarre crew members. Most of my shipmates were hard-working crewmen that I was proud to serve with, but there were some I'm sure were recruited from Folsom Prison. Take the deck division's chief petty officer—he often bullied new recruits and if they gave him any guff, he dragged them off to the rope locker and raped them. Occasionally one of the recruits would successfully fend him off after which he made their lives miserable by assigning them scutt work that included cleaning up latrines. Then there were people like "B.T."—B.T. was all muscle and had the body configuration of a gorilla. He was very proud of the fact that he had a ten-inch penis and would show it off to anyone who was interested and some who weren't. When I asked B.T. why he joined the Navy, he said that he didn't have a "f___ing choice;" the cops had found him raping two men in the back of his truck, and when he went to court the judge gave him the choice of going to prison or signing up for the military. "What the f___," he said to me one day, "why wouldn't I sign up? There is more tender meat here than I'd ever find in civilian life." It was hard for me to believe that a judge would have such little foresight, but if there's one thing I learned, in life nothing is beyond the realm of possibility. For B.T. it was like putting the fox in the hen house.

One day while we were standing at quarters for inspection, B.T. arrived late and half-dressed. When the Lieutenant spotted him he stepped in front of B.T. and told him he was a disgrace to the Navy. B.T. then came to attention, saluted the officer and said, "Sir, although you're dressed in silks so fine your asshole smells the same as mine." For this breech of naval etiquette, B.T. was put on report and made to serve the final two months of his naval career mess cooking. After we were dismissed from quarters I pulled B.T. aside and asked him why he sassed the lieutenant. "What the f___," he replied, "it was worth being put on report just to see the look on his face."

It was during my last year of active duty that I encountered my second Nazi. It was hard to believe that they allowed him to enlist in the Navy and even more difficult to understand why they promoted him to Petty Officer Third Class before his first assignment at sea. After settling aboard ship he proudly announced to me that he had read every piece of Nazi literature he could lay his hands on and was convinced that all the "niggers" on board our ship should be exterminated. Needless to say he was not loved by our black crewmembers, and shortly after he arrived he was assigned to mess cooking where he complained bitterly about having to serve members of an inferior race.

One thing I can say about my tour of duty, I did get to visit a lot of unique places and see a lot of interesting things. While in the North Atlantic I encountered my first polar bear. It happened on one of those rare, calm days with just enough wind to keep the fog from settling. When I first spotted the bear it was standing on a small platform of ice anxiously watching us approach. As soon as we intruded into its comfort zone it slipped into the icy water and started swimming away. The animal was huge and I was glad I was not sharing its domain. The last I saw of the bear, it had climbed up on the arctic ice shelf and was sauntering across the frozen landscape towards some unknown destination known only to bears.

Killer whales occasionally visited us when we were collecting water samples with Nansen bottles. I remember one day standing on the survey platform ready to release a lead weight when two of them began swimming under the fantail of our ship. They seemed to be quite curious about what we were doing and each time they ducked under the platform they would turn on their sides and look up at me. Even though they might have been trying to determine if I was something worth eating, I enjoyed watching these sleek creatures performing their aquatic acrobatics just a few feet beneath my workstation.

Another unusual encounter occurred while we were collecting water samples over the Puerto Rican Trench. It happened at night during the month of October. The floodlights erected on the fantail had attracted a large population of squid. Some of the animals were two to three feet long and most of them were actively feeding on fish that had also been attracted to the surface by our lights. During this feeding frenzy, I was instructed to drop our Nansen bottles to the fifteen hundred meter level to collect water samples. Everything went according to plan until I tried to retrieve the bottles. When I put our large hydraulic winch into gear the bottles simply wouldn't budge, and the winch began to groan under the tension as I tried to pull up the bottles. I knew the water was far too deep for them to be stuck on the ocean floor, but they were definitely hung up on something. When the winch failed to retrieve the bottles on the second try I called the bridge and asked them to move the ship forward at about seven knots.

"What's going on down there?" the officer on the bridge asked.

"I'm not sure, sir. It appears that our Nansen bottles are either hung up on something or something has grabbed hold of them."

"They can't be hung up on the bottom," the officer replied. "We're over the Puerto Rican Trench and the water is nearly five miles deep. Are you sure you're not hung up on the prop?"

"I'm sure we're not, sir. The wire is hanging straight down."

"Is the winch broken?"

"No, sir, it's not. I just had the ship's mechanics look at it."

"All right. We'll move ahead at seven knots. But let me know when the bottles are free."

"Aye, aye, sir."

Several minutes went by before the wire slackened. After contacting the bridge to let them know we were free, I engaged the winch and began retrieving the bottles. Everyone on the fantail, including me, was anxious to see what had happened. What we pulled out of the ocean left us with our mouths agape. All of the Nansen bottles were clumped together and intertwined among them was the twenty-foot arm of a giant squid. Since everything we did was classified I don't know if this discovery was ever reported to the scientific community, but I do know one thing— there are definitely giant squid living in the Puerto Rican Trench.

During my tour of duty I also got to see some dramatic natural wonders: calving glaciers off Greenland, huge icebergs drifting along the arctic ice shelf, and erupting volcanoes. Perhaps the most phantasmagoric event I witnessed was the eruption of Surtsey's sister volcano off the coast of Iceland. It happened during the 1964 geophysical year. I remember reaching the volcano at night, gliding through a sea of pumice that was floating on an ocean of bioluminescence. Over our heads wavy ribbons of multicolored lights from the aurora borealis snaked their way across the sky while large balls of molten lava were being jettisoned from the bowels of the ocean. We weren't allowed to have any cameras, but I would have loved to have had one that evening. It was a photographic moment I'm sure I'll never see again.

Several times while I was on active duty I went back home to see how my folks were doing. The city still smelled the same but it was a lot more congested than I remembered. I didn't talk too much about my life aboard ship. I suspected Dad knew why. I'm not sure Mom and the rest of my relatives would have believed some of the stories I had to tell anyway. I also noticed that there was a lot more activity in the streets at night than when I was growing up. One evening I remember being woken up by a loud commotion outside the saloon across from the apartment building where my parents lived. When I looked out the window I saw two guys beating up on a young man who had just left the bar. Despite my parents' protestations I went down to see if I could help him out. By the time I got there he was lying in the street half-conscious and the two guys that had attacked him had fled. Blood was running from their victim's nose and there was a large gash across his forehead. I tried to get him to go back inside the saloon but he refused. The last I saw of him he was staggering down the street with my handkerchief tied around his head.

Dad said a lot more stuff like that was happening over at the bar, especially on Friday and Saturday nights. Mom wanted to move out of the building, but they couldn't afford a new place. For the first time I began to worry about what might happen to my folks if they stayed where they were. I had escaped, but it was a different story for them. Their whole life was tied up with the store, and for the moment there was no place else for them to go.

One of the best things that happened to me when I was in the Navy was meeting my future wife Bernice. Bernice was a language arts teacher who had attended Trenton State College. We got together through the efforts of mutual friends and met on a blind date in New York City. It wasn't love at first sight, but we courted less than six months before we began making plans to get married.

Unfortunately, the Navy wasn't too keen about my wedding plans and when I requested weekend leave to tie the knot it was rejected. "Why?" I asked my division head when he passed along the news. After giving me a sympathetic look, he just shrugged his shoulders and ordered me to see the base Chaplin. The next day, I found myself standing outside the Chaplin's door for half an hour before he invited me into his office to give me a forty-five minute lecture on the pitfalls of marriage. When he finished, he stood up, placed his hand on my shoulder and asked me to reconsider. "Think of what it would be like if they ship you out to the Vietnam. It will be hard on the two of you."

Actually, we had thought about what the circumstances would be like if I were shipped off to Nam, but decided to go ahead with our plans anyway. So that Thursday, without witnesses or family, Bernice and I headed to Elkton, Maryland, where a justice of the peace married us. It was not the kind of wedding we hoped to have and I certainly didn't look forward to spending my honeymoon aboard ship but in the end everything worked out just fine.

Lewes Episodes

During my tour of active duty I pretty much made up my mind that I wanted to return to graduate school and get my doctorate in marine biology. When on leave I talked it over with Dad and he agreed it was a good idea. My chances of getting a good job were better with the advanced degree as were my odds of finding a job I really liked.

Near the end of my tour I applied for an early release so I could go back to school. In April of 1966, I was admitted into the doctoral program at the University of Delaware, and in June, I was given an early release from active duty. My parents and Bernice were elated with my good fortune since America's involvement in the Vietnam War was intensifying and they were very concerned that my tour might be extended.

As Bernice and I left Philadelphia and headed south towards Lewes, we chatted happily about the future and I announced how anxious I was to return to my studies and resume a "normal" life. No more sharing the head with ten other guys or listening to B.T. boast about his manhood. Bernice had picked out a cozy apartment near the University's marine lab and I was ready to move in and relax. Everything went fine for the first couple of weeks and then strange things began to happen. One evening when I was headed out to our car to pick up a package, our landlady invited me on to her porch. She said she wanted to tell me something and was hoping I could spare a moment. When I came in she introduced me to one of her male neighbors and proceeded to tell me what a handsome young man I was. I was a little embarrassed by her comments, but in order to be polite I said I was glad she thought so and proceeded to leave. At that point she grabbed my arm and invited me to sit down and have a drink. Now I got antsy. I had no idea what her neighbor thought about the situation. All I wanted to do was get out of there before something unpleasant took place. The trick was how to do it without creating a scene.

"Thanks for the offer," I replied while tactfully removing her hand from my arm, "but my wife and I are planning to go out for the evening."

"What a pity," she sighed as she brushed back her hair, "but any time you'd like to sit down and have a drink, please feel free to stop by."

Back in the apartment, I told Bernice what had happened and she suggested maybe the woman had too much to drink. Maybe, I thought to myself, but I wasn't so sure alcohol was her problem. She seemed really offended when I removed her hand and I could tell by her disappointed expression that she wasn't going to give up easily.

The next incident happened when I was at work at the marine lab. The gas for our stove had run out so Bernice contacted our landlady hoping that she'd replenish the fuel. Annoyed by Bernice's request, the woman stomped into the apartment, strode over to the oven, and placed her hands upon her hips. "What's the problem, dear?" she inquired as she glared at Bernice.

"The oven ran out of fuel," my wife replied as she anxiously looked at the woman.

"Don't be ridiculous, my dear, the woman scoffed as she bent over the stove. "It has plenty of gas and I'll prove it to you." Lighting a match, the landlady lowered it over the gas outlet, and smugly announced that everything was working just fine.

"But there's no flame on the stove," Bernice responded.

"There certainly is," the woman said indignantly, " I don't know what's wrong with your eyesight, but I can see it quite clearly."

When I came home Bernice was visibly shaken by what had happened. "She became very upset when I told her I couldn't see the flame and there was nothing I could do to convince her that there wasn't any gas in the stove."

At this point we realized that our landlady had some serious mental health issues. Dealing with unusual people in the Navy was one thing, but dealing with a mentally challenged landlady was something else entirely. After talking it over, Bernice and I decided it was time for us to start looking for another place. Our decision was reinforced when the landlady introduced us to her own version of the midnight horror show. It started several days after the gas stove incident. Bernice and I had gone to sleep at eleven, and about an hour later loud organ music began reverberating from the landlady's upstairs apartment. It reminded me of those ominous renditions you hear during a vampire movie and continued for hours. Neither of us slept as the music droned on. Then it suddenly stopped. Now what? We didn't have to wait too long for our answer. Footsteps creaked across the floorboards followed by the turning of a doorknob. The door to the upstairs porch opened and for a brief moment it was absolutely silent. Was our landlady coming down to pay us a visit? What would we do if she did? Next a series of gunshots rang out. My God, I thought, she's going to kill us. As we reached for our clothes, the neighborhood dogs began to bark and the door to the upstairs apartment slammed shut. By now both of us were wondering if we would escape with our lives. Nothing else happened that night and the next day we thought about calling the police. After thinking it over, however, we decided our landlady would deny everything and the police would suggest we find another place to live. It took us nearly a week but we finally found new living quarters. The owners seemed normal and the apartment was nice, so we gave them a month's deposit and told them we'd move in as soon as possible. Now all we needed to do was get out of our current accommodations without getting killed.

Just when we thought things couldn't get worse, they did. On the third evening of organ music, our landlady marched down the stairs and unlocked the door between her house and our bedroom. Shocked by her sudden appearance, Bernice and I jumped out of the bed and asked what she was doing. "I wanted to see you," she grinned as she headed toward me. This woman is crazy I thought. Insisting that she get out of our bedroom and give me the key, the landlady glared at us and dangled the room key on her finger. "I don't think so," the woman smiled sweetly, "it's my house and you have no right to ask for it." Now what should I do I thought as I looked over at Bernice. I had no idea whether our landlady was harboring a weapon, so I changed my tactic and suggested we'd talk in the morning. She reluctantly agreed and left with the key.

"Suppose she changes her mind comes back later?" Bernice asked.

I hadn't thought of that, but Bernice was right; we needed to find some way of keeping her out of our bedroom. "Let's tie a rope from the bedpost to the doorknob." Searching through the apartment, we found an old clothesline and secured it to the bed. That night neither of us slept, fearing another invasion by our gun-toting landlady, and when the morning came I hesitantly paid her a visit.

"Come in," she said sweetly as I knocked on the door. "It's so nice of you to join me for breakfast." Taking a chair across from her, I accepted a cup of coffee and asked if she could see her way to letting us have the key to our bedroom. Smiling across the table she apologized for her behavior and said she'd think about it. I told her I'd appreciate that and made a hasty retreat to talk to Bernice about speeding up our plans to move.

Finding the right day to move out proved to be a challenge. Bernice was convinced that the woman would shoot us if she saw us packing. So we waited for the landlady to leave the house. It took several days, but when Bernice spotted her driving off with some packages, she called me at the marine lab. As fast as I could, I drove to the house to pick up our belongings and pack the car. Fortunately for us, our escape proved uneventful and from that day forward we never had a problem with our living arrangements in Lewes. And, I'm grateful to report, we never again met up with our night roaming, gun-toting organist.

During my first summer in Lewes as a doctoral student I decided to do my research on the striped killifish. It is a hardy species of baitfish that lives in nearshore waters along the east coast of the United States where it is an important food source for wading birds and commercially important species of fish like the summer flounder. Not a lot was known about the natural history of this species. I knew that they laid their eggs in shallow water near the edge of salt mashes and that egg laying began in April, but I had no idea how long their spawning season lasted, what the incubation time was for their eggs, or what the optimal environmental conditions were for the development of their embryos. My plan was to collect and study the fish in their natural environment and compare those observations with a range of environmental conditions I proposed subjecting them to in the laboratory.

Dad turned out to be a willing helper with my research. When I was in Lewes my parents, together with my Cousin Lottie and her husband Al, would spend their summer vacations a short distance away in Rehoboth Beach. Dad joined me in the field on several occasions during work on my master's degree and I looked forward to him working with me once again. Whenever the opportunity arose he would drive up to Lewes where we would head out to some of the nearby wetlands. Wearing waders and armed with mosquito spray, seines, and plastic buckets we would wade along the shoreline and slog into the swamp hoping to catch and tag fish. Dad seemed to love the work. No matter how difficult the conditions, he never complained. Heavy rains may have made it hard for him to see through his glasses, but he plodded along behind me sometimes in knee-deep muck with pencil and clipboard to record my observations. Not even the hoards of mosquitoes and biting flies that sometimes descended upon us when the wind stopped blowing made him relinquish his job.

It was during these outings that I came to realize what a deep concern my father had about the natural environment. Several times while we were trudging through the wetlands he would lift his head into the breeze and inhale. "There is nothing like the sweet smell of a marsh," he would say. "If only people could see how beautiful marshes are, maybe they wouldn't be so eager to destroy them."

I had to agree. Despite the bugs and viscous mud that pulled at our waders, marshes were magical places. They teemed with life and were important nurseries for many species of marine life. Today, when I think back, some of my fondest moments during those years took place when Dad and I were working together in the Lewes marshes engrossed in the peacefulness of our surroundings. In one way Dad was helping me fulfill my dream, and in another way I was helping him fulfill his.

During our collecting trips Dad and I noticed that the fish populations near the beach during the day were relatively low while their number increase dramatically at night. After observing this phenomenon at a number of locations along the Delaware coastline, Dad and I decided that nearshore fish populations were making regular inshore migrations during the evening to feed. Initially, I thought about doing a research project on this migration pattern, but ultimately gave up on the idea when I started working on the University's research vessel, *Wolverine*.

However, I felt there was a practical aspect to our discovery that I could to take advantage of. I decided if a large number of fish moved inshore during the evening, trying to net them might be a way to save on my food bills. It wasn't something to do on my own, so I started trying to convince other hungry graduate students to help. I thought getting them interested would be easy, but most thought I was crazy when I suggested the idea. After persistent badgering, I did get a couple of them to join me. I remember the first evening. When we arrived, the near shore waters were boiling with life and in no time at all we netted several buckets of weakfish and summer flounder. My hypothesis about fish migrations had been proven, and after that outing I seldom had any trouble putting together a team of hungry students.

On occasions when Dad was in Rehoboth he would join me on one of my night seining expeditions. Sometimes it was near Indian River Inlet and sometimes we seined the shoals on the north side of Cape Henlopen. A low spring tide during a new moon turned out to be the best time for us to do it. A specially designed hundred-foot seine replaced the fifty-footer I initially used. I had extra weights placed at the bottom of the net and I increased its height to six feet. The extra weight on the bottom made the net more effective in catching flounder and the added height prevented weakfish and other species from jumping over the top.

Dad and I both wore waders when we seined. They protected our feet from stingray barbs and sharp shells but they didn't protect us from leaping fish. On several occasions after we encircled a large school we were bombarded by fleeing fish, and in a couple of instances some of them leapt into our waders. This always came as quite a shock. In the darkness we never knew what was flopping around inside our protective gear. Once it turned out to be a small weakfish and another time a two-foot smooth dogfish.

Night seining under a starlit sky at Cape Henlopen was always exhilarating. We never knew what kind of fish we were going to catch or what kind of nocturnal animals we would encounter. Generally, Dad and I began seining around ten thirty p.m. By then the fish had completed their inshore migration and we could hear them splashing at the surface as they began to feed.

Sometimes we would go to the beach a half hour before low tide to watch the stars. There were no lights to interfere with our view of the Milky Way, and when we looked up into the night sky we would often see meteorites streak across the heavens. It was late but we were never alone. Often we would hear creatures on the prowl. Raccoons and opossums regularly wandered into the intertidal zone scavenging for food, and if we watched closely we would occasionally catch glimpses of ghost crabs prancing about picking up morsels left behind by the receding tide.

My parents' vacation in Rehoboth also gave me a chance to learn what was happening with some of the folks back in the city and more importantly go fishing or crabbing with Dad. Most of our fishing took place on the west side of Indian River Inlet where we concentrated on catching summer flounder, and if nothing was biting, we headed over to the grass flats to rake up some hard clams.

These outings provided a break from my studies. There was one trip, however, that gave me more than a few anxious moments. A thick fog had settled over Indian River inlet and there was a strong incoming tide. As we drifted along in our rented boat, Dad spotted something purple floating alongside, and before I could tell him not to touch it, he scooped it up with our net and turned to show it to me. I'll never forget the excruciating look that came over his face when he lifted the Portuguese man-of-war out of the net. Needless to say, I didn't need to tell Dad that he was in big trouble. Before I could do anything, he flung the creature overboard and scrunched up on the front seat of the boat. My first concern was that he was having a heart attack. I could see that he was in a great deal of pain and I knew I had to do something fast. When I bent over to examine him I discovered several places on his arm where the man-of-war's tentacles were still sticking to his skin. Using a tweezers that I had in our first aid kit, I lifted these off and poured freshwater from our cooler over the affected areas. This appeared to give Dad some relief, but I knew I needed to apply heat to his arm in order to destroy the protein toxin that was causing his discomfort. This meant getting Dad back to his cottage, pronto. Now, everything I did seemed to take place in slow motion. Starting the motor took too long, the boat trip back was agonizingly slow, and every traffic light we stopped at seemed to last an eternity. When we finally arrived at the cottage, Dad was feeling a little better, but it wasn't until he soaked his arm in hot water that most of the pain subsided. Dad never again attempted to mess around with any jellyfish and several days later, after he fully recovered, he informed me that the pain from the Portuguese man-of-war sting was the most excruciating he'd ever experienced. This didn't stop him from fishing, clamming, and crabbing, however, and by the following weekend we were heading up Canary Creek Marsh in Lewes to catch some blue crabs for dinner.

In addition to doing research on killifish I also received a fellowship to study the fish populations in Delaware Bay. All of this work was done aboard the top-heavy vessel *Wolverine*. The project called for us to do fifteen-minute trawls in different sectors of Delaware Bay throughout the year. Before each drag we collected a water sample with a Nansen bottle and recorded salinity and water temperatures. After the trawl we dumped our catch onto the deck and identified and measured random samples of each species of fish.

I liked working aboard the *Wolverine* and so did my fellow graduate student Ron Smith, but some of the students we hired to assist us found the work grueling, especially when it was rough. In turbulent weather, the boat would rock from side to side and the fish would slosh across the deck in a thick layer of slime making it very difficult for us to complete our survey. I don't know if they would allow graduate students to do this kind of work today. There was definitely an element of risk. If you didn't pay attention, it was easy to get your leg entangled in the trawl lines and find yourself hanging upside down. You also had to be careful not to get knocked overboard by the bulbous, cod end of the net when the ocean was choppy. When we brought up the net it might contain several hundred pounds of marine life, and our haul would swing back and forth across the deck like a giant battering ram before it came to rest. On these occasions I thought about the dangers faced every day by commercial fishermen and the risks they took bringing their catch to market. The price we pay for fish in the market comes nowhere close to compensating the risk fishermen take.

There were also times when the catch itself was a safety issue. On several occasions we captured large sharks. They turned out to be difficult to get out of the net and none of them appreciated being dragged out of the water and dumped on the *Wolverine*'s deck. Their jaws constantly snapped as they flopped across the fantail, and the only thing we could do was try to ascertain their sex and estimate their size before tossing them overboard. Of all the sharks we captured, angel sharks were the most disagreeable. Whoever decided to call them "angels" certainly did so with tongue in cheek. These large, flat-headed creatures snapped at everything. I remember one time when a particularly vicious specimen chomped out huge hunks of wood from the *Wolverine*'s gunnels as it flopped back and forth across the deck.

Stingrays were also a major part of our catch, especially during the summer months. All of them had to be counted and a sample measured and sexed. The trick was not to get pierced by their poisonous spines. This meant we had to remove the spines from the ones we were going to measure. Neither Ron nor I were ever stabbed by their poisonous barbs, but there was one graduate student who had a stingray spine driven under his kneecap when he knelt down to get a blood sample from a shark. I wasn't on board that day, but I remember the *Wolverine* returning to the dock with the crew waving frantically for us to get help. The screaming student had to be carefully lifted from the boat with his leg bent back and transported to the hospital. He was able to walk again, but his experience instilled in me a deep respect for these animals.

When I took Dad and Al out on the *Wolverine* with me one day my father asked what I learned from the survey work we did. After giving some thought to his question I told him there were two important things: first was that the fish population in Delaware Bay was rapidly declining, and second that the bottom trawlers like the one we used to do our surveys were harmful to the benthic environment. "They destroy the marine habitats on the bottom of the bay and they crush a lot of non-commercial species when we hoist the net on board," I added sadly.

"Do you think, as a result of what you've found out, they'll stop using trawlers in the bay?" he inquired.

"Not any time soon," I admitted after giving his question some further thought, "but maybe in the future. There needs to be better management of our fishery resources, but I don't think that will happen until our coastal fisheries come close to collapsing. Too many people's lives depend upon commercial fishing and there are too many political issues involved for it to work differently."

Dad shook his head. "It's too bad that things will have to get to that point before we do something," he sighed. "It doesn't look like things will bode too well for people or fish in the future."

Spinnerisms

I'd never considered living in Florida, but after spending nearly two years in the North Atlantic with the Navy, I knew I wanted to work someplace south of the Mason-Dixon Line. Unfortunately, in 1970, there weren't too many job opportunities for a recently graduated Ph.D. in marine science. The Vietnam conflict was still sucking the country dry, both spiritually and monetarily, and a lot of research funds that had been going to universities were now being directed towards the war effort. Even job opportunities abroad had dried up.

That's why I was so excited when one chilly Tuesday morning in late November I received a letter offering me a job I'd applied for as a aquatic ecologist for the Deltona Corporation on Marco Island, Florida. It was Deltona's plan to convert Marco Island and some of its surrounding wetlands along Florida's southwest coast into a twenty-four square mile resort community. This was not the type of job I had hoped to start my career with, but after twenty rejection notices, it was a job, and the pay was reasonable—a comfortable $9,000 a year.

At the time I first heard about the opening, I was totally unaware of what an aquatic ecologist did for a development corporation like Deltona, so before I applied I'd called them. George Spinner, my future boss, spoke to me. George's gruff, but enthusiastic presentation made the job sound both meaningful and interesting. To this day, I remember his sales pitch: "This is the first time anything like this has ever been done by a development corporation in Florida. Deltona is hiring its own group of experts to answer the concerns that the Army Corp of Engineers and some environmental groups have regarding their development of Marco Island, and you'll be part of this team. In addition, you'll play an important role in telling the company where development can take place and where it can't."

Somewhat cautiously I'd asked, "Just who will this team of experts consist of, and what are their credentials?"

"I'll be heading up the team," George announced proudly. "I'm a marine biologist and I used to be the manager of the Bombay Hook National Wildlife Refuge in Delaware. Then I headed up a research group for National Geographic. It was my job to put together a detailed assessment of U.S. coastal wetlands and identify which ones were threatened by development. People at Deltona were so impressed with my work for National Geographic they called me up and asked me to head up this project. I spoke to Frank Mackle, the president of Deltona, himself. Before I took the job I told him I wasn't pulling any punches. I said that if I found them doing something that wasn't right I'd put a stop to it. Frank said he admired my candor and promised to make sure the company did the right thing."

I had to admit I was impressed by what my future boss was saying. What little I knew about developers at that time suggested they had little regard for wetlands. Drain the land and build on it was the general rule back in the 1960s. "And who will make up the rest of the team?" I probed.

"It will include an experienced research biologist from the University of Miami's school of marine science and a local fisherman I've hired as a guide. Since none of the research team will be familiar with the waters around Marco Island, and since we'll be doing a lot of sampling at night, I thought it would be best if we hired someone who was already acquainted with the surrounding wetlands. His name is Bud Kirk; his wife Kappi is the postmistress in Goodland."

Again, I was impressed. Hiring a local guide was a great idea, even if, as George admitted later, it wasn't his idea. In addition, I had to agree that it was leading edge thinking on the part of a development corporation to hire its own team of environmental advisors. Still, I didn't want to rush headlong into the program without doing some additional checking, so I contacted National Geographic as well as a recent associate of George's, Dr. Jay Harmic, who also happened to receive his doctorate under my graduate school advisor. Both reacted favorably when I mentioned George's name and were complimentary about his knowledge and leadership skills. Feeling a lot better about the job, I called George in early December and told him I would accept the position.

Soon after I called George, I phoned my parents and let them know the good news. They were pretty excited. Mom wanted to know how much the position paid. Dad was more interested in what I would be doing.

My wife and I left for South Florida in mid December of 1970. We were to meet George in Miami where I was to fill out employment forms and get introduced to some of the company officials. The trip was pleasant and uneventful. However, a strong cold front followed us south. If you're the type that believes in omens, you might have looked upon the approaching weather as a portent of future events. But I was too happy about my first job to let my mind become consumed with superstitious nonsense. It wasn't too long after we arrived however that the Mad Hatter appeared at my door and my wacky Alice in Wonderland Adventures began with Deltona.

Uh oh, I thought to myself. This is my first day on the job and I'm already in trouble. Back at the Holiday Inn in Miami, George was explaining the events that had taken place since I'd last spoken to him over the telephone and they didn't sound good. The research biologist at the University of Miami had decided not to take the job of chief aquatic ecologist. According to George he was uncomfortable about the role he was going to play and wasn't certain the company would live up to its obligations. George said he tried to persuade him otherwise, but nothing he said made him change his mind. Extremely agitated by the unwelcome turn of events, George's face grew red and his eyes bulged menacingly. "I want you to take his job," he stammered. At first I didn't know what to say. I was hired to assist with the field study phase of the program and identify the fish we collected around Marco. It was the type of job I felt comfortable with since I had done similar work during my graduate studies. In addition, the job would allow me to become familiar with South Florida's subtropical environment under the guidance of someone who knew more about the area than I did. Now George wanted to thrust me into the leadership role. The question was why? Wasn't there a more experienced biologist who wanted the position?

In order to get a better feel for the situation, I asked George who would be taking my place. Raising his arm he waved toward a young man I'd met upon arrival. His name was Chuck Courtney.

Chuck had graduated from the University of Miami with a BS in Biology and had just finished a tour of duty in the Navy. Since he was a Floridian, he knew a lot more about the South Florida environment than I did, but neither one of us could be classified as the type of expert the company claimed they were hiring to make decisions regarding their development. Silence followed as I put together my thoughts. I began to suspect that the whole thing was a ruse. It was becoming obvious that the company really didn't need a team of experts to help them plan their development. What they needed was a group of people who gave them the appearance that they were concerned about protecting local wetlands.

Outmaneuvered and feeling trapped into a situation I didn't like, I thought seriously about saying no to George's offer. In many ways it would have been the right thing to do, but there was also the practical side of the situation that said why not take him up on his offer and buy myself some time. If things looked like they weren't headed in the right direction, I could start to look for another position. After all, I had no job to go back to in Delaware, there was no imminent new job on the horizon, and if I declined, I would have to reimburse Deltona $800 for transporting my furniture to Florida. Burying my reservations, I gave George a reluctant smile and said yes. From that point on I suspected my career with the Deltona wouldn't last very long, but what I didn't know was how weird things would really get working for George Spinner.

Slapping me on the back, George congratulated me on my decision and invited Chuck and our wives out to dinner at Joe's Stone Crab. At six thirty that evening our garrulous new boss picked us up in front of the Holiday Inn and treated us to a life-threatening, white-knuckle drive through the streets of Miami. By the end of the trip everyone except George was looking down at the floor of the car thanking God that we had arrived at our destination in one piece.

During a sumptuous dinner of stone crab claws, George extolled the virtues of the Deltona Corporation and then presented us with another surprise. "Let's go to the Playboy Club," he announced with a demonstrative wave. His wife Julie started to protest, but a stern look from George muted any future comments from her. When we left the restaurant none of us wanted to get into the front seat with George, figuring we had a better chance of surviving a head-on collision if we were packed together in the back. However, George had already made it known that he expected one of his new employees to sit up front so he could talk to them. Thankfully, Chuck agreed to sit next to him. I have to admit I was embarrassed by not speaking up, but at the same time I was relieved at not having the opportunity to become the company's first environmental casualty.

For a second time that evening everyone was treated to a hair-raising trip through the streets of Miami. Tires screeched as we pulled up to the Playboy Club. It was hard for me to believe that we had made it there in one piece. Sighs of relief followed as the car doors opened. Surfacing from the back seat, Alfdis, Chuck's new wife from Iceland, whispered to me she thought she was going to be sick. With a dramatic flair as he opened the door, George ushered us into the club and began ogling the Playboy bunnies and pulling on their fluffy tails. His wife pretended not to notice, but it was hard to ignore his juvenile posturing as an annoyed hostess led us to our seats.

Before returning to our hotel rooms, George informed us that we would have to spend another day in Miami before heading over to Naples. There was more paperwork to be filled out and Frank Mackle wanted to meet his new employees. "But I'm slated to meet the moving van tomorrow at ten a.m.," I sputtered. Waving aside my protest, George informed me I'd have to make other arrangements. "Not likely," I grumbled to myself as my wife and I headed to our room. Why hadn't he informed me of this change earlier? It was now eleven thirty at night and we had no way of getting in touch with the moving company. After a lengthy discussion, Bernice agreed to drive alone across the Everglades to Naples while I took care of business in Miami and had the unenviable thrill of riding to Naples with George. It was five fifteen a.m. and pitch dark when Bernice left the Miami hotel. Later she admitted she was never so frightened to drive alone. Throughout the trip she kept worrying about running into a bear or an alligator. Fortunately, she never saw either. But numerous snakes had slithered onto the highway to get warm after the cold front had passed through. Swerving to avoid them, she still remembers cringing each time she listened to the tires crush one of their scaly bodies into the wet pavement.

Back in Miami, Chuck and I filled out forms and were introduced to Frank Mackle and some of the other Deltona executives. There was a lot of glad-handing and backslapping rendered after which a sumptuous lunch was provided. Later that day George decided to leave for Naples rather than wait until the following morning. Shaking my head at another one of his unexpected moves, I listened as he announced with an air of authority, "This will give us a chance to get things underway sooner."

The drive across the South Florida peninsula, to no one's surprise, was another sweaty palm experience. In an effort to quell our fears, George proudly announced that both he and his wife, Julie, had been to defensive driving school and that we had nothing to worry about. It was hard to believe that defensive driving school had made any impact on him, since at the time he was making this revelation, he was in the midst of passing numerous cars on two-lane U.S. 41 at a speed in excess of 90 mph. Cringing in the back seat, Chuck, his wife, and I barely had the courage to look up as the car narrowly missed hoards of fleeing vultures that were feeding on squashed snakes. I don't know what the record is for driving to Marco Island from downtown Miami, but I'm sure George accomplished the feat in record time. When we pulled up to Deltona's new offices on Bald Eagle Drive, it was just a few minutes before four p.m. and I'm certain that we left Miami at about a quarter to three. Turning around in his seat before shutting off the ignition, George grinned and asked us what we thought of the Everglades, as everyone anxiously grabbed the car's door handles. "It was great," Chuck quipped before scrambling out of the car. In truth, I don't believe I remember too much about the landscape on that trip, and probably Chuck and Alfdis don't either.

The holiday season passed quickly, and by the first week in January Bernice and I were fully settled in our duplex on the outskirts of Naples. Everything seemed to be moving along smoothly except for my relationship with George. I wanted to get out into the field and learn as much as I could about my new environment and the type of development plans Deltona was making. However, George kept a tight leash on Chuck and me and refused to let us out of his sight. Everywhere he went we were told to follow. His behavior only reconfirmed my initial suspicions about the job, so Chuck and I began to dream up ways we could get away from George and do our own assessments of what was happening on Marco. Ordering supplies offsite, longer than normal lunch hours, and abandoning the office when George had to attend meetings were just a few ways we accomplished this. When we returned there was always an endless litany of questions from George. "Why did lunch take so long?" "Why did you have to leave the office?" "Wouldn't it be a lot easier to order supplies over the phone?"

Early on in the project we were introduced to Bud Kirk, our professional guide. This stout, affable, and shrewd gray-haired gentleman was a survivor, one of those pioneers who came to Southwest Florida in the early part of the twentieth century and carved a niche for himself in a beautiful, but tough and sometimes inhospitable environment. Moving to Florida from up north, he entered a world where mosquitoes were so thick during the rainy season you sucked them up your nose and swallowed them. "Back then air conditioning didn't exist and jobs were hard to find," he'd announced shortly after we'd met. And with a great deal of pride he added, "If you wanted to survive in South Florida, you had to be resourceful." Bud had worked as an alligator hunter, a manual laborer who helped construct the Tamiami Trail, gill net fisherman, stone crabber, supervisor at Doxsee's clam factory on Marco, garbage collector, fishing guide, movie consultant, and owner of Kirk's Fish House. He had done them all and now he could add consultant and guide for Deltona's environmental team to his resume.

It was hard not to like Bud and his beautiful wife Kappi. In 1960, shortly after Hurricane Donna had ravaged Collier County and covered most of Marco Island with twelve feet of water, Bud and his family had taken up residence in the sleepy fishing village of Goodland. Situated on the southeast corner of the Marco River, Goodland was home to a number of feisty, independent, gill net fisherman and stone crabbers who made their living harvesting the nutrient rich waters of Gullivan Bay and the surrounding Ten Thousand Islands. Relaxing on the porch of their wooden, Florida-style home, Bud and Kappi would often carry on animated conversations with their neighbors in the late afternoons. Exaggerated reports of a recent fish catch were scoffed at and angry discussions delved into the whereabouts of crab trap poachers. "Poachers should all be shot," one fisherman grumbled.

"Nah, " Bud replied, "they ain't worth going to jail for."

Bud was also a collector of every piece of junk imaginable. Haphazardly stuffed underneath his house was a treasure trove of memorabilia that became the permanent home for an assorted population of frogs, lizards, and snakes. All you had to do was ask him about some of the things he discovered on the island or while he was out fishing and in a flash he'd have you crawling underneath his home looking at glass fishing balls and pieces of Indian pottery.

Whenever the opportunity arose, Chuck and I would join Bud to explore the nearby wilderness that surrounded Deltona's ongoing development. Sometimes we would do it on the weekends, but mostly we would try to get away during the week when George had to leave town. Like many early Florida pioneers, Bud had mixed feelings about the changes that were taking place. He loved the Ten Thousand Islands and the hordes of wildlife that thrived in this enchanted jungle of tangled prop roots and tannin stained waterways. His eyes danced with excitement every time we took off to investigate something new. "Look over there," he'd shout as we passed an oyster shoal. "There's a school of redfish feeding on that bar. If you watch closely, you can see their fins sticking out of the water."

"Do you think things will be the same after Marco's been developed?" I asked him one day as we watched a flock of egrets come to roost on a nearby mangrove island.

"How do you mean?" he asked as he turned and looked at me. "If you're asking me if I think the fishing and the abundance of wildlife will be the same, the answer is no." Then, after a brief moment of silence, he added, "But I suppose that's the price you pay for progress." Bud firmly believed that Deltona's decision to build on Marco would be good for the local economy and what was good for the economy would be good for him and his family. He'd spent too many years scratching a living from Southwest Florida's rugged coastal environment, and his resourceful nature wouldn't allow him to give up an opportunity to share in the easy life that he was sure would soon follow. If I were he, I suppose I'd have felt the same way. But in our hearts we both knew that the

Deltona development was just the beginning of a whole series of construction projects that would take their toll on Southwest Florida's natural resources.

Unfortunately, our premonitions were right. Today, in 2012, the redfish are no longer as plentiful over the oyster bars where Bud used to fish, and the once isolated fishing community of Goodland is continually under siege by developers who want to construct condominiums along its waterfront. Bud and Kappi Kirk have both passed on but some of the residents are fighting the invasion. Regrettably, it appears to be a losing battle; expensive homes are turning this colorful fishing village into a newcomer's version of Shangri-La.

My real problems with George began when Deltona completed construction of our laboratory and office spaces. By this time George had begun to loosen the reins and we began to spend more time in the field setting up sampling sites. It became clear that there was one person George didn't want us talking to and that was Bernie Yokel. A tall, bear-like figure, Bernie's weathered features, impish grin, and infectious laugh belied his fiercely argumentative behavior when it came to defending Florida's environment. He'd begun his career as a physical education teacher on the islands of Guam and Saipan, where he'd soon become enamored with the beauty and diversity of aquatic life associated with the region's coral reefs. Infected with a desire to learn more about marine ecosystems, he decided to return to school and get a graduate degree in marine science. Back in Florida, he enrolled at the University of Miami where he came under the tutelage of notable scientists like Durban Tabb and Claire Idyle who were deeply concerned about the damage being done to Florida's aquatic ecosystems. It didn't take long for Bernie to adopt his mentors' passion for preserving Florida's wetlands, and when an opportunity presented itself for him to conduct research on the coastal wetlands of Southwest Florida, he grabbed it. Selected by the Collier County Conservancy in 1970 to become the director of its newly established research station at Rookery Bay, Bernie designed a series of baseline research studies that enabled him to evaluate the health of the region's coastal ecosystem. Initially, the Deltona Corporation helped support Bernie's baseline studies and agreed to run a similar series of studies near Marco Island where development was taking place. The primary goal of these studies was to measure the impact, if any, that Deltona's development was having upon Rookery Bay wetlands, as well as the coastal waters surrounding Marco.

Since I was in charge of setting up the baseline research studies for Deltona, I felt that I needed to spend as much time as possible with Bernie to make sure our sampling procedures and sampling sites fit the parameters established by the University of Miami research team. Unfortunately, George had different ideas. He made it clear in distinctively colorful terms that I was in no way to meet and discuss things with Bernie unless he was with me. George distrusted Bernie and believed he was going to try to undermine the company. He was also concerned that I would be influenced by Bernie's thoughts regarding the environment and would react in a way that was detrimental to Deltona's plans. I must admit that, in a way, he was right. Bernie's concerns about coastal development and the impact it would have upon the environment were valid. However, I was determined to do the study the way it was initially outlined. And that involved using sound research techniques that would allow Deltona to make the most appropriate decisions regarding their development on Marco Island.

On one of my white-knuckle drives to Miami with George, he tried to get me to agree that we should dispense with Bernie's services after about a year. By then, he argued, we could conduct our own surveys without Bernie looking over our shoulder. "After all," he grumbled with red-faced intensity, "it's costing Deltona a lot of money to support Bernie's research and that money could be spent better elsewhere." It wasn't too difficult to figure out what George was up to, and I wasn't about to play his game. Without Bernie sticking his head inside Deltona's tent, there would be no one but us to make sure the company was living up to its agreement. Fully aware that my company loyalty was being tested, I took several moments to collect my thoughts while the Everglades landscape blurred past my window.

"I'm uncomfortable with that suggestion," I finally replied. "The company is getting a lot of positive publicity from this joint venture and if we dump this cooperative effort after a year, it would appear it isn't sincere about protecting the environment."

When I finished, George shook his head and gave the gas pedal an extra push as he passed a line of campers.

Over the next couple of weeks, the staff and I went about the tasks of setting up the laboratory and pinpointing the locations of our sampling sites around Marco Island. Part of the reason for the big push was to get ready for a public relations gala the company had planned. Local and regional newspapers, as well as correspondents from *Newsweek* and *Time,* had been invited to attend the opening during which George and other Deltona officials would declare their concern for the environment by welcoming in a new era of cooperation between developers and environmentalists. On the day of the event, George instructed Chuck and me to remain at the laboratory to answer any research questions the reporters might have. He anticipated they would show up shortly after lunch and then depart to look at other aspects of the project. Once they left we were to meet with company officials at a jacket and tie affair at the yacht club at six p.m.

Arriving before noon, Chuck and I did some last minute straightening up and waited for the press to make their appearance. The hours dragged and by four thirty we were certain that something had gone wrong. Chuck and I made phone calls to company executives and George's home trying to find out if something had happened. No one had heard from George, but everyone promised to have him give us a call if they saw him. Eventually I sent Chuck home to pick up his wife for the six o'clock event, locked up the lab, and went home to change.

As I walked through the door of the yacht club shortly after six, a Deltona executive pulled me aside and warned me to steer clear of George, but his warning came too late. My boss's menacing figure confronted me as I turned around. Snarling his displeasure, he informed me with a series of colorful expletives that I had just used up eight of my nine lives. I thought for sure that he was upset with me for leaving the laboratory before the press arrived so I began stammering out my excuse. Before I got halfway through my explanation he waved his hand for me to stop and glared at me with eye-bulging anger. I never felt so intimidated in my life. If the reason for his anger wasn't because I had left the lab, what could I have done that made him so upset? Not knowing what else to do I waited quietly for his response.

"It's those f___ing fish," he finally snarled.

I had no idea what he was talking about, but I didn't want to generate any more displeasure. "What about them?" I asked.

"None of those f___ing fish that you stored in the lab are identified by their common names." He was right. The fish we had collected during some of our initial sampling trips were only labeled with their scientific names. "I want those f___ing fish identified with their common names ASAP," he hissed before turning his back on me and stomping off into the dining room. Incredulous, I turned and looked at the Deltona executive standing off to one side. After shrugging his shoulders and rolling his eyes, he took another sip from his drink and disappeared into the crowd. Later, I learned from someone who was at the press conference that a couple of reporters asked George the common names of the fish that were lining the shelves in our lab and when he couldn't identify them, the press began to snicker.

For my remaining two months at Deltona, George's bizarre behavior never ceased to amaze me. On one occasion he passed nine cars on the two-lane St. Petersburg Bridge while telling Chuck and me how he had once spent several weeks recovering from a massive heart attack. I wasn't sure why he told us this, but after getting to know George better, I decided he said things like this because he enjoyed scaring the hell out of us.

On another equally uncomfortable trip to Miami, George related to me an amazing story about his past that left me speechless. According to George, when he was working for the Bombay Hook National Wildlife Refuge in Delaware, he wanted to create a series of duck ponds to attract birds during their fall migration. Since there was no money to undertake the project, he called up a friend at the Dover Air Force base and asked him to conduct a training run over the refuge. George claimed he marked out the locations for the duck ponds and the Air Force crews "accidentally" flew over the refuge and released their bombs. "This is the type of creative thinking we need to use when dealing with Deltona's environmental problems," he said to me. "We have to think outside the box."

I had no problem thinking outside the box, but his example of creative thinking seemed, to say the least, a bit extreme. For a brief moment I thought George's story was a practical joke, but when I looked over at him there was no telltale smirk on his face. Finally,

I asked him if his experiment worked out the way he expected it to. "You're damn right it did," he replied, "and it saved the taxpayers a lot of money." According to George, it appeared his bosses didn't appreciate his creative thinking as much as he thought they should since he wound up being banished to an outpost in Montana working for a boss he hated. I guess the federal government hoped he would quit after his reassignment, but somehow George managed to step in the right manure pile and wound up getting a job with National Geographic.

At Deltona you could never tell what was going to happen during the workday. Sometimes I would start off with a normal routine and find myself in an unbelievable situation by the end of the day. One memorable experience took place in January. We had just picked up a new boat and were giving it a test run when the engine stopped running. Nothing we did got the motor started so Bud suggested we paddle the boat close to shore and walk it to Goodland. Chuck balked at that idea and reminded Bud that we were nearly three miles from town. In response Bud jumped into the water and suggested we do the same. "If we don't do something," Bud replied, "well be out here all night. Don't worry, I've done it before." Reluctantly, Chuck and I jumped into the water and started pulling on the boat while Bud related a story about the time he got his mullet skiff stuck in the backwater. He said it was low tide and he felt he could take a shortcut across some oyster bars. What he didn't anticipate was how sharp the oyster shells really were, and about half way back the tattered sneakers he was wearing fell apart and he proceeded barefoot the rest of the way. Bloody and in pain, Bud finally limped up to his house where his wife Kappi came to his rescue with needle and thread. "She sewed my feet up good as new," he proudly announced as we shoved Deltona's boat along the mangroves. At this point, the sun was close to setting and I was beginning to think that we would be in the same predicament as Bud when Vernon Sweet, a Sundown Patrol pilot, spotted us from the air. Vernon radioed one of the local fishermen and within half an hour we were scrambling aboard his boat. I'm not sure what Bud and Chuck were thinking as we were being rescued, but I was happy we were not still trekking back to Goodland awaiting Kappi's smiling face holding a needle and thread in her hand.

Another incident happened the day I decided to test our new bottom trawl. Weeks had been spent getting its specifications just right so that its configuration was similar to the one Bernie was using in Rookery Bay. Anxious to see how it worked, I collected Chuck and Bud and headed towards the south end of Marco Island on a calm, sunny February morning. The collecting device was a small cone-shaped net about fifteen feet across at the mouth. Inside the back end of the net was a mesh liner that allowed us to capture small specimens that would have escaped through the net's larger outer mesh. The idea was to pull the trawl over different benthic habitats for fifteen minutes and then retrieve the specimens for identification and analysis in the laboratory. Comparable sampling sites were chosen near places where coastal development was taking place as well as locations where Deltona was not involved in any construction. By comparing the samples from different locations, over a period of time, we were to find out what impact, if any, Deltona's development had upon coastal marine life.

The site selected for our first trawl was in a deep slough that entered the north end of Gullivan Bay. After tossing the net over the stern and lowering the wooden doors that were designed to keep the mouth of the net open, Bud gently eased the boat's throttle forward as Chuck and I organized the collection bottles and sampling trays. Less than five minutes passed before we felt this violent thump that brought the boat to an abrupt halt. Bud was concerned that we had snagged a large tree, so he stopped the engine and we began to pull up the net. It took all three of us to inch the net toward the surface and we were pretty winded by the time the wooden doors appeared at the stern. Looking over at me, Bud shook his head and said, "I don't think we're hung. I think we've caught a large fish, maybe an eagle ray. I can feel something pulling on the lines." I couldn't imagine how a large eagle ray could have swum into the opening of our small trawl, but I'd seen stranger things happen when I was working on the *Wolverine*. Reaching over the stern, Chuck and I struggled to get the net closer to the boat so we could see what was in it. None of us was prepared for what happened next. The tail of a giant fish waved at us from the back end of the net and slammed into the stern of the boat. After seeing the tail, there was little doubt about what we'd captured. It was a mammoth goliath grouper. The question was how to get it out of the trawl without damaging our new net. The fish was too big to bring into the boat without the assistance of a block and tackle. The only thing we could do was beach it and see if we could pull it out head first from the back end of the net. This task was going to be formidable. The fish was nearly six feet long and must have weighed over three hundred pounds. It was also wedged so tightly in the narrow mesh liner that it would be nearly impossible for us to peel off the net without special tools.

After unsuccessfully struggling for more than hour to get the fish out of the net with the tools we had on board, we decided to drag it back to Bud's dock in Goodland. As fate would have it, just as we started to drag the fish back to Goodland, a Deltona photographer saw us struggling with the creature and started taking pictures. When we told him we were taking the fish back to Goodland, he decided to tag along. It didn't take long for word to spread about the fish we'd captured, and when we pulled up to Bud's dock half the town of Goodland and George were waiting for us. Photographers and reporters from the *Marco Island Eagle* and *Naples Daily News* had been called, the fish was hoisted out of the water with block and tackle, and publicity photos galore were taken. One reporter asked George what he was going to do with the fish. Not wanting to miss a good public relations opportunity, George told him we were going to fillet the fish and give it to a nursing home. At this point Bud tried to pull George aside and tell him that the fish was too tough to eat, but George brushed him aside and instructed Chuck to call the local nursing homes and find out if any of them wanted it. Of course there were health regulations about where nursing homes could get their food and Chuck tried to tell George that he might have a problem getting them to take it. But George just shook his head at Chuck's comment and told him to get on the phone and start making the "damn calls."

Meanwhile Bud laid out the fish and began to fillet it. Initially, George just sat back and watched, but then he started to needle Bud about the lousy job he was doing. All of this was taking place in front of Bud's Goodland neighbors and you could see George's insults were getting to Bud. His face grew redder with each slice of the knife until, totally exasperated, he stood up and handed his knife to George and asked him to demonstrate how he should fillet the fish. George was a bit flustered by Bud's retort but had no choice except to step in and take over. Grabbing the knife from Bud's hand, he bent over and started butchering the fish. Needless to say, George's lack of skill didn't go unnoticed by the people of Goodland, who soon began to chuckle at his pathetic efforts.

About ten minutes into George's disastrous fillet demonstration, Chuck returned to the dock and reported that he still hadn't found anyone willing to take the fish. George grumbled about Chuck's incompetence and told him to call up his wife Julie. George wanted Julie to bring their condo bed sheets to Bud's dock so he could use them to wrap up the fillets. When Julie arrived George was in the process of skinning the fish. Unfortunately for George, his ability to skin fish was just as bad as his filleting technique. Bud had tried to make some suggestions to help George out, but George refused to listen. Pulling Julie aside, George handed her a pair of ice tongs and instructed her to keep the animal's skin taut as he separated it from the grouper's flesh. Julie tried hard to keep tension on the skin, but every time George made a mistake he blamed his wife for his blunder and began cursing at her. At this point I was too embarrassed to stick around, so I went into the fish house to see if Chuck had found anyone who would take the fish. Fortunately, he had.

After the fillets were cut up into smaller pieces George asked Chuck to deliver them to the nursing home, but Chuck skillfully avoided George's request by telling him he needed to drive his wife to the doctor. Bernice had our car so George said he would take them to the nursing home himself. Large hunks of fillets were placed into plastic bags filled with ice and then wrapped in bed sheets that were piled into the trunk and back seat of George's car. Unfortunately for George, it was a good twenty-five mile drive to the nursing home, and by the time he reached his destination the mid-afternoon heat had melted the ice and puddles of bloody water had seeped into the floor of his vehicle. The following week George was still grumbling about the stench in his car, and on our next trip to Miami I used the offensive odor as an excuse to drive separately.

That night I telephoned Dad and told him the story about the fish we had caught. He couldn't believe there were fish that big in

Florida and was anxious to see a picture of the one we'd captured. During our conversation he informed me that he and Mom were coming down for a summer visit. At this point I didn't want to tell him how tenuous my job situation was, so I told him I was pleased to hear they were coming and I'd set up some opportunities for us to go fishing.

The first major environmental challenge against Deltona's Marco Island development came from the National Audubon Society. It targeted the canals being dug on the island. At that time developers in South Florida created waterfront property by uprooting mangrove forests and replacing them with a network of canals. Fill from the waterways was used to raise the level of the surrounding land so that houses could be built. This provided the new homeowners with waterfront property where they could dock their boats.

Environmental groups like Audubon argued, and rightfully so, that the elimination of mangrove swamps took away important nursery areas for marine fish and invertebrates. In addition, they accused the company of creating canals that did not provide adequate tidal flushing and were not dug appropriately. Ideally, Deltona's canals should have been dug to a uniform depth. Audubon's concern was that Deltona was creating deep pockets in the canals and that during tropical storms these pockets of anaerobic sediment would be flushed into the surrounding environment and cause a massive die-off of marine life.

Not knowing if the accusation was true, George arranged a meeting with the person in charge of designing and constructing Deltona's canals. He was a tall, lanky, rugged looking former Army Corp of Engineers Colonel who loved to smoke highly odiferous Cuban cigars. From the look on the Colonel's face, when we walked into his office, you could see he was not pleased to see us. The Colonel scowled as George reached out to shake his hand, and the muscles in his jaw tightened as we seated ourselves across from him in his neatly arranged leather chairs.

"Tell us about the canals Deltona is digging," George began.

George's inquiry was initially greeted with silence. Then the Colonel asked George what he specifically wanted to know about the "f___ing" canals. Taken back by the Colonel's caustic response, George stammered out the list of concerns outlined in the

Audubon letter. When George finished, the Colonel removed the cigar from his mouth, flicked its ashes into an empty receptacle, and gave us a contemptuous sneer. Grumbling a litany of complaints about tree huggers, he rose from his desk and invited us into his conference room. The walls of the rectangular meeting area were covered with maps showing the locations of existing and future canals. Blue lines went in every direction. It was obvious the colonel knew that a straight line was the shortest distance between two points. Sweeping his arm towards the wall, he confronted us with the enormous task of plotting the canals. Yes, the canals could be redesigned so that tidal flushing would be improved, he grumbled, but making sure the canals were dug to a uniform depth was another matter. That task would need the approval of top-level executives. Not sure why, I bared my ignorance and asked him for an explanation. Now the Colonel knew he was dealing with a group of country bumpkins. With the grin of a Cheshire cat he pounced upon my ignorance and vigorously tapped his finger against one of the diagrams. As I moved closer so I could see what he was pointing to, he explained that the canals had to be dredged to a sufficient depth so that large boats could navigate in them. However, he added, it was not always possible to keep the canals at a uniform depth because the fill that was removed from some areas was not suitable to build homes on. In these situations he had to dig deeper, sometimes to a depth of twenty or twenty-five feet, in order to obtain enough good fill.

Now we had the answer to our inquiry. The criticism leveled by Audubon regarding the depths of the canals was accurate—a fact that Chuck and I later confirmed when we took depth readings in different waterways. Since we were the company's environmental advisors, it was our job to let the company know what they needed to do to correct the situation. However, a company's success is based upon how much profit it generates. Redesigning the canals so they would generate better tidal flushing and keeping them at a uniform depth were not difficult problems to solve, but the solutions involved spending money. New straight lines would have to be drawn, new waterways would have to be dug, and fill would have to be trucked in when they couldn't get enough from dredging the canals. After our meeting, I asked George if he thought the company would be willing to spend the extra money to correct the problems. "They damn well better be," he grumbled as we drove back to the lab. "They brought us here to tell them how to do things properly and that's what we we're going to do."

The second environmental problem that arose involved Deltona's proposed development of an area called Marco Shores that was part of a 9100-acre section of land known as the Collier-Reed tract. This land had been purchased from the Collier Corporation in 1969. At that time Deltona was fully aware that the Colliers, in joint agreement with the National Audubon Society and the Conservation Foundation in Washington, D.C., had already developed a schematic for this land that showed very limited dredge-and-fill activity. A good portion of the property was wetlands and some of it, like Marco Shores, was situated close to the Collier County Conservancy's Rookery Bay. Neither the Conservancy nor National Audubon wanted any dredge-and-fill development taking place in these wetlands, and both environmental groups made their feelings known to Deltona. Deltona had assured both groups that no plans had been finalized for this area and that before any decisions were made regarding this property they would get input from both agencies as well as their own environmental research team. I had no reason to believe any differently until a rumor was passed along from inside the company that Deltona had finalized its plans for Marco Shores and had begun selling lots. In addition, the rumor suggested that Deltona had deliberately ignored the jointly agreed upon plans between Collier and National Audubon and had submitted their own schematics which called for the creation of an extensive canal system. Word also was being circulated that the company knew their proposal was headed for trouble but felt certain they had enough political clout in Tallahassee to overcome any permitting problems.

Interested in learning where Deltona's plans currently stood, Chuck and I dressed in business suits and went over to the company's sales office. Since we hadn't been working for the company long enough for anyone to recognize us, we felt certain we could get the information we needed without anyone catching on to what we were up to. When we entered the office one of the company's sales people greeted us enthusiastically, and I indicated our interest in purchasing some waterfront property. He responded by telling us that most of the choice pieces of waterfront land on Marco had already been sold so he tried to interest us in other pieces of property. When I insisted that we were only interested in waterfront land he told us to wait a moment while he talked to his supervisor. After a few minutes he returned and told us he thought he might have something that would be of interest. Waving us through a door at the back of the sales office, he ushered us into a room whose walls were covered with maps showing future development locations on and around Marco Island. One of those maps showed a detailed layout of the company's plans for Marco Shores. There were still a number of choice sites available on Marco Shores if we were willing to live off the island, he noted. I could feel my heart begin to pound as he went on to describe the amount of development that was proposed for Marco Shores and the commitments the company had from various hotels to purchase property once Deltona had its permits. "How certain are you that Marco Shores will be developed?" I asked after he finished his sales pitch.

"Absolutely certain," was his response.

After I left the sales office, all sorts of unsettling thoughts started swimming through my head. Some centered on the company and a lot focused on George. Deltona was definitely not one of those "build and leave" corporations like Gulf American that had developed Cape Coral, and they took great pride in making sure they gave their buyers a good product. But it was also evident that they had made a conscious decision to cross an ethical line when they decided to sell property they might not get permitted. I also wondered how much George knew about Deltona's plans for Marco Shores. If he knew about it, why had he kept us out of the loop? Was he trying to keep it a secret? Waiting a few days to allow my blood pressure to return to normal, I asked George if he'd heard anything about Deltona's plans to develop Marco Shores. George expressed ignorance and announced that if the company were trying to circumvent his efforts he would make them pay. George's past behavior had not filled me with a lot of confidence so I wasn't so sure he was telling me the truth. That night I updated my resume and started some discreet inquiries about another job.

Meanwhile, Deltona received more letters about the low oxygen levels in the canals and decided to hold a top-level executive meeting in their "war room" in Miami. George, Chuck, and I were invited to attend, and George was asked to give his assessment of the situation. It was the first time I had ever participated in a meeting of this nature and I didn't have a clue what to expect. When we arrived Billy Vessels, a former All American and Heisman Trophy winner from Oklahoma, was standing guard at the door of the plush conference room. Chuck later told me that Billy had been hired by Bob Mackle to act as the family bodyguard after Bob's daughter had been buried alive and held for ransom.

After we seated ourselves around the table, Frank Mackle began by reading the latest accusations Audubon had leveled against the company. Then he looked over at us and asked if there was any merit to the charges. I knew that there was, but George had told us beforehand to keep our mouths shut. He said he'd studied the issue and he would address the accusations. Pounding his fist against the table, George glared at the Mackles and announced in very profane language that there absolutely was merit to their charges. A little shocked by George's profanity, Frank Mackle hesitated a few seconds before asking George what he thought was creating the low oxygen levels in the canals. "It's the f___ing manatees," George announced. "They're sucking all the f___ing oxygen out of the f___ing canals." I couldn't believe what George had just said. Looking around the table it was obvious that no one else could either. At this point, Chuck, who was about to burst out laughing, excused himself and went to the restroom.

Finally, Bob Mackle stammered, "But, George, manatees are born aren't they?"

George's face began to turn red when he realized the blunder he'd made. Wiping the sweat from his brow, he turned towards Bob Mackle and said, "You're damn right they are. But the f___ing things are eating up all the f___ing algae clinging to the sea walls." More stares of disbelief focused on George. At this point I could envision the company people asking themselves what they'd gotten themselves into. Fortunately, before the situation got too embarrassing, one of the company executives stepped in and suggested that the research team conduct a study that would address the allegations. Like a drowning sailor reaching for the last life preserver, George grabbed at the idea and promised everyone he'd have this fact-finding study underway and completed in a week.

As head of the research team, I was given the unenviable task of designing the investigation. This included determining the bottom profiles of several canals, ascertaining the oxygen concentrations at different depths in the canals, as well as carrying out a twenty-four-hour study to compare the salinity, pH, and water temperature in both canals and natural areas. It took the better part of a week to set everything up. Comparable sampling sites in canals and natural areas were selected, trial time runs initiated, and a date set to undertake the investigation.

We began our twenty-four-hour study on a Friday morning. The weather forecast had projected a cold front coming through late Saturday morning, so I figured we had plenty of time to complete our research before bad weather set in. I had also learned from my graduate school days that no field investigation ever proceeds without glitches, so I had tried to set things up so that we didn't experience too many problems. Initially, everything went according to plan, but as darkness and fatigue settled in, the time it took us to take our water samples and the time it took us to travel between sampling sites increased significantly so we were always running behind schedule. By two o'clock in the morning we were really feeling the strain. Then the cold front arrived. Sheets of rain, strong winds, and lightning engulfed us right in the middle of one of our sampling stops. On top of that, the tide was going out and we wound up having to trudge through thick mud to get to one of our sampling stations. I just didn't have enough field experience in Southwest Florida to realize that a strong outgoing tide pushed by strong winds could completely drain the water from shallow bays. That run took us twice as long as we anticipated, and when we reached the laboratory utterly exhausted, it was time to take our next series of samples. I don't know how Chuck felt when we finished the study on Saturday morning but I was numb with fatigue, and my workday had just begun. I spent the rest of Saturday and nearly all of Sunday analyzing the data and preparing a report for Monday morning.

I was still numb with fatigue when I arrived at work on Monday, but I was proud of the fact that I had finished the report and that it was ready for distribution. I wasn't so sure how happy the company would be with my findings, but the data would certainly help them with future decisions regarding their canals. There were, as the Audubon letter suggested, irregularities in the bottom contours of the canals and, in the deeper sites, there were places where the circulation was so poor that extremely low oxygen concentrations had developed. In the natural areas we also found low oxygen readings in deep channels, especially during the evening hours when no photosynthesis was taking place. In the natural areas, strong wind and wave action from storms would change the shape of these channels over time and eradicate these dead zones. With Deltona's canals, the situation was also correctable. It would involve redesigning the canals so there was greater water movement and plugging up some of the deep holes. I have to admit that what we didn't discover were herds of manatees grazing upon fields of algae growing along the sea walls.

Unfortunately, George was in a sour mood when I walked through the door on Monday morning. It was quite obvious that Bud and Chuck were anxious to stay out of his way and both seemed relieved when George ordered me to have them work on an outside project. To say the least, I was ill prepared for what happened next. As I took a seat across from George his face grew red, his eyes bulged, and he slammed his fist against the top of the desk. "You've just used up the last of your f___ing nine lives," he snarled. Absolutely astonished by his outburst, I tried to figure out what he was talking about. Had he found out about my visit to the sales office? Had he run into some problems with Chuck and Bud that I didn't know about? Somewhat shaken by his aggressive behavior, I raised my hands in a questioning position and asked him what the problem was. "The f___ing fish," he yelled.

What fish? I thought to myself. We hadn't caught any fish during our research investigation. "You didn't finish labeling those bottles of fish with their f___ing common names and guess who showed up this weekend?"

"*Newsweek* and *Time*," I groaned. He was right; I hadn't finished the job, but I was too exhausted to give a damn.

"You're fired," he snarled as he swept the pages of my research report off the top of his desk. At that moment something snapped inside and I lost my self-control. Standing up, I looked down at George and told him he couldn't fire me because I quit. Then I reached across the desk and grabbed George by the collar. Staring directly into his face I told him he was the biggest asshole I'd ever met. And that was the end of my career with Deltona.

Before I left, I picked up my report, which I mailed to the company. I assume the study was of some value since Deltona referenced it in their annual report.

What Now?

Out of a job and no income. Things could be worse. After I left George's office I stopped by Rookery Bay and informed Bernie Yokel of my change in employment. He congratulated me and said that if he heard of any job openings he'd get in touch. Then I headed home to tell my wife the bad news and begin some job inquiries.

Jobs were still scarce but a few opportunities did crop up. Bernie passed along my plight to Joel Kuperberg who was working for the governor. The only job opening Joel had was as a state inspector ferreting out illegal dredge-and-fill activities. Apparently there were quite a few of these operations taking place throughout the state and an effort was underway to stop them. Joel and I talked briefly over the phone about the position, and then he sent me up to Bradenton to talk to a guy who had just quit his job as an inspector. When I approached his house I noticed the curtains were drawn and his wife was extremely nervous when she opened the door. She relaxed a little when I told her who I was but said she wasn't sure her husband would want to see me. I told her I'd driven over a hundred miles to talk to him and hoped he could give me some insights into the job. After talking with her husband, she reluctantly agreed to let me in. The poor guy turned out to be an emotional wreck. It became clear after talking to him that ferreting out illegal dredge-and-fill operations was risky business. During his short career he had received numerous death threats and there were scattered bullet holes on the outer wall of his house. Later that day I called up Joel and politely declined his offer.

The state's research lab was hiring people, but the best job they had available was a position as a bottle washer. Although I had a lot of experience at home doing that sort of thing, I also declined that position, stating I felt a little over qualified for the job. The most exciting employment opportunity came from the federal government. I had several meetings with people from the Environmental Protection Agency. They were planning an ecosystem analysis of the Big Cypress Swamp and its estuaries and were interested in having me work on the fisheries component of their study. I received my GS rating and things looked good for a while. I was recommended for the job, but just as I was about to begin work, the position was given to someone inside the agency who wanted to be transferred to Naples. The loss of this opportunity was a bitter disappointment. I had really looked forward to doing some valuable field research in the Ten Thousand Islands and Big Cypress Swamp, especially since I felt the project would play an important role in helping protect some of Collier County's natural resources.

It was during this period between jobs that my parents came down for their summer visit. When they arrived they told my wife and me that they were thinking about selling their business and retiring. Mom wanted to move to Cape Cod but Dad wanted to retire some place where it was warm. I thought Dad's suggestion about moving to a warmer climate was more realistic. I couldn't imagine Mom living in a place that had only three months of summer. Her arthritis was bad when I started college and over the intervening years it had steadily gotten worse.

During my parents' visit we took them on a tour of Naples and suggested that they might want to move here. As I discussed some of the pros and cons of this move, I made it clear that I was still looking for a job and that once I found one Bernice and I would probably move out of Naples. My parents said they clearly understood my situation, but after seeing Naples they declared that this was where they wanted to spend their retirement years; by the end of their vacation they had purchased a small trailer in a mobile home park called Harmony Shores on the south end of town. There were number of fruit trees in the park left from an old orchard, and it was situated close to a tidal creek where Dad could launch a boat. For people who had spent almost their entire lives living in a small apartment in a congested city it was like moving into the Garden of Eden.

After my parents returned to New Jersey I decided I needed to find temporary employment until a more attractive job offer came along. My landlord said there was a job opening at the Big Cypress Nature Center and suggested that I go over and check it out. The Center was located east of Goodlette-Frank road just south of Golden Gate Parkway. At one time it had been the beachfront home of Julius Fleischmann. In the late 1950s Julius donated his home as well as some land north of Caribbean Gardens to Nature Centers for Young America (N.C.Y.A.) to create an interpretive facility. The N.C.Y.A. had been successful in setting up several other nature centers in Florida and was anxious to have the Naples Center become one of its premiere operations. Later, when N.C.Y.A. merged with National Audubon, ownership of Big Cypress Nature Center was taken over by the latter organization.

In order to get the Fleischmann house to its new location the Jaycees cut the building into three sections and reassembled it on the property north of the Caribbean Gardens. No money had been given to help operate the Nature Center, but the public school system paid the Center $4,700 to conduct nature education programs for local school children. Gene Trainor was hired as the Center's first director in 1960. Gene was successful at getting community contributions as well as having local groups use the facility as a meeting place. On January 18, 1960, Mrs. Ted Below, Sr. held the first organizational meeting of Collier County Audubon at the Center, and on February 15, 1961, Alexander Sprunt, Jr. gave the first Collier County Audubon lecture at the facility. Everything seemed to be headed in the right direction for the fledgling Center. Prominent people from the Naples community were actively involved in its operation, the Center had its own women's league, and local residents like Dr. Baum contributed to its wildlife exhibits.

However, the winds of success shifted quickly. At a meeting in Everglades City on May 21, 1961, a newly elected school board withdrew the school system's monetary support for the Center stating that the public school children did not make adequate use of its programs. With no school funding and financial support from other community organizations gradually disappearing, its director left for another job. For nearly a decade the only activities provided by the Center were summer camps. This continued until 1969 when the Nature Center board was able to regain school funding, get monetary support from United Way, and acquire a decreasing endowment from the Fleischmann family. Bill Brannan became the Center's next full-time director, and in 1971 Wayne Parker replaced him.

When I got to the end of the washed out lime rock road that led to the Nature Center, I was greeted by the squawks of Nellie, a festive Amazon parrot. The bird had been donated to the Center by Collier County Audubon and was being housed in a large metal cage on the northwest side of the Nature Center porch. As I headed down the walkway I noticed a group of children gathered around the cage begging the parrot to say something. "Cutie, cutie caballero," the parrot obligingly responded as the children laughed and tried to mimic its speech. Next, the parrot attempted to give a rendition of "Three Blind Mice," but it was never able to articulate the last word so it kept repeating "three blind" over and over again. More squeals of laughter arose from the children as I opened the Nature Center's screen door and stepped inside to meet its director.

Wayne Parker interviewed me for the job. He was a tall, soft-spoken, easy going former schoolteacher who loved the outdoors and seemed excited about expanding the Nature Center's activities. Wayne was looking for someone to take over the Center's naturalist job, a position that involved teaching a series of five-day nature and conservation classes to all of Collier County's fourth grade public school children. In addition, the naturalist was supposed to help run summer camp programs and after-school classes. When Wayne finished the interview, I told him I liked the idea of teaching children about the local environment. I said I felt that if they grew up understanding how precious their natural resources were, the better our chance would be to preserve Southwest Florida's environment. It was nice to be on the same wavelength with someone even though it didn't look like I was going to get the position. It turned out Wayne had already interviewed a person from Ohio who was the number one candidate. I told him I understood, thanked him for his time, and said that if the other candidate didn't work out I was still interested. About a week later Wayne called and said that his other candidate had taken another job and that if I was still interested I should report to work the next day.

Elated at finding a job, I showed up early the next morning on the Nature Center doorstep to learn more about the naturalist position. I was quickly informed that school was going to start in a week and that there was a lot I needed to do to get ready. This included acquiring a chauffeur's license, learning how to drive a school bus, learning the locations of all the public elementary schools in the county, distributing program booklets, preparing teachers for the field trips, and purchasing a couple of Nature Center uniforms. Somehow I managed to get all these things accomplished, but the thing I had the most difficulty with was developing a series of activities for nine- and ten-year-old children.

I had forgotten what it was like to be nine years old and my head began to spin with all sorts of questions. How do you teach nature to someone this young? How do you keep them interested for five hours? And most of all, how do you keep them under control during a field trip? The night before my first class I had nightmares about children being dragged off by alligators or bitten by poisonous snakes. When I woke up that morning to the sound of the alarm, sweat was pouring off my brow and I could feel my heart pounding. It was time for me to face the dragon.

The lonely forty-five mile drive along the dark two-lane road that led to Immokalee did little to bolster my confidence. Reminding myself of the children's story "The Little Engine That Could," I kept repeating, "I know I can, I know I can." After parking at the administrative center I walked up to the front desk and asked for the keys to the school bus. "What bus?" was the secretary's surprised response.

"The one for the Big Cypress Nature Center program." Somewhat confused by my reply, she scurried down to the assistant superintendent's office. Anxious minutes passed. Had they forgotten that I was coming? I looked up at the clock. I was supposed to be at Highlands Elementary School in fifteen minutes. Finally the secretary reappeared with the assistant superintendent in tow. There were no extra buses for the Nature Center program he informed me. In a state of panic I pleaded my case. I needed a bus so I could take the children on their field trip. "Are you qualified to drive a school bus?" he inquired. Pulling out my wallet I showed him my chauffeur's license.

"We might have one available at the maintenance shed," was his cautious response. Calls were made, directions given and I hastily scrambled across town to pick up the vehicle. I was already five minutes late for class when I pulled up to the maintenance shop. Parked off to one side, the bus looked like it had just been towed from the junkyard. Dented fenders and broken windows were the least of its problems. Inside, a large hole ran down the center aisle and most of the seats were filled with cinder blocks. There was no time to complain. I moved the cinder blocks to the back of the bus so the children would have a place to sit and headed off to the school. The gearbox turned out to be an even bigger problem. Every time I shifted, the bus lurched forward and cinder blocks fell off the seats. Hopping down the highway, I arrived at Highlands Elementary twenty minutes late with some of the cinder blocks threatening to fall through the hole in the floor.

The teacher wasn't too happy that I was late, but after I explained the situation she gave me a sympathetic smile and welcomed me to her class. The moment of truth had arrived. Giggles arose after I introduced myself. They had never heard of anyone by the name of "Mr. Smells" before so I wrote my name on the board and tried to explain how to pronounce s-c-h-m. More giggles followed, so I gave up on that idea and started to talk about the plants and animals that lived in Florida's wetlands. I was certain lecturing to them wouldn't work so I had devised all sorts of devices to keep their attention throughout the week. I used a slide show with role play activities, brought in live animals, used a sight and sound game so they could recognize the noises made by different swamp animals, and blindfolded them and had them use their sense of touch to identify different plants and animals from a "habitat box." It was pure magic. Everything I did seemed to work—everything that is except the bus trip to and from the field trip site. The children had to straddle the large hole that ran down the center aisle of the bus in order to get to their seats and the teacher began to panic when the bus lurched forward every time I shifted gears. The children, of course, loved it. As cinder blocks toppled to the floor after each bump, they laughed and bounced up and down in their seats. The teacher had a different take on the situation and at the end of the day she pulled me aside and demanded I find a better bus. I apologized about the condition of the bus, but told her that it was the only bus the assistant superintendent could spare. Grumbling, she stomped out of the room and said, "We'll see about that!" The next day when I went to pick up the bus I was pleasantly surprised to receive the keys to brand new, spotlessly clean vehicle. What wonderful magic had this teacher preformed? When I showed up at the school I made sure I thanked her for her help. Greeting me at the classroom door, she smiled and said, "You can be assured that it will be the last time my husband will ever jeopardize the life of the children and me with a broken down bus!"

Immokalee is a poor, rural agricultural area in the northeastern part of Collier County. Large farms surround it and its population increases dramatically during the winter dry season with migrant farm workers and their families. I enjoyed teaching in this community. The children were eager to learn and they taught me a lot of interesting things about the surrounding wetlands. But I was also naïve about the school population and the community. I recall one day being on a field trip with a very well behaved class of children. As usual I began by asking them questions about the different plants and animals we were seeing. When none of the children responded, I asked the questions again and some of them started to laugh. It was then that I noticed the teacher trying to attract my attention. "What is it?" I whispered as I stepped off to the side.

"I should have told you sooner," she said with a look of embarrassment, "but none of these children speak English. They're migrants from Mexico and they just arrived a week ago."

"Do you speak Spanish?" I asked.

"Not much," was her sheepish response, "but the school system is earnestly looking for bilingual teachers."

"Are there any parents who could act as interpreters?" I inquired.

"Not yet," she informed me, "but they hope to have someone on board real soon." I don't believe the children learned a lot about nature that day, but I'm certain they had more fun than they did picking vegetables on the weekend. On several occasions in later years when I was teaching migrant children, they arrived in class so tired after working in the fields they would fall asleep in class. This was not a problem the school system could solve quickly, but they did hire two bilingual teachers so they could communicate with the children.

Another eye opener was the discovery that many of the young black children seldom traveled outside Immokalee. I distinctly remember my first trip to the beach with a group of fourth graders in the fall of 1971. They were hot and thirsty when I pulled into the beach parking lot, and all of them wanted something to drink. Before I could haul out the extra supply of water, a group of black children ran down to the Gulf and began gulping down seawater. The shock on their faces when they discovered that it wasn't fit to drink was something to behold. Spitting the water out on the beach, they raced back to the bus and told me that the lake was polluted. When I turned and looked at the teacher in disbelief she shook her head and said she wasn't surprised by their reaction. "They didn't let black people on the Naples beach until two years ago. They probably think the Gulf is a giant freshwater lake."

Often when I arrived at school the children would inundate me with animals and plants they'd collected. Most were delivered in jars and boxes that had air holes poked in the tops. The majority of the specimens were harmless, but a few had the teachers racing for the nearest exit. I distinctly remember one fourth grader who dumped two healthy pygmy rattlesnakes on top of the teacher's desk and wanted to know if they were poisonous. Needless to say the snakes were not happy about the way they were being handled and began striking at everything that moved. Within seconds the class was in total chaos. The teacher raced out the door looking for the principal, the girls started screaming and ran to the back of the room, while one boy tried to impress his classmates by attempting to grab one of the snakes behind the head. Without thinking, I grabbed the fearless youth by the back of the shirt, pulled him away from the lethal fangs of the enraged snakes, and dumped the angry duo into a wastepaper basket. Sweat poured from my brow and my heart almost stopped as I raced out of the room with the wastepaper basket and deposited the snakes into a sealed container on the bus. When I got back to the classroom the principal and the teacher had calmed the children down and I began my pre-field trip orientation by telling the boys and girls why they should not pick up snakes.

During one classroom presentation at Immokalee Middle School I discovered the science lab had no running water. So I emptied water from a spigot on the street into a bucket and transferred some if it to the terrarium where I housed the frogs and turtles I'd brought to class.

Many of the children on the field trips never seemed to have enough to eat. When we went on an outing the schools always packed an overabundance of sandwiches. I thought there was no way these children could eat them all. I was mistaken. As soon as lunchtime rolled around they would gulp down every bit of food and ask for more. The magnitude of how really hungry these children were hit home when I came across a black boy dragging a burlap bag across the school lawn. When I asked him what he had in the bag he said, "Ma dinner." Curious as to what he was eating, I asked if I could see what was inside his bag. "Sure," he responded proudly and opened up the bag so I could take a look. To my amazement it was filled with robins. When I asked him where he was bringing them he said he was taking them home for his mother to pluck!

"There's not a lot of meat on them," I said.

"I know. That's why I shot so many."

I was at a loss for words. He was obviously proud of the fact that he was able to provide food for his family and it was equally obvious that it was pointless to chastise him for killing the birds.

Because of the hunger problem, I made sure that I never left any live animals in the classroom overnight, especially gopher tortoises and chicken turtles. On two occasions I had forgotten to bring these animals back to the Nature Center and in both instances they were not there when I returned the next day. The first time one of these animals disappeared I thought one of the children had taken it home as a pet, so I confronted the class and asked the person who had taken it to return it as soon as possible. My request was greeted with silence. When I asked again and promised to look the other way when they returned it, one of the girls in the classroom began to cry. "I told James not to take that turtle," she blurted out.

Wiping tears from his eyes, James sheepishly stood up and admitted he taken the turtle. "I had to do it," he whimpered. "We had nothin' to eat and I was hungry."

Teaching in Naples was a world apart from the classes I taught in Immokalee. Most of the classrooms and buildings were new and many of the children, except those from the East Naples area, came from middle and upper income families. The majority of these children had plenty to eat and none of them as far as

I knew, ever spent the weekend working in the fields picking tomatoes. In Naples, I learned a great deal from the classroom teachers, and with their help I began to design better field trip activities. These were exciting times for me. The children couldn't wait for the naturalist to show up and teachers started preparing follow up activities for our field trips. However, the threat of monetary cuts in the school system's operating budget loomed large and something needed to be done to make sure the field trip programs weren't discontinued.

In the spring of 1972, while I was working at the Everglades School, Wayne asked if I could develop a testing program that would prove the worth of the Nature Center program. I told him I had a good background in statistics but no experience in educational testing. After mulling things over, we decided to visit Bill Hammond in Lee County. Bill had received a federal grant to develop a countywide environmental education program and had incorporated testing procedures to evaluate the success of his project. Bill was, and still is, one of the best environmental educators I've ever met. When we walked through the door of his office he greeted us with a big smile and began a non-stop monologue about the wonderful environmental education activities he was developing. After listening to him, I knew the Nature Center had a lot of catching up to do. I also realized that with the support of the right people there was no telling how successful the Nature Center could become.

Bill generously offered us copies of their tests without hesitation and advised us how we could modify them to address the subject material covered in our activities. It took some doing, but over the summer, with help from Bill and some of his staff, I developed a series of pre- and post-tests to evaluate the effectiveness of the Nature Center's program. The tests were designed to show the student improvement in content as well as in their appreciation of the natural environment.

Meanwhile, back at the Nature Center, Wayne assisted with the after school programs, gave community lectures, and maintained the largest private snake collection I'd ever seen. In fact the entire south wing of the Center housed snakes from all parts of the world. Our scaly residents included a giant anaconda, an emerald tree boa, several yellow rat snakes, an indigo snake, a couple of pygmy rattlers, an Indian cobra, and a water moccasin. Like many of the middle and high school boys who visited the Center, I was fascinated with the collection. Snakes are among the least understood and most maligned creatures. If you want to see a person squirm, just mention snakes and ask them to hold one. Wayne wanted to teach people about snakes and instill in them an understanding of the important roles snakes play in our environment. "Be sure to tell the children how important snakes can be in controlling rats and other pests," he would often say to me before I left for class.

Even though the Center's programs were going well and Wayne and I talked daily about new directions we could undertake, Wayne's love of snakes began to generate problems. Since Wayne's collection included venomous species, the Nature Center board wanted him to keep the door to the back room locked so no child would wander in and get bitten. He agreed to this even though it thwarted his plans to use the collection as a way of getting middle and high school students interested in volunteering at the Center.

Shortly after the board's decision to keep the snake collection behind locked doors I returned to the Center and found Wayne holding a badly swollen and discolored finger. When I asked what had happened he said one of his pygmy rattlesnakes had bitten him while he was trying to feed it and he was on his way to see a doctor. He was very upset about the incident and was worried that it would get back to the board so he asked me not to breathe a word of it to anyone. I promised I wouldn't and offered to drive him to the doctor. He thanked me for the offer but said he could handle it by himself.

Dr. Bailey, the husband of a local radio host, Lynn Bailey, was the physician that treated the bite. Instead of using antivenin to treat snakebite he believed in slicing open the area where the venom had collected so that the toxin could drain from the wound. It was his opinion that the aftereffects of the toxin were far less severe in people treated by this method than they were in people treated with antivenin. When Wayne returned to the Center his finger was swollen and discolored, but the doctor promised him a full recovery with complete use of his right hand.

Wayne took pictures of the wound and the healing process. He thought they might be useful in an education program. When I told him I thought the pictures might defeat his goal of getting people to appreciate snakes he shrugged his shoulders and said it was equally important for people to learn to respect them and leave them alone. Later I used the pictures in a classroom presentation on poisonous snakes. The request for the program came from a concerned teacher in Immokalee. She said most of her children couldn't distinguish poisonous snakes from harmless ones and a rattlesnake had recently bitten one of her fourth graders when he tried to pick it up. As part of the presentation she wanted me to show the children the differences between harmless and poisonous species and emphasize the importance of leaving these creatures alone.

"Do you want me to show them pictures of what a poisonous snake bite looks like?" I asked her.

After thinking it over she said, "Yes, it will make my students think twice before trying to handle one."

With slides, charts, and live examples of commonly seen harmless species in tow, I headed to Immokalee to do my program. I prefaced the program with the ecological importance of these creatures and then told the children why they shouldn't try to pick them up. Next, I showed slides of the different species of poisonous and non-poisonous snakes that lived in Immokalee and ended the program with a an overview of the different types of snake bite treatments including the photos Wayne had taken of his finger. When I got about halfway through the presentation I heard a series of loud thuds as several chairs came crashing down in the back of the room. At first I thought it was just a couple of children fooling around, but when the lights went on, much to my chagrin, I discovered two of the fourth graders had fainted. It appeared that they hadn't eaten all day and the photos of Wayne's open finger were too gruesome for them to look at. Needless to say, I was embarrassed by the entire incident and never used Wayne's photos in an elementary class again.

About a year after I began work, the Nature Center board decided to hire a group of consultants from National Audubon to evaluate the Center and make recommendations concerning its future in areas like fund raising, membership, and programs. After spending about a week with us, they drafted a document outlining their recommendations and sent a copy to the board. Unfortunately for Wayne, one of their suggestions was to remove his snake collection from the Nature Center premises as soon as possible. The difficulty from Wayne's perspective was that he didn't have a place to house the collection. He felt he needed an air-conditioned trailer, but he lacked the funds to purchase one. Conversely, the board was concerned with liability and the threat the poisonous snakes posed to young children. With the passage of summer camp and the arrival of the new school year, the pressure was on Wayne to take action.

During my second year of teaching fourth grade classes I started administering the pre- and post-tests we'd developed with Bill Hammond's assistance. This proved to be a monumental task that occupied most of my weekends and a good bit of my evenings. But the effort proved to be extremely beneficial. A statistical analysis of the data clearly illustrated that our programs were having a significant impact on the children's appreciation and understanding of Southwest Florida's environment.

Often after class I would sit down with Wayne to review the strides we were making and discuss some of the educational activities we might try in the future. Unlike the previous year when we seemed to feed off each other's enthusiasm during these sessions, there were times when Wayne seemed disinterested and depressed. Something had changed but it was difficult to pinpoint what it was. At first I thought the mood swings were due to the board's insistence that he move the snake collection. But as time went on and his mood swings became more pronounced, I decided he was experiencing some psychological problems. I don't know what other people do when they're confronted with this type of illness, but I knew I was unequipped to handle it. I liked Wayne a lot. He was intelligent and creative and the Nature Center had the opportunity to blossom under his leadership, but the forces at work inside him were leading him down a path that was self-destructive. When I tried to find out what was wrong he would dismiss me with a laugh or give me a peculiar look. Soon we were avoiding each other entirely and Wayne became less and less involved with the Nature Center's daily operation. Years later doctors would diagnose the chemical imbalance that robbed this talented person of his future, but it would not come soon enough to save his job.

In the spring of 1973, the Nature Center board asked Wayne to resign and temporarily elevated me to his position. In part, the board took this action because of the problems he had getting rid of the snakes and in part because of his mood swings. It was not something that I wanted to see happen. A change in leadership at this point bore the risk of jeopardizing the Center's future, especially since funding was hard to come by. Since I knew Wayne had been having discussions with United Way and the Collier County School System before he left, I asked him where he thought we stood financially with these agencies. He told me as far as he knew both organizations intended to meet his funding requests for the coming fiscal year. I was pleased to hear this, but when I contacted the agencies they made no bones about the fact that they intended to drop all of their support. Needless to say I was stunned by this revelation. If the Nature Center was going to survive, I needed to act quickly.

With the results of the evaluations of our fourth grade program in hand, I sat down with the school superintendent and showed him what a valuable asset the program was to the area's school children. Then I asked parents and teachers who had participated in the program to write letters of support. Things were shaky for a while, but after receiving some additional support from administrators, the school system agreed to fund the program at the same level as the previous year. Funding support from United Way, however, was an entirely different story. According to them, the monetary request Wayne had submitted was not in line with the services we were rendering. In order for me to get them to consider funding the Nature Center I asked their executive director to let me revise our proposal. Somewhat reluctantly she decided to let me do it. More sleepless nights followed before I managed to draft an operating budget that was to her liking. The next step was to get the request approved by the United Way board. Unfortunately, the day of the board meeting I was going to be on the beach with a summer camp class so I asked one of the Nature Center board members to represent me. "Sure," Harry Nell said, "I'd be happy to help out." Now everything was back on track, or so I thought.

Then came the day of the board meeting. Harry frantically called the Center to say he would not be able make the United Way meeting because his boss had just assigned him an emergency repair job. His telephone call came as a shock. Someone had to defend the proposal and that someone would have to be me. Looking at the clock I realized I only had five minutes to get there and I was covered with sand and seaweed. Flying out the door in a wet bathing suit, I arrived in the United Way office five minutes late only to discover I was at the wrong place. Panic set in. If the meeting wasn't here, where was it? "At the bank on Fifth Avenue South," someone said.

"Can I use your phone?" I asked the person in the office.

"Sure," she replied. I picked up the phone and pleaded with the executive director at the other end to let me give my presentation. Somewhat hesitant, she agreed, but only if I could make it within the next fifteen minutes. My car screeched to a halt in the bank parking lot with only a few minutes to spare. Racing up the stairs, I introduced myself to the secretary and was hastily guided into the boardroom. Out of breath, caked with salt, sand, and seaweed, I seated myself at the head of the table and thanked the board for their patience. I don't know if it was because they felt sorry for me, or the fact that they liked my proposal, but the board ultimately gave the Nature Center all of the monetary support I'd requested. The next step was to turn the Center's future around and implement the projects Wayne and I had dreamed about.

Dad's parents, Angielina Basso Schmelz and Fred Schmelz

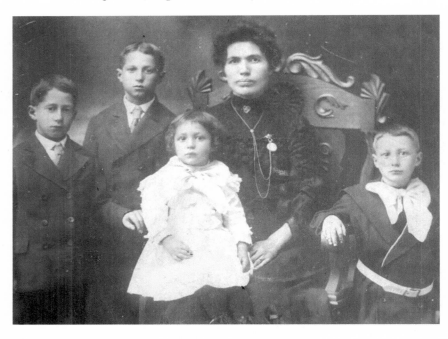

Dad's mother with her four sons. From left to right: Bill, Fred, Henry, and Walter

Mom and Dad at the Palisades across from New York City

Dad and Gary in their Navy uniforms

Chipper

Dad in the store

Dad, Cousin Lottie, and Al next to the "Dream Machine"

Cape Cod bounty

Dad and buddies with their Long Island tautog catch

U.S.S. San Pablo

Gary retrieving Nansen bottle aboard the U.S.S. San Pablo

University of Delaware research vessel Wolverine

Stingray catch aboard the Wolverine

Goliath grouper ensnared in trawl net

Chuck Courtney and Gary with goliath grouper outside Bud Kirk's fish house

Searching for fossils in a quarry

Fossil sand dollars and shells

Aerial photo of Tigertail Beach. Dirt road on left was route driven to Big Marco Pass

Gary leading a group on Tigertail walk

Dad showing sea pork to group at Tigertail Beach

Aerial view of Round Key area of Ten Thousand Islands, location of shark attack on manatee

Aerial view of Conservancy Nature Center

Dad with welcome drink in Long Island, Bahamas

Loggerhead turtle about to be released

Tugboat at Big Marco Pass

Dad and Gary seining for bait at Tigertail Beach

Dad with Topsy

Time Diggers

One of the things I knew I needed to do to make sure the Nature Center was a success was learn more about South Florida's natural environments. If I had a better feel for its different habitats, I could initiate field trip programs and give lectures about them. Until now what I had learned came mostly from books. But books only provided so much insight. I needed to get out into the field and explore the Ten Thousand Islands and Everglades-Big Cypress Swamp ecosystems. Consequently, when my parents arrived in Florida in June of 1972 and Dad started talking about fishing and exploring the Everglades, I saw it as a great way to spend my weekends learning about South Florida's habitats while spending some quality time with my father. The question was what aspect of the Florida peninsula should I concentrate on?

This question was answered when a visitor to the Nature Center brought me some fossils he'd collected from a nearby quarry. I loved to study fossils when I was young and I'd become an avid fossil collector when Dad took us on a vacation to the Scientists' Cliffs in Maryland. It was one of the few times we didn't go to Cape Cod, and I'll never forget the initial excitement I felt as my father and I walked along the shores of Chesapeake Bay hunting the bones and teeth of creatures that lived on our planet millions of years ago. "What kind of animals did the bones belong to?" and "How long ago did they live here?" were just some of the questions I pestered my father about. Poor Dad knew no more than I did, so I insisted he take me to the nearest library so I could learn more.

Shortly after the visitor dropped off the fossils, one of the Center's older student volunteers said there was a great fossil collecting site in LaBelle, a small town situated on the south side of the Caloosahatchee River about seventy miles northeast of Naples. He told me he had visited the site as part of a high school class and thought that a fossil hunt would be a neat activity for the Nature Center summer camp. His idea sounded great so the following weekend the entire staff took off to check the place out. The fossil site turned out to be a huge borrow pit and the number of fossils in it was awesome. Everywhere you stepped there were fossil shells. Even more unbelievable was the condition of the shells. They had been dead for over a million years and, except for their white color, they looked liked they'd died yesterday. Some of the cowries still had glossy exteriors, and the spines on some of the shells were so perfect it was hard to imagine they'd stayed intact when they were scooped out of the ground.

In addition to the shells, there were large numbers of bones scattered throughout the piles. Some were whale vertebrae; others belonged to horses that had become extinct just before the arrival of the paleo-Indians. There were also turtle bones that belonged to creatures the size of Volkswagens and the glossy-black teeth of ancient elephant-like creatures called mastodons. Like a kid in a candy store I gathered up as many specimens as I could and took them back to the Nature Center. Once again there were lots of questions that needed to be answered: How old were the fossils? What did the Florida peninsula look like when these creatures lived here? Most of all I wanted to find out if there were other places like the one in LaBelle where different kinds of fossils could be found.

Shortly after we visited LaBelle, I started taking summer camp children to the quarry, and later in the year I incorporated fossil trips into the Nature Center's public school program. For many of the children, fossil collecting became one of the highlights of our weeklong field trip activities. At the same time, I collected as many books and scientific publications as I could get to learn more. What I discovered was that Florida had some of the best-preserved Cenozoic fossil deposits in the United States. In fact, the upper strata of the Florida peninsula are made up almost entirely of fossils, and in some places these fossils are so close to the surface you can step on them. In the Big Cypress Swamp during the dry season, for instance, slabs of lime rock are exposed that are rich with fossil casts and molds of marine mollusks. These deposits belong to the Tamiami Formation and date back to a time 3.5 million years ago when the Big Cypress region was covered by a shallow tropical ocean.

From 1972 to 1987, Dad and I journeyed through Florida's past together. Dad called people who collected fossils "time diggers" because they were always digging for the remains of creatures older than they were. Florida is a great place to be a "time digger." All you need is a shovel and pick and you're ready to start. A drainage ditch dug around a fruit orchard might lead to the discovery of mammoth bones and take you back to a time when Florida was covered by temperate forests where giant sloths and armadillos shared their environment with hairy mammoths. Piles of dirt filled with fossil seashells near a housing development could transport you to an era when Florida was under the ocean and giant sharks swam in its warm tropical waters.

Whenever a new pit opened up or someone cleared land for a new housing development, Dad and I would get permission from the property owner and head out to see what discoveries we could make. At one location, near the edge of Lake Okeechobee, pieces of petrified wood and the presence of fossil coffee bean snails told us that in the not-too-distant past a mangrove swamp thrived along the lake's eastern shore. Fossil freshwater snails collected from a drainage ditch in LaBelle, together with the remains of horses, camels, and glyptodonts, were evidence of a Pleistocene watering hole that existed in this region during the last ice age. Near Audubon's Corkscrew Swamp Sanctuary, we discovered a massive one-million-year-old coral reef that was once part of a warm tropical ocean that harbored all kinds of unique marine animals.

Dad and I would sometimes drive hundreds of miles to get to a fossil site. Often, we had no specific destination in mind. We would simply drive along back roads and look for a place where they were digging. Many times we would meet up with other fossil enthusiasts. Some were professional geologists and paleontologists from Florida universities, but the vast majority were amateurs. Many were affiliated with shell and fossil clubs that held local shows in which amateurs could exhibit. The rest were interested in finding rare specimens that they could sell.

One thing I learned from the literature and other fossil collectors was that a large number of the specimens we were collecting had never been described. When I became aware of this, Dad and I began recording the location of each collecting site and the date when we collected the specimens. Most of the species we collected were marine mollusks, but there were representatives of many other phyla including crustaceans, bryozoans, echinoderms, fish, and mammals. Dad once asked what I was going to do with all the specimens we'd collected and initially, I had no idea. There must have been several thousand of them in my garage and several hundred more in cabinets in my house. In the 1970s there weren't too many institutions interested in housing collections of Florida invertebrate fossils. The only ones I knew of were the Smithsonian in Washington, D.C. and Tulane University in New Orleans. Eventually, I put some of the fossils on display at the Nature Center and used others in lectures that I gave to community groups. It wasn't until the late 1980s that I began to publish scientific papers naming some of the specimens my father and I had unearthed.

Most fossil collectors like their privacy and want to be left alone as they unearth their treasures. Nevertheless, Dad would sometimes follow them around and ask them what they were looking for. A few would stop and chat but most would ignore his inquiries. I could never anticipate what Dad would say or do when he met up with a fellow fossil hunter. On one occasion he encountered a sixty-year-old woman kneeling on the ground looking for micro-mollusks. It was a hot day and the sweat was dripping off her nose and forehead as she carefully scanned the ground with a lit cigarette dangling precariously from her lips. Sitting down alongside the woman, Dad stared at her until she lifted her head and looked at him. "You know, I used to do that," he said.

"Do what?" the woman asked caustically as she brushed away some gray hair from the side of her face. "Hunt for microfossils?"

"No." Dad replied. "Smoke. It's bad for your health. If you give it up you'll live a lot longer."

Removing the cigarette from her mouth, the woman looked over at Dad and snapped, "It's none of your goddamn business whether I smoke or not. It's not killing you is it?"

Dad acknowledged that it wasn't, but he couldn't resist giving her one last word of advice as he stood up and started to walk away, "You should have that cough checked. It sounds pretty bad."
As I watched, the woman gave Dad an icy stare, took another puff

on her cigarette, and blew the smoke in his direction. Several years later I heard from another fossil collector that the woman had died of lung cancer. Dad didn't say anything when I told him the news. He just looked out the car window and asked if there would be any bones where we were collecting that day.

For the most part fossil collecting in Florida is a reasonably safe activity, but there were some things we needed to watch out for. On cold days snakes liked to warm themselves on the top of fossil piles in the late afternoon. Most of the snakes Dad and I came across were harmless but on two occasions we did encounter large water moccasins. If you decided to dig fossils out of the quarry wall, you also had to be careful not to undermine the site otherwise it would collapse on you and you'd get buried under tons of dirt. Another issue was watching where we stepped. If the mining company was doing a lot of digging, the ground could get very soft, especially after a heavy rain, and Dad and I sometimes found ourselves sinking in mud up to our waists.

On one occasion Dad stopped to let me know he was heading over to help someone out. When I asked him what had happened he told me that a woman was stuck in the bottom of the quarry and he wanted to give her a hand.

"Is she hurt?" I asked as I rose to my feet and brushed myself off.

"Nah, she's just having trouble climbing out of the pit."

Even though it didn't appear to be an emergency, I decided to tag along and see what was up. When I caught up with Dad he was kneeling over the edge of the pit talking to the woman. Reaching down, he lifted up her bucket of fossils and then extended his hand to hoist her out. This proved to be a big mistake. The person asking for assistance weighed twice as much as Dad and when she grabbed hold of him she flipped him headfirst into the bottom of the pit. All types of terrible images raced through my mind when I saw him disappear. His legs and arms were broken, he'd landed on a rock and was unconscious, or worse yet he was dead. As fast as I could, I scrambled down to rescue him. "Are you all right?" I gasped when I arrived at the spot where he had landed. At first there was no response and then I heard a faint moan. I couldn't believe it. Dad had somehow avoided landing on rocks and other jagged structures in the pit and had become immersed in a thick, viscous pool of mud. None of his bones appeared to have been broken; only his pride had been damaged. As I stood there and offered him a hand out of the brown goop, he grumbled about the damn mud then lifted himself up and wiped the slime off of his glasses. Meanwhile, the woman Dad had tried to rescue managed to crawl out of the pit and was standing at the top yelling to us about how sorry she was for all the trouble she'd caused.

During lunch, Dad and I would often talk about the fossils we'd collected and try to envision the evolution of the Florida peninsula. From the people we talked to and the books we read we knew there were never any volcanoes in Florida and that the state seldom experienced earthquakes. We also knew dinosaurs never roamed the state's landscape because a deep tropical ocean covered the entire region seventy million years ago. During this era giant turtles along with many strange varieties of fish swam in its aquatic environment, but none of them left behind fossils that were easy to uncover. Their remains were buried thousands of feet below the surface where they were occasionally recovered from exploratory wells.

A warm tropical ocean covered most of the Florida peninsula for the next thirty million years, and a shallow-water grass flat, like the one that is in the Florida Keys today, replaced the deep-water ocean environment that existed during the time of the dinosaurs. It was a marine habitat teeming with life. Paleontologists discovered the fossil remains of some of these Eocene life forms when they dug the Cross Florida Barge Canal. Large populations of protozoa called foraminifera plus numerous species of invertebrates and fish lived in this grassy habitat. The shallow sea was also home to larger animals like crocodiles, dugongs and whales.

Around 3.5 million years ago a shallow ocean covered the Sarasota area. Marine grass flats, coral patch reefs, and mangrove islands made up part of this aquatic ecosystem. Included among its subtropical and temperate residents Dad and I discovered the remains of whales, walruses, manatees, dolphins, sharks, birds, fish, and numerous species of marine invertebrates.

By the early Pleistocene, the northern half of the Florida peninsula had emerged from the ocean while the southern half remained a tropical marine habitat. Places like LaBelle were fifty to one hundred feet beneath the ocean and a tropical sea still covered most of the Caloosahatchee River system. This warm environment did not last long. Massive ice sheets encroached upon North America. As these ice sheets expanded and contracted the Florida peninsula underwent radical changes in shape and size. With the last ice age twenty thousand years ago, a mile high sheet of ice covered New York City and the ocean receded from Florida's coast leaving the southern interior of the state 390 feet above sea level. During this epoch mammoths and mastodons wandered across the landscape and herds of wild horses grazed on the peninsula's open grassland.

After spending fifteen years studying the geology and paleontology of Florida, my father and I reached one inescapable conclusion—the southern half of the Florida should never have been developed. Today we are experiencing a warming trend and the polar ice caps are once again melting. As they melt, the southern half of the state is being reclaimed by the ocean, and even with aggressive beach renourishment programs costing trillions of dollars, nothing will prevent this portion of the state from turning into a shallow marine platform that will eventually look like the Florida Keys.

One day when Dad and I were discussing South Florida's future he wanted to know if there was anything I could do at the Nature Center to warn people about what was going to happen to the state. "Not a lot," I admitted. "People are not about to abandon South Florida because of what might happen. The only thing that can be done is to educate them about South Florida's future." Eventually, I did this by taking people on Nature Center fossil collecting fieldtrips to show them the geologic record imbedded in the face of quarry walls. Here they observed layer after layer of fossil shells and other marine life. Most came away believing that the sea level would once again rise and cover the South Florida peninsula but none intended to leave. They would take their chances since they didn't see themselves living long enough for these changes to be a threat. In some ways they are just like the woman Dad lectured in the quarry about cigarette smoking. There is no sense giving up what is gratifying for something that might happen. You can only give them the facts and allow them make up their own minds.

New Horizons

My first chore after Wayne left was to hire a naturalist, but I only had enough money for a six-month salary. After that, things would depend on the school board's final approval of our request, which wouldn't happen until late summer. This meant that anyone who took the job would have to do so on a leap of faith. The whole thing was pretty scary, but the risk had to be taken if the Nature Center was going to survive. I went back to my revised operating budget and massaged the figures once again. If we established a membership program and implemented some after school classes, we just might swing it for a year. The next question was who would be crazy enough to take the job. I called Jerry Cutlip, the director of National Audubon's Corkscrew Swamp Sanctuary, and asked if he knew of anyone who might be interested in the position. After giving it some thought he said he thought he did. A young man by the name of Steve Goeser had just contacted him looking for a job. He said Steve had worked for him the previous summer and was a good worker. Needless to say, I was pleased to hear that someone like that was available so I contacted Steve by phone. Yes, Steve was interested in the job and yes, he would be happy to come for an interview. Less than a week later Steve sat in front of my desk answering questions and listening to me describe the naturalist's responsibilities. Steve, however, didn't look anything like the young man Jerry described. He had long, well-groomed, shoulder length hair and a mustache, and the more I looked at him the more he reminded me of one of those stained glass images of Jesus Christ. Times had changed since I had gone for my first job interview, I thought to myself. Was I getting to be an old fart at thirty-three? I also thought about how the Nature Center board and the school administration would relate to him. His references were fine. He had a college degree. Noticing the ring on his finger I asked if he was married. He gave an affirmative nod. "Do you think your wife will like living in Naples?" I asked.

Steve smiled and said "Oh, sure. Do you provide health insurance?"

That was the question I dreaded most. "No, maybe sometime in the future," I replied and went on to describe our tenuous financial situation. "Would your wife be willing to work if things got tight?" I inquired.

"Sure," he replied with a broad, captivating smile.

If Steve was as diligent and hardworking as Jerry said, there was no reason to believe he wouldn't work out. Rising from behind my desk I shook his hand and had one of the volunteers give him a guided tour of the Center including the naturalist's living quarters. After looking at two other candidates I finally called Steve and offered him the position.

Late that summer the school board approved our funding request, and that fall I showed Steve where the public schools were located and introduced him to the fourth-grade teachers. Steve turned out to be a good naturalist. My favorite picture of him was taken by one of the local newspaper photographers. In it he's pointing out something in a tree to a group of fourth graders. The Nature Center volunteers said it reminded them of a picture of Jesus Christ with his disciples.

During Steve's employment as a naturalist, the Nature Center faced major problems caused by the 1973 gasoline crisis. The programs in Immokalee proved to be the most difficult to implement. Steve and all of the teachers who lived in Naples but taught in Immokalee had to spend long hours in gas lines so they could drive four hundred miles to and from school each week. Gas thieves were also a major headache. Often when we went to pick up the bus we found that the gas tank had been drained the night before. No matter how much security the school system provided, the thieves would successfully steal gasoline. Finally, the maintenance people in Immokalee inserted a device into the tank that prevented the thieves from removing the gas. This cut down on our fuel loss but so enraged the thieves that they smashed windows on our bus and punctured its tires.

My biggest concern during Steve's tenure remained getting enough operating funds to keep the Nature Center afloat. Although we had the school board and United Way funds to keep us going, I needed to generate more money from memberships and contributions. On one occasion when my fundraising efforts weren't going as well as I hoped, I sat down with Steve and brought him up to date on our precarious situation and diplomatically urged him to keep his options open. After we finished our talk, Steve said he understood the Center's situation and would act accordingly, but about two months later he came to me and announced he was about to become a dad. When he made the announcement I got a sinking feeling in my stomach and all sorts of questions raced through my mind. Could we get medical coverage for his family? If not, were there other ways we could help him out with his medical expenses? Unfortunately, I didn't have any answers. To complicate things, early on in the pregnancy, Steve and his wife learned the fetus was at risk and would require special medical attention. It was heart-rending news. When I heard about it I went home, slumped down in the living room chair and threw a draft of a grant proposal I was writing across the room in frustration. With no options left, Steve called home, and explained the situation to his dad who offered him a job with his company in Homestead. It meant he would get the insurance coverage he needed to pay for his escalating medical bills, but it also meant that Steve would be giving up a job he really loved. The day he and his wife left was a sad one for the volunteers and me.

Now I needed to find a replacement for Steve. I would have no problems finishing up the school programs by myself, but I still needed time to increase our membership base, submit proposals to community organizations and design adult activities for the upcoming fiscal year. It was Rick Bantz, the naturalist at Corkscrew Swamp Sanctuary, who came to the rescue. Rick was aware of Steve's situation, and when Steve left he stopped by the office and said he would like to work for us. He liked the idea of working with children and didn't think he'd get a chance to do that anytime soon at Corkscrew. To say the least, I was thrilled. I knew from past experience that Rick was an excellent naturalist and that he loved children. But at the same time the Sanctuary's director and I were friends and I wanted to make sure that if I hired Rick it wouldn't affect our relationship. I called Jerry that afternoon to let him know that Rick had applied for the naturalist position at the

Nature Center. Jerry was aware of Rick's desire to work for us and felt he would make a fine addition to our staff. He said he was sorry to lose him, but that he also understood Rick's desire to become more involved with education. I thanked Jerry for his comments and told him I would offer Rick the job.

I couldn't have had a better person to replace Steve. "Ranger Rick," as he came to be known by the fourth graders in the county, was idolized by the children and whenever he showed up at a classroom he was mobbed by youngsters who struggled to hang on to his uniform. In some ways I liked to think of him as Collier County's first "environmental rock star."

With Rick conducting fourth grade programs I started addressing a number of other Nature Center issues. The first involved starting up a membership program and expanding our after school and adult activities. In order to accomplish this I printed up and circulated membership application forms, designed and distributed a quarterly newsletter, and created and implemented adult lectures and weekend field trip activities. With the money obtained from these efforts I hired a secretary/receptionist.

The next changes involved the Nature Center's building and grounds. When families visited the Center there were no exhibits, other than a large Everglades diorama, and there was no signage on our nature trail. In order to fill this void I got permission to hire a second naturalist. Bernie Yokel gave me the name of someone he thought could fill this position. He was working as a volunteer at Rookery Bay and had a Master of Science degree in biology.

Dave Addison showed up in my office for an interview several days after I talked to Bernie. Dave was a tall, somewhat reserved individual who had moved to South Florida with his wife after serving two years in Vietnam and attending graduate school. His hope was to find a job in the Naples area where he could make use of his education and try to forget the war. During our discussion, I learned that Dave was a skilled craftsman and an enthusiastic outdoorsman, both of which were attributes I knew the Nature Center could use. After interviewing several other people for the naturalist position, I called Dave and told him we had need of his skills.

Besides teaching public school programs and assisting with our summer camp activities, Dave constructed a number of exhibits for the Center. They included two 100-gallon aquariums, one with fresh and one with saltwater fish; reptile displays; and cases displaying local marine life and fossils. Along the nature trail he also put up signs describing the native vegetation, established bird-feeding areas, and constructed a large shade house where visitors got a close up look at native orchids and air plants.

Another Center program that definitely needed a new direction was Junior Audubon. It was one of the activities that Wayne had taken under his wing. The concept of the Junior Audubon program was a good one—get middle and high school age students interested in protecting the environment. The program was implemented by Nature Center staff and received monetary support from the local Audubon society. When Wayne was at the Center, Sewell and Virginia Corkran were the Audubon representatives who helped supervise the project. When I took over, Bob and Mary-Lou Nadeau had replaced the Corkrans. Most of the activities involved lectures and field trips, but sometimes the students participated in special events like Collier Audubon's annual Christmas bird count or greeting dignitaries like Governor Askew when they visited Collier County. The students said they enjoyed the field trips, but wanted to be involved in something that was more meaningful. After listening to their complaints I suggested they hold a meeting at the Center to decide what new direction they wanted the program to take. The officers of the club agreed but decided to open up the meeting to all interested high school students not just those participating in Junior Audubon.

The idea that gained the most support was the creation of a wild animal hospital. It was a project suggested by Rick because concerned residents were constantly bringing injured wildlife to the Center and we had no way of treating them. With some reservation I agreed to go along with the proposal but only if the Nature Center oversaw the project. The program would address the issue of injured wildlife that were brought to the Nature Center, but it also carried certain risks like liability problems and disease transmission.

After the initial meeting the students held planning meetings, officers were elected, and a brochure was designed and disseminated to make the public aware of the clinic. The acronym selected for our program was A.R.C. (Animal Rehabilitation Center). The students enlisted the volunteer services of local veterinarians since none of the Nature Center staff had the skills needed to treat injured wild animals. Drs. Ned Johnson and Larry Coen were the first veterinarians to volunteer their time. Dr. Johnson was already familiar with treating wild animals through his work with Jungle Larry's African Safari, while Dr. Coen had an interest in treating animals other than domestic pets.

At the time the students decided to get into the wild animal rehabilitation business there was a similar program underway on Sanibel Island. It was called C.R.O.W., an acronym for Clinic for the Rehabilitation of Wildlife. Dr. Coen and some of the students wanted to see how their program operated, so I made arrangements to visit the facility. Their hospital was nothing like I expected. The two women who ran C.R.O.W. operated out of a home in a residential neighborhood. Most of the animals were housed outdoors inside a chain link enclosure at the rear of the house. The enclosure provided shelter from the sun and a wading pool for larger birds like egrets, herons, and pelicans. The house itself served as the hospital, and seriously injured birds were kept in closets to minimize trauma. I, for one, could not imagine how these two dedicated individuals could manage to live in the house. The odor of bird feces and the smell of disinfectants permeated every room, and when we sat down on the sofa to talk to the directors a cloud of bird guano enveloped us. I also decided from our visit that C.R.O.W. had to have some very tolerant neighbors because the houses adjacent to them had dozens of vultures perched on their roofs. When I asked about the vultures they admitted they were a problem. It appeared that the birds knew a good thing when they smelled it, and whenever food for the injured animals remained uneaten the vultures would fly into their enclosure to devour what was left. Another problem with the vultures was that they also used the neighbors' rooftops as a restroom and piles of guano had begun to accumulate on them.

Regardless of the atrocious working conditions, I had to give the two women credit for their efforts to save injured animals. They also knew they couldn't remain where they were and were desperately seeking financial help so that they could move to a new location. Their dream was to acquire several acres of land on Sanibel and build a hospital where the animals could be properly treated and cared for.

We learned a lot from C.R.O.W. including trying to get local fishermen to donate fish and seeing if pharmaceutical companies would donate frozen rats and mice to feed injured raptors. "Also, don't forget to check with local stores like Publix," they suggested. "They throw away lots of food and they might be willing to donate some of it." We'd never thought of most of these things and all of them eventually proved helpful.

Back at the Center we began an aluminum can recycling program to help pay for some of the program's food and medicine. Efforts were also made to get local television coverage of the students' rescue efforts, and almost every week newspaper articles were written focusing on the release of a rehabilitated animal. Within a year, A.R.C. became one of the most heralded and best-funded projects in Collier County. Local businesses donated food, Collier County Audubon donated $1,000 towards its operation, college scholarships were awarded to participating volunteers, and the supervisor of the program received the Outstanding Humanitarian Award for her services.

Once I got involved with the wild animal rehabilitation business I also learned a lot about the dark side of human behavior. In the book *The Life of Pi*, the zoo director sets up an exhibit behind a large curtain that invites the public to see the world's most dangerous animal. When the visitors pull aside the curtain they are confronted with full-length images of themselves. There is probably no act of cruelty that human beings have not committed against animals. In A.R.C. we received pelicans with their bills chopped off, egrets and hawks with arrows stuck in their bodies, mammals and wading birds with their legs cut off, birds with their eyes deliberately poked out, and baby opossums covered with cigarette burns. Seeing this cruelty on a daily basis had a profound impact upon the students as well as the Nature Center staff. Some of the students quit because they couldn't tolerate seeing the cruelty. Others became so upset they wanted people punished for their behavior. All of this placed a tremendous burden on Center personnel. A great deal of our time was spent convincing student volunteers that not everyone was as bad as they thought and that a lot of people really cared about the local wildlife otherwise they wouldn't rescue them.

As the program expanded, I continued to be concerned about health risks and liability problems associated with the program. I stressed these concerns to both the Nature Center staff and the student volunteers, and for over a year we had no problems. Then the heart-rending situation with Seymour the otter forced us to make some major program modifications.

Seymour was rescued from some children who were pelting him with rocks. The abrasions and cuts from the rocks turned out to be minor, but Seymour was also seriously ill with pneumonia. Dr. Coen treated the pup with antibiotics and the student volunteers were successful in nursing him back to health. By the time Seymour was several months old he became the comic mascot of the Center and often romped behind the student volunteers to the pond where he delighted our caregivers with his zany antics.

At times I was totally amazed at Seymour's intelligence. One of the things he loved to do was play pranks on people. One in particular totally captivated me and if I hadn't seen it with my own eyes I wouldn't have believed it. Seymour loved to ambush people, not just anybody, only women who wore sandals and painted their toenails red. As part of this game he would crouch underneath the receptionist's desk and wait for his victim to get within striking distance. Then he would dart out and grab hold of her big toe. He never held on to the toe very long, but the jumping and screaming of his victims were an immense source of pleasure to the otter. Inevitably, as our receptionist tried to calm the victim down, Seymour would lie on his back, slap his paws together, and begin to laugh.

The tragic events that led to Seymour's demise began over a weekend. One of our dependable high school volunteers had responsibility for taking care of Seymour and had invited her boyfriend to join her. Instead of putting her gloves on, she used her unprotected hand to feed the otter a meal of fresh fish. In its haste to grab the fish, Seymour nipped the volunteer's finger and drew blood. The wound wasn't very deep so when it stopped bleeding the volunteer chose to ignore it. Later, the wound reopened and the girl's boyfriend insisted she go to the hospital to have it treated. Once she went to the hospital and described what had happened, the hospital reported the incident as a wild animal bite to the health department. As a result, when I showed up at work on Monday I was greeted by two grim-faced health officials who demanded I turn over Seymour so that he could be examined for rabies. Needless to say I didn't want to do that. After listening to their description of the otter bite, I told them I was certain that the animal did not have rabies and asked if we could quarantine Seymour and keep him under observation for several weeks. The two officials reluctantly left the premises without the otter telling me they'd have to discuss my proposal with their boss. His response was swift and without mercy. Seymour must be beheaded and examined for rabies. The students were horrified and demanded that I refuse to give him up. Newspaper and television coverage of Seymour's plight soon got the community in an uproar. Letters appeared in the local papers asking for the health department to spare Seymour's life. Finally, the head of the Florida State Health Department came to Naples. He was no more sympathetic to the situation than the local officials. He concurred that the animal must be beheaded. A warrant was served and two local health department officials arrived at the Center to pick up Seymour. In front of television cameras and newspaper reporters, the two health officials used bare hands to seize the otter and thrust him into their carrying case. In the process, one of the men was bitten by the otter who was terrified by their rough treatment. When I asked the officials in front of the cameras why they hadn't used gloves to retrieve the animal, they smugly responded that they had had rabies shots and didn't have to worry about contracting the disease. It was a sad day at the Nature Center when the rabies test results came back. As everyone expected, Seymour's test was negative.

You learn something from negative experiences; I know we did from the Seymour incident. For a while we debated whether or not it was wise for us to continue treating mammals. We knew that other wild animal centers were choosing not to work with them because of the potential problems that could arise with rabies. We decided, however, to continue treating them, but under a stricter set of guidelines. Beginning that day, every A.R.C. supervisor or volunteer working with mammals had to get rabies shots and there was strict enforcement of the glove rule. No volunteer was allowed to handle or feed any mammal without gloves and if they failed to do so they were suspended from the program. We also decided to restrict public exposure to our mammals to avoid any further bites. For as long as I was director of the Center, we never had another incident where we had to put an animal down as a result of carelessness.

Concerned citizens delivered most of the injured animals to the rehabilitation center. Whenever anyone rescued a wild animal there was, of course, a certain amount of risk involved. The animal had no idea what the rescuer's intentions were and quite often they bit and scratched the individual who was trying to save them. We made a concerted effort to dissuade the public from picking up mammals because of rabies and also warned them through newspaper articles and television programs about the serious injuries that could be generated by birds' beaks and talons. Most people heeded the warnings but a few brave souls had some traumatic encounters.

I remember one intrepid fisherman who rescued an osprey from drowning. The osprey had apparently latched on to a fish that was bigger than it could handle and was dragged underwater. Somehow the fish was able to escape, but not until the bird was totally exhausted. When the fisherman saw the bird floating on the water he guided his boat alongside and rescued it. Much to the fisherman's consternation the osprey showed its appreciation by locking its talons into the man's leg. I'll never forget the desperate look on the fisherman's face as he staggered up the Nature Center walkway with the bird still attached to him. It took nearly fifteen minutes to calm the bird down and get it to release its grip. Every minute we struggled with the bird, I empathized with our Good Samaritan who gutted out the experience with remarkable courage and patience.

Another animal rescuer had an experience that still leaves me chuckling. This gentleman had discovered a turkey vulture with a busted wing hopping along the side of the highway. Not wanting to pick the bird up with his hands, he took off his jacket, placed it over the vulture, and put the animal in his car. A few miles down the highway he became overwhelmed by the putrid smell coming from the back seat. His eyes began to water and he said he almost vomited. In order to get rid of the smell he rolled down the driver's side window. By the time he reached us we could smell him coming. With a handkerchief over his nose, he opened the back door and pleaded with us to get rid of the bird. Thankfully it hopped out of his car without us having to capture it. From the odor, we had a pretty good idea what had happened. The vulture had recently eaten a ripe skunk, and when our rescuer captured the bird it regurgitated its partially digested meal. I don't know if the bird's rescuer ever got that smell out of his car, but I do know he never showed up with another wild animal.

We changed the name from Animal Rehabilitation Center to Wild Animal Rehabilitation Center because people began dropping off exotics. Some of them had escaped into the wild, while others were pets people had become bored with. By far, the most common non-native species people brought to us were Muscovy ducks. When I first arrived in Naples I thought these birds were cute. Nearly everyone I knew fell in love with them. Then I discovered what a messy nuisance they could become. Put out a bird feeder and they'd consume all of your seed. Leave the door to your screened-in swimming pool open and they'd waddle in leaving behind copious amounts of dung. There was even an instance where one of these ducks decided to nest in a homeowner's attic.

At one point we had so many crippled Muscovy ducks they were using up our food budget faster than we could replenish it. Finally, after talking things over, we decided not to accept any more Muscovies and tactfully refused to take them whenever a Good Samaritan brought one in.

Among some of the other non-native animals that were delivered to our doorstep during the program's formative years were a ten foot boa constrictor, several green iguanas, a large monitor lizard, several species of parrots, a couple of feral pigs, and a friendly, but prankish wooly monkey called Dolly. With the exception of Dolly, we made it our business to find new homes for these creatures as quickly as possible.

Dolly was a playful wooly monkey that loved to romp around the animal rehabilitation compound with our student volunteers. Since the student volunteers loved having her around we housed her in a large cage that was built on the south side of the Nature Center away from the visiting public. Unfortunately, one of the Nature Center's visitors strayed off of our nature trail and discovered Dolly. As luck would have it, it was also a day Dolly was bored from a lack of attention. As the woman bent over to get a closer look at the monkey it grabbed her shiny gold necklace and wig and refused to let go. The screams that arose from the back of the Nature Center put me into panic mode. When I reached Dolly's cage the monkey was jumping up and down and urinating on the woman's necklace and wig. Mortified by the situation I tried to calm Dolly down, but nothing seemed to appease her. As soon as I attempted to get the monkey to give me the necklace and wig she started slinging them from one side of the cage to another. I'd never seen Dolly so upset. Putting on a pair of gloves, I asked the woman to stand back while I went inside the cage to try to retrieve her possessions. It took a lot of coaxing, but I was eventually successful. Fortunately, the woman was good-natured about the whole incident, but I made a decision right then and there to find Dolly a new home.

After completing my second year as director of the Nature Center it was time for me to decide whether I was going remain in that position. These were exciting times at the Center and with the help of staff and volunteers we were really making progress. The board was happy with my performance, the Center's financial situation was fairly secure, memberships were on the rise and the new programs had generated a lot of interest. So one day while Dad and I were sitting on the wooden porch of the Nature Center I asked him what he thought I should do.

"Do you like what you're doing?" he asked as we both watched the sun's late afternoon light blanket the lime rock road that led to the Nature Center.

"Sure," I responded, "but it's not exactly the kind of work I intended to do for the rest of my life. I was trained to be a marine biologist."

"Can you use any of the things you learned in college with your new job?" he asked.

"Absolutely. And if I stay I'll get to use some of the knowledge I've gained from our explorations."

"Then maybe you should stay. Sometimes life offers you an opportunity you just can't refuse and maybe this is one of those times."

After thinking about it some more I realized that Dad was right. This was one of those times. So after our discussion I sat down and began to make even bigger plans for the Center's future.

Swamp Stompers

The massive saw grass prairies of the Everglades and the magnificent cypress swamps along Southwest Florida's coast make up one of the world's most breathtaking ecosystems. When I moved to South Florida I knew very little about this complex environment except for what I read in Marjory Stoneman Douglas's classic *Everglades, River of Grass*.

I still remember my first journey into this expansive wetland. It was at night along a puddle-filled lime rock road during the height of the rainy season. The Nature Center's director, Wayne Parker, said the Everglades was a great place to collect snakes, so a couple of the Center's student volunteers and I hopped into his four wheel drive jeep and headed off into the swamp's inky interior. For me, the outing was a unique opportunity to learn something about the region's snake population. For the students, the idea of hunting snakes at night was too cool an adventure to pass up.

During our drive Wayne informed us that most snakes are nocturnal and that our best chance to see them was at night after a heavy rain. That night the conditions were perfect. We had just experienced some powerful thunderstorms and there were all kinds of critters hopping and scurrying across the highway. After about an hour we turned off the main road and headed slowly north on a poorly maintained lime rock trail. I'll always remember the possessed look on Wayne's face as his headlights illuminated the road in front of us. No snake was going to escape detection. His eyes shifted from one edge of the road to the other, and as soon as he spotted the slightest movement he slammed on the brakes and skidded to a halt. My job, he said, was to capture snakes and put them into one of his pillowcases. When I asked whether or not he knew which ones were poisonous, he just laughed and promised he'd only send me out after harmless ones. The first snake we encountered was a mud snake. It was fairly docile and when I picked it up it coiled its cool red and black body around my arm and made no attempt to bite. The next one we sighted was a large green water snake. When I jumped out of the car and cornered the snake it was clear it wanted no part of me. I was also pretty sure I didn't want any part of it. The snake repeatedly struck at me as I tried to pick it up, so I tried to maneuver it into a position where I could toss it into the pillowcase without being bitten. "Grab him behind the head," Wayne kept yelling at me as the snake inched closer to its escape route. Finally, I lost my sanity and followed Wayne's instruction. I missed and the snake sank its needle-sharp teeth into my hand. I grimaced in pain as the blood oozed out of my wound and the reptile shifted its lower jaw from side to side. "Hold on to him," Wayne shouted as he leapt out of the jeep. "Try not to move your hand; otherwise you'll damage its teeth." Never mind the snake's teeth, what about me? I thought to myself as Wayne loosened the animal's grip. That was the last time I went snake hunting in the Everglades. From that day forward most of my treks into the swamp were during the day, and I can assure you most of them were a lot more pleasurable than my initial outing

By the time Dad and I started exploring the Everglades-Big Cypress region it was only a vestige of its former self. The scenic, meandering Kissimmee River had been straightened to reduce flooding on adjacent cattle ranches, the custard apple swamps surrounding Lake Okeechobee had been replaced by huge sugar plantations, wildfires continued to eat away at the thin veneer of nutrient rich soil, and the region's massive six-hundred-year-old bald cypress trees had nearly all been logged for lumber.

Since I was still learning about this ecosystem, the first outings city folks like my father and I took into the swamp were limited to short hikes and canoe trips. We started by borrowing one of the Nature Center's newly donated canoes and used it to fish and explore the southern half of the Turner River Canal situated off Route 41 just east of Ochopee. The canal was created to drain the Big Cypress Swamp, and despite the fact that it was manmade it was still a scenic waterway to explore. Five o'clock was our wake up time. This allowed us to be on the Turner River Canal just as the first rays of light illuminated the horizon. The cool morning air during the dry season always invigorated us and heightened our spirit of adventure. As we paddled along the canal's tranquil waters we were frequently greeted with a chorus of sounds generated by creatures whose ancestors had sung the same hosannas to the rising sun for thousands of years. At first light pig frogs, hiding behind a forest of cattails, would begin with deep-throated croaks while sleepy-eyed wading birds added to the chorus with guttural complaints from the treetops. Next came the twitter of songbirds followed by the persistent din of insects. Collectively, they generated a discordant wilderness symphony that was music to our ears.

In our initial explorations we were mostly interested in catching largemouth bass. Halfway down the tree-lined waterway Dad and I would cast our surface plugs towards the shoreline hoping to attract the attention of one hiding in the shadows of the cattails. Ever vigilant, these bass would suspend themselves above the weeds waiting to dart after unsuspecting prey. Sometimes it was the flash of a golden shiner and sometimes it was the silver glitter of our lures that got their attention.

Casting towards the banks of the canal was often challenging for Dad and on occasions led to some interesting situations. One morning his lure wrapped around some branches just beneath a green heron nest. When he jerked on his line its hooks embedded in the tree and he couldn't shake them loose. This required that we maneuver back to the tree to untangle the mess. Upset with our early morning intrusion, the young birds announced their displeasure with a series of angry squawks. Dad, of course, expressed his own dissatisfaction as he reached up into the tree and tried to untangle his line. As he did, the herons started regurgitating copious amounts of half digested fish on top of my father's head. Dad's response to this indignity was a second barrage of colorful expletives during which he threatened to ring the herons' necks. At one point I wasn't certain he'd ever succeed in freeing his lure. Twice he nearly tipped the canoe over as he yanked on the tree limb. Ultimately his hooks pulled free, but when he turned around I couldn't help but laugh. He looked exactly like someone who'd received the worst end of a pie-throwing contest.

Perhaps the most bizarre experience we had while fishing in the Turner River Canal was the day Dad hooked a yellow rat snake that was crawling among the branches of a cypress tree. Unaware that he had snagged the reptile, he jerked the line to free his lure and out flew the snake with its tail end attached to one of his hooks. Both of us ducked as the snake zipped over the canoe and landed a short distance away in the canal. Thrashing about, the frustrated snake repeatedly struck at Dad's lure in an attempt to free itself. The question that I faced was how badly did Dad want his lure back. I suggested we cut the line, but Dad wasn't about to let the snake swim off with his prize Rapala. "I'll drag him back to the canoe," he said, "then you grab him behind the head and I'll unhook him." Somehow I remembered doing something similar once before.

"All right," I reluctantly agreed as Dad slowly began retrieving his line.

"Don't let him get in the canoe," Dad began shouting as the snake gave up attacking the fishing lure and began striking at me when Dad pulled him alongside the canoe. Yeah, sure I thought to myself, and what if I miss. My first two attempts failed, but on the third try I managed to get a firm grip on the creature so Dad could remove the hook. I was never happier to see a snake returned to the wild and I'm sure the snake was equally glad to be rid of us.

By about ten o'clock, on most days, the fishing activity along the canal would taper off and the two of us would spend the rest of the morning enjoying the scenery as we drifted into the more open recesses of the swamp. Along the edges of the canal, egrets and herons would poise themselves over the tannin-stained water looking for shiners and frogs to eat. And when the light and wind conditions were just right, mirror images of these birds reflected off the water's surface.

Towards noon, alligators and turtles would begin to crawl up onto the banks of the Canal to sun themselves. Some of the alligators were in the ten to twelve foot category. They never bothered us while we were in the canoe but we always kept a wary eye on them as we drifted along. Most of the turtles we saw were black and yellow striped peninsula cooters. Sometimes, when the cooters found a broad log in the middle of the slough, they would pile on top of one another until they created a teetering tower of sun worshipers. At the first sign of our approach, this living tower would comically collapse and a host of confused cooters would tumble into the canal frantically colliding with one another as they beat a hasty retreat into the deeper recesses of the swamp.

Otters were our favorite animals to watch. Occasionally we would spot them frolicking along the edge of the slough or chasing one another in the saw grass. During the latter half of the dry season they would often have their pups with them and they were frequently curious about what we were up to. Sometimes they would swim up alongside the canoe and watch us fish, and on a couple of occasions they tried to grab hold of the bass we were trying to retrieve.

The wet prairies and cypress swamps that flourish along Florida's west coast all gradually merge into the shallow water mangrove forests that stretch across the southern portion of the Florida peninsula. On the west coast, this maze of mangroves forms a region called the Ten Thousand Islands. Here freshwater moving south mingles with the saltwater from the Gulf of Mexico and creates a nursery area for marine life. Millions of sport and commercially important species of fish and invertebrates spend their time as juveniles in this transition zone. When the weather was especially nice Dad and I would paddle down the Canal to this mixed region of saw grass and mangroves. As we glided along we were always amazed at the amount of life that it harbored, especially at the end of the rainy season. Everywhere we looked, the mangrove prairie was dotted with watery pans swirling with juvenile snook, redfish, snapper, as well as small shrimp and crabs. As expected, this soup of marine life attracted large numbers of wading birds and small mammals all of which feasted upon this smorgasbord of food.

In the late 1970s and early 1980s, Dad and I began hiking into the deeper recesses of the Fakahatchee Strand. At that time most people didn't explore this awesome wetland portion of the Big Cypress Swamp. The majority of it was inaccessible to hikers and the single lime rock road that led into its interior was filled with potholes and covered with water during the rainy season. Despite these obstacles, my father and I always tried to spend several weekends each year trekking through this subtropical forest.

When Dad and I first entered the heart of this swamp we journeyed into a deep slough where dozens of royal palms, many exceeding a hundred feet in height, stood as sentinels over bald cypress trees and tropical hardwoods. It was in this region that early naturalists identified forty-eight different species of orchids, some of which existed nowhere else in the United States. Many of these orchids clung to the gnarly branches of custard apple trees and it was not unusual for Dad and I to discover five or six species growing on a single tree. The swamp was also home to all kinds of air plants. It was often impossible for us to count the number growing on one trunk, and like the resident orchids, a single tree often possessed as many as a half dozen species.

The resident animal population in the Fakahatchee, although not as diverse or as abundant as its plant life, was equally fascinating. Among the denizens of this forest, we discovered the endangered Florida panther, Everglades mink and Florida wood stork as well as more common species like black bear, river otter, whitetail deer, opossums, raccoons, and numerous species of birds, reptiles, and fish.

Insects and spiders were abundant in the swamp, but mosquitoes were the most challenging. They were prevalent during the rainy season and for the most part thrived around the edges of roads leading into the swamp. Once we waded into the cool, waist-deep water of the slough, we noticed a dramatic decline in their numbers. This was because the swamp had its own mosquito control program in the form of mosquito fish. There were uncountable numbers of these tiny fish in the swamp's murky water and they kept the adult mosquito population under control by feeding on their larvae.

Butterflies were among the most spectacular and colorful insects in the Fakahatchee. They came in almost every color imaginable and included orange and black ruddy daggerwings, the tropical black and yellow striped zebra heliconias, orange julias, eastern and tiger swallowtails, southern buckeyes, orange and black queens, and viceroys. During the rainy season Dad and I would often spot dozens of yellow and black male tiger swallowtails along the lime rock road leading into the swamp extracting salt from its surface. Sometimes we would also see large clusters of them collecting on the bodies of dead animals searching for salt. In every forest death nurtures life, and in the Fakahatchee the death of a wild animal enabled the tiger swallowtails to perpetuate their species.

If you suffer from arachnophobia, stomping through the Fakahatchee Strand could be a little frightening. In some places the spiders created a thick canopy of webs. None of the spiders Dad and I encountered were harmful and most were interesting to study. Two of the largest species we came across were the black fishing spider and the golden orb weaver. Golden orb weavers construct large circular webs that extend between the branches of trees, and Dad and I used sticks to clear a path through their webs as we hiked through the swamp. The female of this species grows to three and a half to four inches, while the males are runts that reach about a half-inch in size. Often we would see several male spiders clinging to the periphery of the female's web. For the males this was a precarious position. They benefited from the food the female's web ensnared, but they also had to be careful that the female did not eat them. Mating was also risky business. The males had to be extremely cautious when they approached the female; if she wasn't in the mood to mate or was hungry, there was always the chance he would wind up on her dinner plate.

Perhaps the largest spider we encountered in the Fakahatchee was the fishing spider. Dad and I saw specimens that reached over four inches. It is basically a harmless creature that scurries up and down the trunks of large trees, its black hairy body making it almost invisible in the swamp's shaded interior. My father and I discovered that this spider liked to eat mosquito fish, and their favorite mode of capturing them was to dash down the trunk of a tree to pluck them from the water while the fish were feeding on mosquito larvae. Dad and I were always amazed at how quickly they snatched up their prey, and when we waded through the swamp we often tried to see which one of us would be the first to spot one grabbing a meal.

During one of our initial hikes into a deep slough, Dad had his first encounter with a fishing spider. After we had wandered around for about an hour, Dad placed his hand up against the trunk of a bald cypress tree to rest and suddenly felt the cool hairy legs of a large black fishing spider crawling across his arm. Even though the creature is harmless, its substantial size can catch you by surprise, especially when you come face to face with one on your shoulder. All of a sudden I heard Dad cry out and start jumping around in the water. At first I thought something had bitten him, but when I saw the fishing spider scurry across his chest and leap onto a cypress knee I couldn't help but laugh. I was glad that it wasn't me the spider decided to crawl across. After this incident I noticed that Dad was very careful where he placed his hands when we were moving through a slough.

Hiking through the swamp was always a challenge. Even during the dry season, when the swamp was more accessible, we had to be careful about what we were doing. I remember the first time we tried to explore one of the Fakahatchee's deep sloughs just before the beginning of the rainy season. It was the first time we tried to do this and we thought it would be easy. There would be no water to wade through and there would be no bugs to pester us. After driving about five miles along the lime rock road into the heart of the Fakahatchee, we got out of the car, put on our backpacks with our lunches, and hiked a mile along an overgrown, elevated tram built by Lee Tidewater Company. Upon reaching the slough, we left the trail and headed into the heart of the swamp thinking that we would have no problems relocating our entry point. Unfortunately, we were not as well prepared for this outing as we should have been.

Fascinated by a forest blanketed with epiphytes we soon lost track of where we were. It wasn't until midday when we stopped to eat lunch on the fallen trunk of a cypress tree that Dad asked if I could remember which direction we needed to take in order to get back. I was hoping to use the position of the sun to help guide us out, but it had become overcast, and now I wasn't certain which direction we should take so I told Dad all we needed to do was follow the small slough to our right and it would take us back to the tram. Unfortunately, my path-finding instincts needed a lot of tweaking and after an hour following the slough we wound up where we started. Next, we headed through the brush in the opposite direction. Another hour and a half passed and we still hadn't found the tram. By now Dad was not happy with me and I was beginning to get the uneasy feeling that we might not make it out of the swamp that day. By sheer luck and another hour of wandering around, we discovered the lime rock road near where I'd parked the car. Dehydrated and exhausted, we trudged back to the vehicle thanking our lucky stars we didn't have to spend the night in the swamp. After that experience I never went hiking in the Fakahatchee, with Dad or anyone else, without taking a compass and some ribbons to mark our trail. Of course today you can use a GPS, but I still take tape to mark my path just in case the batteries fail or I lose the GPS in the swamp.

During the rainy season Dad and I used hiking sticks when exploring the swamp. With so many submerged cypress knees and logs it was almost impossible to wander around in the Big Cypress region of the Fakahatchee without some kind of support. Of course, you might wonder why someone would be crazy enough to want to wade around in a swamp in the first place. For us the answer was simple. During the height of the rainy season this region reached its pinnacle of splendor. The once brown and twisted leaves of resurrection ferns rejuvenated themselves and formed a blanket of green on the deeply furrowed branches of the custard apple trees. Blossoming epiphytic air plants clung to the limbs and trunks of every tree, and moonflowers formed a canopy of white flowers along the outer edges of the forest. Best of all, it was during this season the epiphytic orchids that lay dormant for most of year sent out their flower spikes. This was the season of rebirth. *Breathtaking* is the best word to describe it. Frilly ghost orchids clung to the pond apple trees and the flowering spikes of maroon and yellow clamshell orchids suspended themselves from overhanging branches, while night fragrant orchids grew in tight clusters on the trunks of pop ash trees.

At one time the cypress forests and custard apple swamps extended to the eastern edge of what is now the City of Naples. Today, only fragments of this primeval forest still exist. In the mid 1970s a local developer in the area offered to sell the Nature Center some land southeast of Naples where we could build a new interpretive facility. The site was located off Rattlesnake Hammock Road on the edge of a custard apple swamp. From the description I was given, the wooded area sounded like an ideal location for a nature center so Dad and I headed out to see what was there. When we reached the slough, the water level was high and it was obvious that we would need our walking sticks, compass, and orange tape. In addition, the water movement through the slough was fairly strong so we had to proceed very slowly. Everything was going just fine until Dad tripped over a log and tumbled forward into the water. Somehow he managed to keep

178 *Journey to the Edge of Eden*

his glasses on and right himself just as I was about to reach over and grab him. When I asked if he was all right he sputtered, "Yes," and started to move forward. As he did, a large log floated to the surface and Dad put out his hand to shove it aside. To Dad's surprise the log didn't move; in fact it snorted at him. At this point the expression on my father's face was one of wide-eyed disbelief. "Holy shit," he shouted as he tried to turn and run in the opposite direction. The "log" Dad had tripped over was a six-foot alligator and it didn't seem particularly pleased that it had been stepped on. I don't think I'll ever forget my father's frantic shouts as he stumbled out of the swamp. As for the alligator, it didn't seem the least bit interested in chasing Dad. When I finally caught up with my father and suggested we try another route into the custard apple swamp he just looked at me like I was crazy and stomped back to the car.

When Dad and I finally returned to the Rattlesnake Hammock property the water levels were much lower and we found a less arduous route into the slough. It turned out to be a breathtaking wilderness whose rich diversity of plant and animal life far exceeded my expectations. The trees were festooned with all kinds of orchids and other air plants and there was an abundance of deer and other wildlife in the surrounding forest. Unfortunately, the Nature Center couldn't afford to purchase the property but I did get permission from the developer to use it as an outdoor classroom. After some additional explorations, I started leading Nature Center field trips into the slough during the dry season as part of our wilderness adventure program. Everyone we took there was enthralled with what they saw and it soon became one of our most popular activities—that is until I got a surprise call from the police. I was informed that over the weekend someone had driven a huge truck alongside the slough and used a chain saw to cut off nearly all the limbs of the custard apple trees. There was hardly an orchid, air plant, or fern left when I drove over to see the damage. It made me sick to look at the devastation and made me even sicker to realize that I was partially responsible for what had taken place. In all probability, someone who'd participated in one of our field trips had decided to make a quick profit from our discovery. After that I decided never to tell or show anyone the locations of the special places Dad and I discovered in the swamps of South Florida.

Tigertail Wonders

As beautiful as the Fakahatchee and Everglades are, all of us have one special place where we love to escape. For Dad and me it was Tigertail Beach. Deltona donated Tigertail to Collier County in 1969. It is situated at the north end of Marco Island and the current story is that it is named after the Seminole chief Charley Tigertail. Another story I heard when I was working for Deltona was that aerial photos of the beach reminded the island's planners of a tiger's tail.

There was no parking lot at Tigertail's main entrance when I first discovered it in 1970, just a narrow path that meandered towards the Gulf through a coastal hammock and a mangrove creek that you had to wade across at high tide. Once across the creek, you arrived at a sandy beach that stretched for a mile north towards Big Marco Pass.

A part of the Ten Thousand Islands, Tigertail is a microcosm of some of the habitats found in this region. It has a nearshore muddy bottom with shoal weed, a deeper offshore area with turtle grass, the remnants of a mangrove creek, and large stretches of sandy shoals. It was during one of my early fishing trips to this location that Dad I decided that this stretch of beach might be an ideal outdoor environmental classroom for Nature Center school programs and adult field trips. However, in order for me to turn it into one I needed to learn everything I could about Tigertail's habitats. This task would turn out to be a lot more challenging than I anticipated since it meant being able to identify the different life forms that were part of each community as well as understand the relationships that existed between them. When I told Dad about my plans to do a detailed study of Tigertail, he became very excited and offered to help. He said it would be like the times we spent in the Delaware marshes doing research on killifish. Shored up by his enthusiasm, we started making more visits to Tigertail on the weekends to learn everything we could about its different environments. Tide charts were studied; seines, buckets, and dip nets were purchased; and identification guides of South Florida marine plants and animals were acquired. After arming ourselves with all the tools we needed, Dad and I engaged ourselves in a task that turned out to be an eight-year educational adventure.

Considerable thought was given to where we should begin this study. I thought maybe we should start with the dune and hammock environments that bordered the Gulf but Dad thought we should begin with marine habitats. After further discussion I chose one of the grass flat communities. We took the plunge during a spring low tide at seven in the morning. To this day I remember standing bleary-eyed on the shallow mud flats thinking about what I had gotten us into. I knew the sea grass bed that I was standing in was shoal weed, but I knew very little about the environment it grew in or the type of life that lived beneath it. So what should I do next? It took me entirely too long to realize that I was sinking in the answer. The best place to start was with the mud in the lagoon. Bending over, I grabbed a handful of this viscous goop and did something most people never do—took a deep whiff. Not too surprisingly it smelled like rotten eggs. The foul odor was hydrogen sulfide gas produced from the decay of marine plants and animals. Ironically, it was the same odor many Marco Islanders would later try to use as proof that the lagoon was polluted.

I knew from my training as a marine biologist, that the mud oozing between my fingers had life in it, but I never realized how much. Spreading it out across the palm of my hand I uncovered several worms and a couple of bivalves. For some reason Dad had decided to bring a metal strainer with him that day so I placed a handful of mud into it and washed it with seawater. The results were incredible! In one handful of mud there were a half dozen different species. If the concentration of life in one handful of mud was uniform throughout the entire shoal grass community, then I estimated the amount of life living in the sediment at Tigertail was in the billions. No wonder so many birds came to feed on these shoals at low tide. The flats offered a smorgasbord of food that required little effort to procure. It was also the reason so many birds used the nearby beaches to breed. Some of the life forms we identified in the mud included juvenile pointed Venus clams, juvenile southern quahogs, bamboo worms, and large numbers of burrowing brittle stars.

The presence of juvenile quahogs came as a pleasant surprise to my father and me. We knew that at one time there were huge populations of adult clams in the Ten Thousand Islands. In fact, one of the largest beds stretched from Coon Key, east of Goodland, south to Pavilion Key. Initially, clam diggers used rakes to extract these clams from shallow water and on good days they harvested eight to ten bushels. Later, on Marco, Captain Bill Collier invented a dredge that could harvest five hundred bushels of clams in twelve hours. Unable to compete with the dredge, the individual clam fisherman either went out of business or sought employment with Captain Bill. No marine resource is inexhaustible, however, and that was certainly true for the Ten Thousand Island clam population. By 1947, nearly all of the clams had been harvested from the region and the Doxsee clam factory on Marco Island was forced to shut down. Therefore, our discovery of juvenile clams at Tigertail was good news. It suggested that a sufficient number of adult quahogs had survived to be able to replenish their decimated beds.

In later trips to Tigertail we used a coring device to look at the different layers in the mud. Most of the life forms that lived in the mud occupied the upper layers of sediment away from the organically rich, but oxygen depleted zone where the hydrogen sulfide gas was produced. A few species, however, adapted to the deeper layers. They included burrowing brittle stars and great cleft clams.

The shoal grass growing in the mud is a short, thin flat-blade grass whose tips are usually broken. This plant possesses a root-like structure called a rhizome and one of the important functions of this grass is to stabilize marine sediments. The plant can tolerate near freezing temperatures in the winter dry season as well as temperatures in excess of 90° F during the hot, summer rainy season. Shoal weed is also able to survive in very saline conditions where the salt concentrations in the water can reach forty parts per thousand. During the day my Dad and I discovered that these plants saturated the shallow waters off Tigertail with oxygen, enabling fish to move into the shallow water to feed. At night, however, these same plants used up the oxygen in the lagoon, and many of the fish that entered this habitat during the day retreated to deeper, more oxygen rich waters offshore.

Besides stabilizing the sediments of the near shore environment off Tigertail, this dark green mat of grass provided shelter and food for many species of invertebrates and small fish. Dad and I dragged our dip nets through the grass to see what we could capture. Our efforts were rewarded with numerous specimens of grass and broken-back shrimp as well as southern spider crabs.

At the base of the shoal weed we also discovered large numbers of juvenile pink shrimp and blue crabs. Our studies showed that the shrimp reached their peak of abundance during the month of October, after which they migrated into the Gulf's deeper waters to spawn. Blue crabs were most abundant during the rainy season. Their larvae were washed into the grass flats during the dry season where they metamorphosed into their adult form. These young crabs used the grass beds for cover, feeding and shedding their exoskeletons, until they reached maturity. Like the pink shrimp, their numbers dwindled after the month of October. In August and September, Dad and I would often see the crabs mating in the shallow water along the shore, and by October most of the mature females had disappeared and migrated offshore to produce a new generation.

In order to see what was swimming in the water above the grass, Dad and I dragged a thirty-foot seine through the water. Among the small fish we collected were the molly-like mosquito fish, the stocky sheepshead minnow, the chubby Gulf killifish, and the slender longnose killifish. All of these fish were capable of tolerating the extreme temperature and salinity fluctuations as well as low oxygen levels that could be characteristic of this habitat. We also discovered quite a few transient species. To our surprise, they included the juveniles of a number of economically important species such as spotted trout, grey and lane snapper, striped mullet, and Gulf flounder.

Offshore, in slightly deeper water, Dad and I found a narrow region of turtle grass. The rectangular blades of mature grass were about one foot in length and three quarters of an inch wide. This grass grew in less turbulent areas where there was more protection from wind and waves. I knew that this plant produced flowers that were pale white and about one inch in diameter. The flowers had no true petals, and the male flowers were situated on the same plants as the females but higher up. At Tigertail the turtle grass flowers appeared at the end of the dry season and throughout the rainy season, but it took Dad and me a long time to find them. We were finally successful on one of those rare days when the water was crystal clear and there was very little wind generating ripples on the surface. Wading side by side through the grass, we moved against the incoming tide and carefully scanned the beds. The total number of flowers we discovered that June day was two, so we surmised that the number of flowers in bloom at any one particular time was exceptionally small.

Turtle grass plays a number of important ecological roles in Tigertail's marine environment. Their broad leaves reduce the velocity of tidal currents so that particles of debris being transported in the water column sink to the bottom of the lagoon. Subsequently, these nutrient rich sediments create an ideal habitat for a wide variety of marine life. In addition, by reducing the amount of suspended material in the water, the grasses also increase the amount of light that can reach the bottom thereby creating an environment that is more conducive to photosynthesis and plant growth.

Among the things Dad and I observed about turtle grass was how much plant and animal life clung to the grass blades. Scientists call these life forms epibionts. Over 113 species of algae alone have been reported growing on the blades of turtle grass. Using a hand lens my father and I discovered a couple dozen different species of epibionts when we examined the turtle grass leaves. In addition to algae, they included sponges, tunicates, bryozoans, and hydroids. Once again we tried to guesstimate how much life lived on the grass blades at Tigertail by calculating the average number of life forms on several plants, multiplying that number by the number of plants found in a square meter, and then multiplying that number by the number of square meters of grass growing in the lagoon. Our results were astonishing. In the few acres of turtle grass present at Tigertail during our study we estimated that there were several million epibionts.

Just like everywhere else in the Gulf and Ten Thousand Islands, the amount of life we found in the grass beds varied with the season. After several years of observation we found that the life attached to the grass leaves was most abundant during the latter half of the rainy season. Once the westerly cold fronts of the dry season arrived, the shallow water along Tigertail became turbid and the water temperature over the grass beds plummeted. As a result, the area occupied by the grass beds shrank dramatically and there was a corresponding decline in the population of epibionts and other life forms. Throughout the coldest portions of the dry season the beds remained in a near dormant state, only beginning the process of rejuvenation when the warmer, less turbulent weather arrived in late April and May.

Among the larger sedentary life forms we discovered in the turtle grass beds were barnacles and tunicates. Relatives of shrimp, the barnacles bonded themselves to hard substrates like seashells and driftwood. One day when Dad and I were planning to study the grass beds, I placed a glass jar into one of our buckets and promised to show him how barnacles collected food with their feet. When we got to the beach I thought we'd find some right away but it took quite a while before we discovered a cluster attached to a small cockleshell. After wading ashore, I placed the shell into a jar, filled it with seawater and held it up to the sun so we could watch the barnacles perform. Perhaps it was the intensity with which we were looking at the jar that attracted a family's attention. Whatever it was, they strolled over and stopped to ask what we were doing. "Observing how barnacles eat," I remember my father answering in an authoritative voice.

"Can we see them?" one of the children asked. Turning over one of our buckets, I placed the glass jar on top of it and stepped back so everyone could take a look. As soon as I did, Dad began a running commentary about how barnacles lived upside down in their shell and waved their legs around to trap particles of food. "Are you a professor?" one of the children asked when he was finished.

"No," Dad replied, but from the expression on his face you could see that he was proud to think that they thought he was. For the next hour Dad told the family all about the things we were studying and how important all the plants and animals we'd observed were to each other as well as to us. It was his time to stand in the spotlight. I'd never seen him as enthusiastic as he was that day, and I often reflect about what wonderful teachers parents and grandparents can be. I have no doubt that that was one of the reasons volunteers were such a valuable asset to our education programs.

Tunicates were abundant at Tigertail. Belonging to the phylum Urochordata, they are more closely related to us than they are to crabs and shrimp. When Dad and I looked at a juvenile under a microscope it looked like a tadpole. When we examined it closely we could see a tiny nerve cord, small eyespot, and a primitive "backbone" that ran through their tails. Studies have shown that juveniles swim around until they find appropriate places to attach themselves. Once they locate a suitable shell or rock, they stand on their heads and cement themselves to it by secreting a sticky glue-like substance. When attached, the juveniles metamorphose into adults by absorbing the backbone and other structures in their tails.

We discovered two species of tunicates at Tigertail. One was the pleated sea squirt. They grew in lumpy clusters and had shiny bodies that slipped from our hands when we tried to pick them up. Like its common name implies, this animal released a stream of water whenever we squeezed it. Dad loved to show this creature to his friends. After telling them how this slippery lump was one of their distant relatives, he'd ask them to take a closer look at its "mouth" and laugh when they got a face full of seawater.

The other common tunicate species at Tigertail was the sea pork. These animals grow in rubbery mat-like colonies and come in a variety of colors. After a cold front passed through Dad and I found quite a few of them washed up on to the beach. Most people had no idea what these rubbery masses were when they discovered them. On several occasions Dad and I came across people standing around poking at them with sticks. Whenever we encountered them they would ask us what the colorful lumps were and ultimately be astounded when they learned they were animals. In a few situations we even found individuals who thought the lumps were "whale vomit" and had started collecting them to bring them to perfume manufacturers. Most of these folks returned the lumps to the ocean when we told them what they were, but a few thought we were trying to talk them out of their treasure and insisted on carting them off. I suspect these people were very disappointed when they didn't get ten dollars an ounce for their rubbery lumps.

By far the most interesting gastropods Dad and I discovered living on the grass flats were sea hares. Two species periodically showed up in the lagoon. One was the ragged sea hare; the other was the Brazilian sea hare. Sea hares are snails without an external shell that get their name from their soft, rabbit-like head. The ragged sea hare possesses a cream-colored gelatinous body covered with finger-like outgrowths known as papillae. At Tigertail they grow to a length of eight inches and feed on the blue-green algal film that covers the sand in the sea grass beds. The Brazilian sea hare has a brown body with irregular blotches of yellow and white. It reaches a length of eleven inches and has a wing-like mantle that enables it to swim. Both species showed up at Tigertail at the end of the rainy season and the early part of the dry season (October through December) when they laid their sticky, spaghetti-like, gelatinous eggs in the sea grass. Throughout our study we never observed anything feeding on the sea hares and we often wondered why. Ultimately we discovered that they have skin glands that secrete unpalatable chemical compounds that protect them from predators. We also observed that both species produce a purple, ink-like substance that some investigators suggest confuse and frighten off predators.

In order to capture and identify the larger vertebrates that fed over the turtle grass beds at Tigertail we used the Nature Center's hundred-foot seine. This was a project that Dad and I couldn't handle alone so we always enlisted the help of friends and Nature Center staff. Our usual plan was to arrive at Tigertail just prior to sunset during an incoming tide. This gave us just enough light to unfold the seine and scout out the areas we wanted to drag the net over before it was too dark to see.

Whenever big fish moved in over the grass beds we would hear a powerful swoosh followed by an eruption of mullet. This always marked the beginning of a feeding frenzy and none of us could resist its allure. The "big ones" were calling to us, and as fast as we could we'd pick up the net and drag it out into the lagoon. And big ones were what we often caught seining through the turtle grass at Tigertail. Some of my staff and neighbors would wade out into chest deep water with me while Dad and a few of the other guys would work the shallow end. The idea was to pull the net in the direction of the incoming tide. As we walked along we could feel the fish strike the net. Sometimes, when the big ones hit, the force of the blow was so powerful it nearly pulled the brails out of our hands. The more fish the net ensnared, the more jerks we would feel, and when the belly of the net began to boil we knew it was time to close the trap. At that point, Dad and his helper would stop pulling the net while those of us at the deep end would quickly drag the seine towards the beach.

There were times when we would capture half a dozen five- to ten-pound snook. This happened mostly at the end of the dry season when the snook were moving into the passes to spawn. Besides snook, we netted an assortment of other fish including spotted sea trout, redfish, grey snappers, Gulf flounder, mullet, black drum, and sheepshead. Hard head catfish, Atlantic needlefish, ladyfish, crevalle jacks, Atlantic guitarfish, southern stingrays, and a variety of sharks rounded off the catch. Most of the sharks avoided our net, but there were times when we caught a few, particularly whenever the large fish were crowded together in a feeding frenzy. Seining on these nights sometimes proved to be pretty dicey especially for the people at the deep end.

I remember one evening when I was by myself at the deep end pulling the net through chest-deep water. The mullet were hopping over the net trying to avoid being eaten and schools of bait fish were breaking the surface all around me. Suddenly Dad and his helper began shouting at me and pointing to something. With all the activity taking place I couldn't make out what they were saying. I thought maybe they wanted me to swing the net towards shore so I waved back and started in. Just as I did, I spotted the large dorsal fin of a shark heading straight towards me. Sharks are unpredictable and I had no idea what this one was about to do. So when the dorsal fin veered in my direction I thought, Oh shit! From the shape and size of the fin it looked like a bull shark. These sharks have a reputation for occasionally taking a bite out of swimmers, so when I saw it my anxiety level spiked. The shark had apparently joined in the evening's feeding frenzy and my only hope was that it was more interested in eating fish than it was in taking a bite out of me. Thankfully, it veered off at the last moment. Back on the beach I breathed a sigh of relief and thanked Dad for his warning. Needless to say, that was the last seining run we did that evening.

Except for a few plants there was very little visible life on Tigertail's sandy beach. It was a highly unstable environment that changed from day to day as well as with the seasons. As Dad and I walked down Tigertail one day I remember turning towards him and asking him where he thought this sand came from. His response was that it came from the Gulf. That had been my initial thought when I first looked at the sand on other Naples beaches I had visited, but I knew the answer wasn't that simple. When I asked Dad where he thought the sand in the Gulf came from, he scratched his head and said he guessed it came from the beach. He wasn't entirely wrong; the sand along Florida's Gulf coast is constantly moving. Waves perpetually sweep a portion of our beach sand offshore, and prevailing currents eventually carry it south onto another section of beach. But Florida doesn't have any rocks that can be broken down into silicon dioxide which is what most of Florida's west coast beaches are made of. Therefore, the sand making up the beaches on this coast must come from someplace other than Florida. That place, it turns out, is the southeastern coastal plain and southern Appalachians of the United States. It has taken tens of millions of years for the rocks in these areas to erode and the eroded sediments to be swept into river systems like the Mississippi. Transported south, the sand is ultimately deposited in the Gulf of Mexico where, after millions of years, the prevailing currents carry it south to Naples and Tigertail Beach. So when my father and I walked on the sandy beaches of Naples and Marco Island we weren't just walking on sand, we were walking on eroded fragments of rock that had glistened in the afternoon sun when dinosaurs roamed our nation's tropical forests. Dad would often joke with me about traveling through time as we trudged through the sand at Tigertail. And laughingly, I would respond by saying that if we put our ears close enough to the beach maybe we could hear the roar of dinosaurs at their moment of extinction.

When Dad and I first visited Tigertail its beach was located on the east side of the lagoon. Today, the sandy beach is on the west side of the lagoon and stretches northward in the form of a mile-long spit. Adjacent to the beach was a shallow sandy shoal with its own characteristic life forms. Among the more common species my father and I observed were the keyhole sand dollars, Florida fighting conchs and Atlantic horseshoe crabs.

Live sand dollars are covered with dark brown or purple spines and possess flattened external skeletons that enable them to slide beneath the sand in search of particulate matter and glass encased plants called diatoms. The sand dollars' thin edges and the holes in their skeletons help prevent them from being cast ashore by storms. Nevertheless, large numbers were often washed up after a cold front and Dad and I would watch as treasure-hunting beachcombers scoffed up the bleached skeletons.

The second most frequently seen marine creature on Tigertail's sandy shoals was the Florida fighting conch. Thousands of these active snails were also cast ashore after winter storms. Because of their beautiful colors shell hunters loved to collect them and Dad and I would often encounter people returning from the beach with bags full. When Dad saw this he would often engage them in a conversation and suggest that they let them go. A number of the people he talked to had no idea that the shells housed live animals. If people would let him, he'd place the shells into a pool of water so they could see the animal's mouth and eyestalks. Many were amazed by what they saw. Through these mini-educational sessions Dad got most of the people to release the live shells they'd collected, and sometimes a few of them would even thank him and shake his hand after he explained why it was important to let them live.

Almost everyone who regularly walks the beach along the eastern seaboard and the Gulf of Mexico has seen horseshoe crabs. Relatives of the spider, these large, tan-colored invertebrates with a horseshoe shaped head and long pointed tail were one of the first creatures I saw crawling up onto the shore in New Jersey when Dad took me fishing. Horseshoe crabs have roamed our oceans since before dinosaurs dominated our planet. It has been suggested that their success as a species is due to their simple body design and their ability to mass-produce offspring.

At Tigertail, Dad and I observed horseshoe crabs coming ashore to lay their eggs in April and May. When this happened a spectacular feeding frenzy took place. As we watched them burrow into the sand to lay their eggs, shrieking hoards of shore birds gathered around to devour the grainy mass of caviar. Along with the birds, schools of longnose and Gulf killifish slithered amongst the sticky masses sucking the eggs into their distended bellies.

Eventually, snook and redfish were attracted to this feeding bonanza devouring hundreds of killifish as they popped out of the sand. Minute after minute the feast continued as more and more crabs crawled ashore to lay their eggs. Hours passed before the egg-laying ritual stopped and the crowds of predators dispersed. The real miracle is that enough fertilized eggs hatch to sustain future generations. But succeed they do—just as they have for the last 450 million years. In about four weeks, during the next spring high tide, the tailless larval crabs would hatch and be washed into the Gulf to become part of the plankton community. Should anyone doubt the ecological importance of these life forms, all they need to do is visit the beach today when these crabs are breeding.

After molting, the juvenile horseshoe crabs take up residence in shallow intertidal waters off Tigertail. Here they feed on worms and nematodes. Dad and I could always locate them by the trails their tails left behind in the sand. The tail of the horseshoe crab is completely harmless and is used to turn the crab upright after it's been turned over. But some of the people we encountered thought it would sting them and were shocked when Dad picked one up by this lance-like appendage.

Whenever Dad took his friends down to Tigertail in April and May to show them some of the wonders we'd discovered, they would inevitably come across horseshoe crabs. Most of his friends had seen them before, but he would always challenge their knowledge by asking them if they could tell the difference between a male and a female. Whenever he posed this question they would give him a strange look and think that he was trying to play some kind of joke on them. "It's no joke," Dad would announce as he reached down and grabbed an adult crab by its tail. Then with a lot of fanfare, he would look at the crab's underside and tell them the sex of the animal. More dubious looks would inevitably follow until he let them in on the secret. The first two legs in an adult female crab always end in a set of pincers, while the first two legs in a male crab always end in a set of hooks. To the more curious guests his next question would be, "Why do the male crabs have hooks?" When they couldn't answer, Dad would promptly reply, "It's because the male needs them to hang on to the female when they're having sex."

Like the marine plants and invertebrates in Tigertail's lagoon, Dad and I noticed the diversity and concentrations of fish over the sandy shoals also varied throughout the year. In the cold months of December through March, sheepshead and southern kingfish would move close to shore to feed on food washed up by dry season cold fronts. In April, as the water temperature steadily rose, there was a gradual rise in juvenile baitfish. This increase in baitfish generated a corresponding rise in large predatory species like snook and Spanish mackerel. By July and August when the baitfish reached their peak concentrations, we regularly observed black tip, bonnet head, lemon, and bull sharks on the shoals together with snook, redfish, mackerel, and snapper. By the third week in October, these near shore fish populations reached their maximum levels of abundance and then dwindled dramatically with the arrival of December cold fronts. Some of these larger species moved offshore while others retreated into the deep holes of the Ten Thousand Islands.

At Tigertail there was always a plethora of bird life. From April through July least terns and black skimmers nested on the mile long sand spit. In the winter dry season numerous species of shorebirds migrated to the region's shallow flats to fatten up on the lagoon's rich supply of food. Sanderlings, snowy plovers, least sandpipers, dunlins, greater yellow legs, and short-billed dowitchers were just a few of the birds Dad and I saw prowling the shoreline. In addition to the seasonal visitors, there were always a fair number of year-round residents, including reddish egrets, tri-colored herons, great blue herons, snowy egrets, and brown pelicans.

One of the most important things Dad and I learned from our observations at Tigertail was how all of the different life forms depended on each other for their survival. The sea grass that washed up onto the sandy beaches during a winter storm provided nutrients to the dune plants that were responsible for slowing down beach erosion. With a more stabilized beach environment, the shore birds began to nest and raise their young. The droppings from these birds added more nutrients to the coastal habitat as well as to the turtle grass and shoal weed environments. With additional nutrients, the expanded dune vegetation provided a home for many species of insects, birds, reptiles, and amphibians, while the enlarged areas of sea grass provided food and shelter for numerous species of marine life.

Once Dad and I identified and understood the interdependence of all these life forms and the contributions they made to each other we came to realize that Tigertail wasn't just a place but a living, breathing entity. It didn't have arms and legs and a heart like we do. But it nurtured and gave birth to new life every day. Its component parts were its nutrient rich mud, sea grass beds, mangrove forest, sandy shoals, and plankton-filled water.

The studies and observations Dad and I made at Tigertail were never published, but I used most of our findings in the Big Cypress Nature Center and Conservancy field trip programs for children and adults. The children's programs were run through the Collier County Public Schools and were given to every fourth and seventh grader. Nearly twenty-five thousand students participated in these field trips over a period of twenty years and I'm certain their experiences made a lasting impression on them. I can say this because years after the program was terminated due to a lack of funds, former students approach me and tell me what an important influence these trips had on their lives.

Today, Tigertail has been set up as a county park and is listed as one of the top twenty beaches in Florida. In 1978, the Conservancy of Southwest Florida gave $30,000 to the County to help establish the park, and the Florida Department of Natural Resources provided $100,000 in matching funds. Tigertail is a great place to take children to study marine life. It is also a great place to fish and look for birds. What I'll always remember about Tigertail is walking along its beach in the early morning with Dad, the two of us enjoying the sunrise and anxiously awaiting our next discovery as we walked along its beaches and waded out into its lagoon.

The Ten Thousand Islands

In addition to Tigertail, Dad and I wanted to explore some of the more remote areas of the Ten Thousand Islands. This coastal area can best be described as an enormous shallow-water wetland dominated by salt tolerant trees called mangroves. As far as I am aware, no one has completely studied this immense ecosystem, and its furthermost recesses remain as much a mystery today as do the deepest parts of the ocean or the most inaccessible parts of the Brazilian rain forest.

Collier County's portion of the Ten Thousand Islands stretches from Vanderbilt Beach south to the northwest border of the Everglades National Park; it is protected and regulated by five state and federal agencies. They include the Fakahatchee Strand State Preserve, the Ten Thousand Island Wildlife Refuge, the Big Cypress Preserve, the Florida Panther National Wildlife Refuge and the Rookery Bay National Estuarine Research Reserve.

Exploring and fishing in the Ten Thousand Islands were always pretty challenging for Dad and me. In the entire time Dad was in Florida, we only saw 3-5 percent of this wilderness. It possesses hundreds of miles of meandering waterways and mangrove shoreline that form a web-like mosaic where current day recreational fishermen can still get lost.

Commercial netters know a lot about these backwaters and how difficult it is to find your way through them. The contours of this labyrinth change on a daily basis. Trees are constantly being blown over becoming hazards to navigation, bays fill up with silt, and oyster bars expand and clog up once navigable channels. The maps they sell you in marinas are of some help. They give you a general idea about the depth and locations of certain channels, but you cannot rely on them for detailed information about oyster bars, hidden logs and other structures. Today you can use a GPS to mark the location of hazards and hidden channels, but you still have to periodically go back to check if they are still there and find out where new ones have cropped up.

During the rainy season, just after sunset and just prior to sunrise, the mosquitoes rise up and sing their song in this enchanted forest. Dad and I called the music they generated the hum of life. According to one estimate there are seventy-five species of mosquitoes that live in Southwest Florida, but salt marsh mosquitoes are the dominant species in the Ten Thousand Islands. It is probably an underestimate to say there are trillions of them living in the mangrove swamps during the rainy season. In the early morning while boating in the open waters of Gullivan Bay, Dad and I would often watch hordes of these insects envelop the region's mangrove islands. Whenever that happened it created a magical illusion in which the islands seemed to undergo a gradual metamorphosis. With the rising sun, the islands' silhouettes would contract from fuzzy amorphous balls into sharply outlined clusters of islands as millions of mosquitoes retreated into their shady coastal canopies.

These feisty, blood-sucking insects quickly gained a nasty reputation from the early explorers and naturalists who visited the Ten Thousand Islands, and it is mainly because of them that the coastal areas of Southwest Florida were one of the last places in Florida to be developed. However, despite their reputation, the mosquitoes are an important component of the region's food web. Both the larvae and the adults are a major source of food for numerous species of marine life as well as many other creatures that live in this tangled forest of spider-like prop roots.

About five years after Dad moved to Florida he called me up and said he wanted to chip in with me to buy a boat so we could fish and explore the Ten Thousand Islands. Neither of us had a great deal of money at that time, so whatever boat we decided to purchase had to be inexpensive. Ultimately, we went to Sears and bought a fourteen-foot aluminum johnboat. Since we were going to be fishing in the backwaters we also bought a nine horsepower short shaft Evinrude outboard. The whole rig, together with a trailer, only cost us around $1,200, but for Dad it was his pride and joy. For the first time in his life he was part owner of a boat and he could go fishing almost anywhere he wanted.

Since neither one of us had any experience fishing in the Ten Thousand Islands, Dad and I purchased a map and started asking residents about the best places to fish. The map was easy to get, but not surprisingly most people we talked to were reluctant to tell us the locations of their favorite fishing holes. So off we went to explore the jungle of tangled roots and winding waterways to see if we could discover our own secret places.

Whenever we ventured into the backwater we were awed by the magnitude and diversity of bird life. As we motored along the meandering channels at low tide we would often see hundreds of birds feeding on the mud flats. And towards dusk, when the sun was just about to slip below the horizon, the spectacle of wading birds and pelicans returning to roost in the mangroves was absolutely amazing. There was so much life it was hard to believe that there were times when the bird population was even more plentiful. But descriptions provided by eighteenth century naturalists left little doubt that the bird populations were now only a mere vestige of what they once were. In the late eighteenth and early nineteenth centuries plume hunting resulted in a sharp decline in their numbers, and during the twentieth century coastal development radically altered their breeding and feeding grounds. When Dad and I watched the birds fly over at dusk, we often wondered what it must have been like to see these creatures returning to roost before man impacted their populations. The sound generated by their flapping wings and their guttural utterances as they clamored into the tops of the mangrove trees by the thousands must have been a wonder to behold.

During our initial explorations of these wetlands we became very interested in the feeding techniques of birds, in part because observing them helped us locate good fishing spots and in part because I had learned to incorporate what I observed into Nature Center programs. If wading birds like snowy and great egrets were lined up on the prop roots of red mangrove trees, it was a sign that redfish and snook were feeding along the bank. And if cormorants were diving over the grass flats, it was a sure indicator that trout were nearby.

On rare occasions, we discovered birds whose feeding behavior was strikingly different from other members of their species. The first unique feeding activity we observed was that of a tri-colored heron in Gullivan Bay south of the tiny fishing village of Goodland. Normally, these birds captured food by stirring up the bottom with their feet and spearing fish with their bills. On this occasion, however, the tri-colored heron squatted in the water and situated itself so that its body produced an elongated shadow. While in this position the bird waited for a school of small fish to congregate along the edge of its shadow line and then leisurely plucked fish out of the water with its beak. There was no wasted energy and it proved to be a far more effective technique than the hit-or-miss wading method we'd observed being employed by other members of its species.

We saw another deviant feeding behavior while fishing off of a sand bar at Cape Romano. Shortly after we anchored, we spotted an osprey perched on a dead tree limb in the middle of a nesting colony of terns. At first Dad and I paid little attention to the bird, but then we noticed that instead of diving into the water for fish it was diving into the colony of birds. Curious about what the osprey was up to we moved the boat closer and discovered it was attacking the colony of young chicks. To our amazement we watched it grab one of the newly hatched birds and fly back to its roosting area to devour it.

During our explorations we discovered that reptiles were fairly abundant in the Ten Thousand Islands. They ranged from large crocodiles to smaller species like green anoles and ring neck snakes. The first one we encountered was a brown mangrove water snake. It spends its entire life swimming amongst the mangrove islands where it feeds exclusively on fish. It is a harmless species and unlike most snakes, doesn't lay eggs but gives birth to live young. One day, while Dad and I were fishing in Addison Bay, we actually saw one of these snakes slither into the mangroves with a fish in its mouth. While we watched, the snake swallowed the fish and Dad wanted to know why the snake had crawled out of the water to consume its prey. It was one of those thought-provoking questions that I didn't have an answer to, so when we got back home I looked it up. It turned out mangrove water snakes are incapable of swallowing their prey underwater. My research also revealed that these snakes have to drink freshwater in order to survive. Until then I hadn't thought much about snakes needing to drink. The question was where did a mangrove water snake find freshwater? I had assumed they crawled into the interior of one of the elevated islands and drank from pools of rainwater. However, my father said he later observed one lapping up droplets of water from the leaves of a red mangrove tree after a heavy downpour.

Yellow rat snakes are excellent climbers and are fairly abundant in the Ten Thousand Islands. On a couple of occasions while we were fishing we observed these snakes swim across a creek, crawl into our johnboat, and slither off into the mangroves, where we could see them feeding on small crabs and insects. When they grow larger, however, their ability to climb mangrove trees enables them to feed on small birds, and on several occasions we actually saw them settling in with nesting colonies.

When mangrove barrier islands are destroyed by development, snakes and other animals are displaced and have to seek out new places to live. While these creatures are looking for a new home they often have unfortunate encounters with humans. One such incident involving a yellow rat snake took place while I was working at the Big Cypress Nature Center. I was sitting at my desk talking to Dad when I received a frantic call from a woman who reported that a snake was hanging out of her air conditioning vent. To make things worse the vent was situated over her dining room table and her guests were just getting ready to sit down to dinner. "You've got to do something," she pleaded over the phone. "Can't you send someone over here to get rid of it?" Normally I didn't respond to this type of call, but when Dad heard about her plight he suggested we go over and try to help out.

After inviting us into her condominium on Gulfshore Boulevard North she showed us the snake hanging precariously over the dining room table where it was just about to plummet into a bowl of mashed potatoes. "How could this happen?" the woman screamed as we whisked the snake into a pillowcase. When I explained to her that rat snakes were excellent climbers and that somehow this one had crawled up the wall of her building and gotten into her duct system, she began threatening to call up her condominium association to make sure it would never happen again. I don't know if the condominium association was able to help her, but Dad thought her encounter with the snake was pretty humorous.

"I can just see that snake covered with mashed potatoes slithering across her dining room floor," Dad chuckled as we left her condo.

Diamondback rattlesnakes are the only poisonous reptile that we observed in the Ten Thousand Islands. For the most part, they live on high ground on barrier islands, but on occasion we found them swimming in open water. We never personally had an experience with a rattlesnake, but we did observe a hilarious encounter two boaters had with one in the Gordon River. It happened on a Sunday morning near the north shore of Key Island. Two fishermen were motoring up to the pass when they came across a large diamondback swimming from Key Island to a cluster of mangroves on the opposite shore. For some reason these men decided they wanted to kill the snake. Perhaps they thought they were being good Samaritans, but Dad and I thought they were crazy. Pulling up alongside the snake, one of the boaters stood up and began slapping the reptile with his oar. The snake wanted no part of them and began swimming as fast as it could in the opposite direction. However, the reptile's pursuers were relentless and whatever way the snake swam they would cut him off and resume slapping him as hard as they could. For about ten minutes we watched this idiotic scenario when all of a sudden the snake somehow wrapped its body around the oar and got thrown into the boat. Now it was the fishermen who were in trouble. Clamoring into the bow of the boat, both of them began screaming their fool heads off while the angry snake coiled itself up and began striking at its tormentors. It appeared that the two fishermen never heard our shouts offering to help because they both jumped into the channel and began swimming towards shore. Fortunately, we were able to catch up with their boat, drag it ashore and flip the snake out with one of their oars. As for the two fishermen, they were a bit embarrassed but very grateful to get their boat back. The only complaint they had when we left was that their wallets were soaking wet.

One of the largest reptiles that lives in the mangrove forest is the American crocodile. Nearly hunted to extinction in the early part of the twentieth century, it clings to survival in remote areas of the Florida Keys and the backwater areas of the Ten Thousand Islands. Along Florida's west coast a number of them currently live in the mangrove swamps behind the Marco Island airport, while others have been spotted along the banks of the Blackwater River, Rookery Bay, Naples Bay, Seagate Beach, and Sanibel Island. Bud Kirk once told me that during April and May in the 1940s and 1950s he often observed them swimming out in the Gulf of Mexico south of Cape Romano.

The Florida crocodile is not as aggressive as its African and Australian cousins but reaches a respectable size of fifteen feet. Small mammals, turtles, birds, and fish are its primary sources of food. The Florida crocodile's major problem with people results from unintentional encounters with pets. Like alligators, these reptiles do not see any difference between eating a raccoon or someone's poodle.

While working at the Big Nature Center, the staff and I had several encounters with crocodiles. Most of them occurred while exploring mangrove creeks in the Ten Thousand Islands or leading field trips along the Blackwater River. The most interesting encounter I had took place in 1977 along the mangrove creek next to the Harmony Shores Mobile Home Park where my parents lived. The creek was a great place to catch blue crabs so one morning Bernice, Dad, and I headed down to the waterway to catch dinner. Throughout the morning the action was pretty good and by noon we had filled a five-gallon bucket with these tasty crustaceans. During our lunch break my wife noticed one of the crab lines had become taut and was beginning to head down creek. Hearing her shouts that she had a big one, I ran over with the dip net and waited for her to retrieve the line. That never happened. About halfway in, the line stopped moving and no matter how hard Bernice pulled, the line refused to budge. When I suggested that perhaps it was caught on something she shook her head and said she could still feel something tugging on it. My first thought was that it was a large snapping turtle. We had had large ones grab the bait before when we were crabbing in the creek. But when Bernice took hold of the line with both hands and gave it a hard yank, a seven-foot crocodile rose to the surface. We both stared at the creature in disbelief. "What should I do?" she yelled as the reptile opened and closed it jaws in an attempt to swallow the fish head. Reaching over, I cut the line and watched the reptile swim to the opposite shore with its prize.

When I talked to some of the people at Harmony Shores they told me that the crocodile had been hanging around the trailer park for several months. They thought it was an alligator and the fishermen who cleaned their catch at the dock had made a habit of feeding it scraps of fish every day. When I told them that it was crocodile and they should stop feeding it, they became defensive and grumbled that they didn't feel they were doing anything wrong.

I knew a crocodile taking up residence that close to humans was not a good scenario so when I went to work Monday morning I called the newly formed Crocodile Recovery Team located on Florida's east coast. After I described my encounter, they told me they didn't believe it was a Florida crocodile and suggested it probably was an exotic that had escaped from a local tourist attraction called Jungle Larry's. I was pretty sure they were wrong so I asked them what kind of proof they needed to conclusively identify it as a Florida crocodile. They said close-up pictures of the scutes on the animal's head. Later in the day the Center's naturalist Dave Addison and I sat in my office and discussed ways we could get the close-up pictures. He decided to use a telephoto lens, but to get the best shots we needed the animal resting on the bank in bright sunlight. Dad watched the animal for several days and discovered it liked to sun itself in the afternoon on a neighbor's lawn across from the trailer park. This was just the break we needed. The following weekend Dave approached the animal while it was sunning itself and took the pictures. He didn't get the close ups of the head scutes, but he did get some good full-length body shots.

I sent off the pictures but it was several weeks before I heard back form the recovery team. They confirmed my suspicions and told me they were anxious to remove the animal from its current location. Unfortunately, they were not equipped with a boat and wanted to know if we could supply them with one. I told them the Center didn't have a boat but I'd be happy to let them use one of our canoes.

The following day they showed up at the Nature Center with a noose attached to a long pole and headed off with Dave to capture the crocodile. Just as I anticipated, as soon as they approached the sunbathing croc, it slid off the bank into the creek. Dave and one of the recovery team members waited in the creek with the noose. Their plan was to lasso the crocodile while it was in the water and drag it up onto the bank where the rest of the team could secure it with ropes. The crocodile, of course, had a different idea. The noose never got properly secured around the animal's head, and once it felt the rope tighten it took off down the creek towards Naples Bay dragging the canoe and its occupants with it. Fortunately for those in the canoe, the noose came undone or there's no telling where they might have wound up. Disappointed at their failure to capture the crocodile, the recovery team returned to the east coast and asked us to keep an eye out for it. Dad watched for a month but as far as he could tell the crocodile never returned to the environs of Harmony Shores.

Nearly a year passed before I received a call about another crocodile sighting. It was from a woman who claimed she had seen a crocodile swimming in the water off of Seagate Beach. When I suggested it might be an alligator, she emphatically informed me that she knew the difference between the two species and what she saw was a crocodile. I told her I was interested in her sighting because of my encounter with one at Harmony Shores and I'd appreciate it if she could take a picture of the animal.

She showed up about a week later on the Nature Center doorstep and was bursting with excitement. "I took the picture just like you asked," she said and waved the photograph in front of my face. "My husband told me it was the best picture I've ever taken." Her husband was right. When I looked at her photograph I was absolutely stunned by the image she'd captured. There, sunning itself on Seagate Beach, was a crocodile, and lying no more than five feet away, was a woman sleeping on a blanket totally unaware of what had just crawled up to join her. This was no doctored photo. It was the real deal. And although the woman promised to send me a copy, she never did. She said her husband wanted her to publish it in the newspaper, but I never saw it show up in any of the local publications.

When I told Dad the woman's story he just sat there and laughed. "I can't imagine anyone ever publishing that photo," he said. "Can't you just see it appearing in a chamber of commerce promotion encouraging tourists to visit Naples? I can see the caption: 'Enjoy the sun-kissed sands of Naples while getting to know your neighbors'."

Even though the Ten Thousand Islands can be an extremely hostile environment there are some mammals that manage to survive in this mosquito-infested jungle. Terrestrial species include fox squirrels, opossums, wild hogs, raccoons, river otter, and an occasional Florida panther. Raccoons are by far the most abundant. At low tide, especially early in the morning, Dad and I would observe these masked denizens foraging for food along exposed mangrove roots and oyster bars. Feeling around with their paws, they would gingerly pluck out small crabs and shrimp that lived wedged between the tight clusters of oysters and barnacles.

Nearly all of the raccoons Dad and I saw in the mangroves were skinny. I presumed this was because of the harsh environment. Food is not as easy to capture as you might think and the animals are constantly being attacked by hordes of sand flies and mosquitoes. Dry season cold fronts probably bring these creatures the greatest amount of relief. The fronts lower the air temperature and reduce the biting insect populations while casting ashore vast amounts of food in the form of mollusks and crabs.

Bottlenose dolphin and manatees are year-round residents in the deep channels and bays of the Ten Thousand Islands. When the dolphins are actively feeding they will sometimes drive the fish up against the shoreline and generate a tumultuous feeding frenzy that can be breathtaking in its scope and intensity.

One morning Dad and I experienced one of these feeding frenzies while fishing from the shore along one of the deep channels that entered Gullivan Bay. We had fished this location many times before and knew that the oysters that grew along the bottom provided an excellent feeding ground for sheepshead and grey snapper. As the water level began to fall we noticed quite a few dolphin collecting in the channel. Initially, they just darted around chasing fish, but as more and more food collected over the oyster bed they began slapping their tails on the surface. Then, with stunning swiftness, the dolphins began herding the fish and driving them towards the shoreline where Dad and I were standing. Taken by surprise, neither one of us had time to escape the bombardment of mullet that erupted from of the water. They flew in every direction as we ducked and tried to flee. To our astonishment, soon after the mullet finished bombarding us, we found ourselves facing the snapping jaws of several partially beached dolphins. Dad wanted to try and push them back into the water, but I told him to wait and see what happened. Within seconds the stranded animals began twisting and flipping their bodies until they finally maneuvered themselves back into the channel. From the number of scars on their bodies it was obvious that they had employed this type of feeding behavior before.

Lots of research has been done on dolphin behavior, but during the fifteen years that Dad and I fished in the Ten Thousand Islands we observed some unusual activities that you seldom see reported. One day while fishing for grey trout in the Gulf, Dad spotted a pair of dolphins jumping out of the water tossing something into the air. Curious about what they were doing, I started up our engine and headed towards them. When we first arrived they submerged and failed to reappear. Thinking that we had scared them off, I suggested to Dad we head back to our fishing spot when all of a sudden one of them leapt out of the water with a crown of Sargasso weed draped over its head. Shaking the weed free as it flipped over, a second dolphin leapt out of the water and grabbed the Sargasso weed in its mouth. For nearly ten minutes we watched this delightful game of catch. Sometimes they would grab the seaweed in the mouth and at other times they would flip it around with their tails. We only experienced this behavior once, but we did observe a similar game of catch with grey trout. It occurred with a small pod of dolphin that was feeding off of Clam Pass. One of the dolphins grabbed a trout in its mouth and then flipped it into the air while another leapt into the air and swallowed it.

Perhaps the most unusual encounter we had with a dolphin occurred while we were heading out of Goodland towards Coon Key. As we left the marina and motored towards the channel Dad spotted an adult headed towards our boat. Many dolphins are just curious about boaters and often want to swim alongside. To our surprise this one became very aggressive and started ramming its body into our vessel. The first time it happened we thought we'd accidentally run into the animal so the next time it approached I swerved to avoid it. This time the dolphin rammed our boat even harder. Thinking that the dolphin perceived us as some kind of threat, I began maneuvering our boat every which way to avoid hitting it. For the rest of the trip to Coon Key the dolphin continued to try to slam its body into our vessel only breaking off its pursuit when we reached the open water of Gullivan Bay. I know pods of dolphin will sometimes attack and kill sharks, but this was the only example I knew of where a solitary animal attacked a boat. It is possible that this creature had a bad encounter with another boat, or perhaps it was suffering from an illness. I doubt I'll ever know the real reason for this animal's behavior, but as human interactions with wild animals increase, I'm sure that people will experience even more puzzling incidents.

There are quite a few manatees in the Ten Thousand Islands and Dad and I often encountered them while we were fishing. These ponderous, slow-moving aquatic relatives of the elephant loved to graze on the grass flats in Gullivan Bay during the summer. Sometimes, in the early morning, Dad and I would see as many as ten or twelve of them moving across the shallow flats with the incoming tide. And, if the water was especially clear, you could see schools of fish hovering around them feeding on the marine life they stirred up.

Crocodiles and alligators are listed among the manatees' natural predators, although Dad and I never observed an attack. Sharks were a different matter. On one occasion we saw several bull sharks attack a calf in the grass flats south of Round Key. There were several adult manatees and a young calf feeding in shallow water off shore when an eight or nine foot bull shark began circling the animals. Sensing the danger, the adults formed a tight circle around the youngster. That seemed to work until two more large sharks showed up. Darting into the pod, the sharks eventually created enough confusion to provide an opening where they could attack the young manatee. It was a horrible site. Before the adults could regroup, the sharks tore at the flesh of the young calf leaving it severely injured. The adults eventually did regroup and resume their protective shield, but I doubt the calf survived this savage attack.

Manatees can also be curious about humans. One day while we were out fishing in Gullivan Bay we found ourselves surrounded by a half dozen of these animals. As we drifted along, one of them kept following our johnboat. It was a behavior we hadn't seen before, so instead of returning to the edge of the grass flats to start another drift, we just waited to see what the manatee would do. Very slowly it edged closer until it was right next to the bow of our boat. Then, for some inexplicable reason, it lifted its head up and rested its chin on the edge of the boat next to Dad. Both of us were amazed. At first neither one of us moved because we were afraid we would scare it away. Then Dad decided to reach out and pat the animal on the head. When he did, the creature did nothing but lay there and watch us. Both of us thought this was pretty neat so Dad stroked the animal's head again. This time the manatee lifted its head and belched. The obnoxious gas released from the bowels of this animal defies description. Dad grimaced and waved his hand in front of his face while I covered my nose and started up the engine. As far as I was concerned we couldn't get away fast enough, but I didn't want to injure the animal. Dad came to the rescue by gently nudging the creature's head off the bow while I slowly backed away. It took some time before the creature's fowl odor dissipated, and if there was one lesson we learned that day, it was never to get too friendly with a manatee.

No one I know of is crazy enough to be in the backwater when a hurricane is approaching, but Dad and I were out once during the passage of a double cold front, and we considered this the second most frightening thing any boater can experience. We were fishing among the mangrove islands on the east side of Gullivan Bay. It started off clear and sunny. From the morning forecast we knew that there was a stalled cold front just north of us and we also knew that a second, more powerful front, was moving in behind it. But the weather prediction we'd heard was that the front would not pass through for another twenty-four hours. Consequently, Dad and I still felt we could get a good day's fishing in before the weather changed. As we predicted, the fish were biting pretty well, something they always seemed to do just before a cold front passed through. By eleven o'clock we had caught several good size sheepshead and a number of snapper and I decided we should head to another one of our favorite fishing spots. Just before we took off Dad pointed to a line of clouds that formed the leading edge of the first cold front. It was arriving sooner than projected, but I still thought we had plenty of time to try our fishing hole before heading back to Goodland. Dad wasn't so sure and suggested we start back before the storm caught up with us. My gut told me that he was right, but I couldn't resist the temptation to give the fishing hole a try. So off we went, Dad anxiously watching the sky and me thinking about all the fish we would bring home.

Fishing turned out to be great. Within a half hour we had landed five more keepers and I wanted to stay and catch more. Not Dad, he pointed towards the mouth of the creek and started to pull up the anchor. There was a wall of rain racing towards us and the wind had picked up considerably. Starting up the engine, I began to think about the best route back to Goodland. I knew I didn't want to cross Gullivan Bay. It would be far too rough and with the wall of rain about to descend upon us it would be almost impossible to spot the shallow shoals. Maneuvering through the narrow channels between the mangrove islands was our safest bet. I knew the islands would protect us from the wind and that the ride back would be a lot smoother.

What I didn't take into account was the influence the wind would have on the outgoing tide. Not too long into our return trip I was certain that my plan wasn't going to work. The wind-driven tide was causing the water to drop at an accelerated rate and the channels that normally had enough water for us to navigate were dry. I needed to find a deep-water route back or we weren't going to make it.

Pulling up to an oyster bar along the edge of Gullivan Bay, I surveyed the open water and cringed. The bay had been whipped into a maelstrom of four to five foot waves. Now I faced the decision of heading into the frothy white-capped open water or spending the night in the mangroves. Dad didn't say a thing. He just looked at me and shook his head. I knew what he was thinking. I had to make a decision or there wouldn't be enough water in the channel to get into Gullivan Bay, and spending the night in the mangroves with below freezing temperatures and the wind blowing thirty miles per hour was not a desirable option. Before heading out, I reached in the back of the boat and grabbed our life preservers and thought about the time our boat capsized in Cape Cod.

Getting out into Gullivan Bay was a nightmare, but getting back to Goodland was pure hell. The boat almost capsized when we reached the mouth of the channel. The waves were pushing us sideways and at one point we were inches away from being tossed up on a worm reef. Then the real fun began. The wind had picked up even more and all we had was a nine horsepower engine to buck the waves. Once we reached open water we bounced around like a cork and there were several times I was convinced that we would be tossed sideways and capsize. Meter by agonizing meter we made our way to the channel near Coon Key light. It seemed like it was taking an eternity to reach the mouth of the channel and throughout the trip Dad kept bailing and giving me that look that said I told you so. By some miracle we managed to reach the entrance to Sugar Bay where I pulled behind some mangroves so I could help Dad empty the water out of the boat. There were nearly three inches in the johnboat and all I could think about was how close we came to not making it home

Besides the winter storms, Dad and I also had to keep a watchful eye on the weather during the summer rainy season. From the middle of June through the middle of October thunderstorms develop in the afternoons along the Southwest Florida coast so we always tried to get back by two o'clock. However, sometimes even our most carefully laid plans went awry. Usually it was a change in the wind direction that was the culprit. If the wind was coming out of the east in the morning we could expect the typical afternoon pattern of rain, but if it changed to the south the thunderstorms would appear along the coast in the morning.

No one wants to be out on the water during a rainy season thunderstorm. Even if you are five miles from the nearest cloud, a lightening bolt can appear from nowhere and fry your carcass in a microsecond. In fact more people have died from lightning strikes in Florida over the last one hundred years than they have from shark attacks. When Dad and I fished the Ten Thousand Islands we experienced some pretty scary things. Once, while we were standing in the boat, the hairs on our arms and head stood straight up as an electrical storm approached. In another instance, Dad cast his line out and it never hit the water. When Dad and I looked up we saw his line suspended in midair by a field of static electricity.

As frightening as these events were they weren't as scary as the day we got sandwiched between two merging storms. We were fishing on the grass flats south of Cape Romano when we spotted a thunderstorm approaching from the south. As it drew closer we decided to leave the flats and head back to the boat launch. What we didn't anticipate was the development of a second thunderstorm to the north and east of us. As we were heading back, the storm to our south merged with the one from the north and we found ourselves sandwiched, along with ten other boats, in a torrential downpour where lightening was striking the surface of the water every few seconds. Blinded by the rain, and scared out of our wits by the constant zap of lightening bolts we were left with no choice but to maintain our course and pray that we didn't get struck by lightning or run into one of the other boats. It was a fifteen-minute hellacious experience that I never want to relive.

Early on, Dad and I discovered that July and August were the worst months to fish in the Ten Thousand Islands while October through May were the best. We also found that fishing in the deep channels in the summer during the rainy season was never very productive. About the only thing we caught in the channels were hardhead catfish. Armed with poisonous spines, these interesting but unpalatable creatures were difficult to get off the line and occasionally inflicted painful wounds if mishandled. Dad learned this lesson the hard way when he tried to unhook one and his hand slipped. As I watched, the fish's pelvic fin pierced his t-shirt and stuck in his stomach. Fortunately, the hook came out of the fish's mouth, but the spine remained deeply embedded in my father's belly. I cringe whenever I think about that fish flopping around while Dad hollered at me to do something. "Cut the damn thing off with the pliers," he shouted. Tearing through the tackle box I finally found the pliers and broke off the spine. I could still see the rest of the spine sticking through Dad's shirt, but at least I had detached the fish. Now what should I do? Dad wanted me to remove the spine, but I suggested we leave it where it was and I take him to the hospital. Dad didn't think too much of that idea and insisted that I take the pliers and pull the spine out of his stomach. The thought left me weak in the knees, so I tried to reason with him and pointed out that it would be much better to remove it someplace where there was less chance of his getting an infection. It was then that I learned what a tough hombre Dad really was. Without saying another word he reached over, grabbed the pliers out of my hand, and yanked the spine out of his belly. I can still see his tee shirt turning crimson as the blood spurted out through the hole. It was like someone opened a spigot. Fortunately, we had a first aid kit on board and I was able to apply enough pressure to the wound to stem the flow of blood until we got home. Mom, of course, was not pleased with me when she saw Dad walk through the door. After letting us know what she thought about the whole situation she started yelling at me saying it was my job to make sure nothing happened to him. Thankfully, after a brief visit to the emergency room and a week of recuperation, Dad was as good as new and the two of us were once again out getting into trouble.

During the years that Dad and I fished the Ten Thousand Islands we learned that the best areas to fish were the transition zones between different habitats. Ecologists call these regions ecotones. Baitfish liked to collect along the ecotone, and it was in these transitional areas that we found the highest number and greatest diversity of fish. A mangrove shoreline adjacent to an oyster bar is an example of an ecotone, so too is a turtle grass bed bordering a deep sandy channel. For whatever reason, some ecotones produce more fish than others. In addition, each spot has its prime time when fishing is at its peak. Some are only good to fish on the incoming tide while others only produce when the tide is going out. A good fishing guide is aware of this and will only fish these spots during the peak-feeding periods.

Besides fishing the ecotones, Dad and I had a number of other fishing holes where we knew we could catch fish even when the weather conditions were working against us. On a couple of occasions we even improved these spots by converting them into backwater reefs. Dad came up with the idea and it proved to be quite successful. After a storm we'd pick up wood and other debris that had been washed ashore, load it into our boat, and distribute it around our prime fishing locations. In about six months the debris would become covered with benthic marine life and all kinds of fish would collect there to feed.

One of our backwater reefs was located in Addison Bay and there wasn't a day we didn't come home with a good catch from that fishing hole. After Dad died I never went back to fish that particular location, but one time when I was cleaning fish at the marina in Goodland I ran across a fisherman who proudly showed me his catch and told me he'd found a hot spot in Addison Bay. I had no doubt where his hot spot was and wondered what Dad would have said to him if he'd been there.

Dad loved to catch snook in the backwater in the early years. This streamlined fish with golden scales and a dark lateral line was a prized sport fish for local residents and tourists. Besides being excellent to eat, this fish's fighting antics made it one of Florida's most sought after game species. Unfortunately, during Dad's years in Florida we saw a steady reduction in their numbers. From what we were able to determine there were a number of reasons for this decline. For one thing snook are at the northern edge of their range in Florida and the slightest stress placed upon them has a serious impact upon their abundance. Stress factors could be natural ones such as severe cold spells or they could be factors created by humans such as over fishing, pollution, or the destruction of nursery areas. One factor that probably had a detrimental impact on the their population in the Ten Thousand Islands was the alteration of the water flow from the Everglades-Big Cypress region. By interrupting the sheet flow of freshwater, the salinity pattern in this mangrove estuary was changed enough to produce an environment that was less conducive to the development of juveniles.

Another possible man-made factor that particularly concerned my father and me was the five-mile reef that Deltona established off of Marco Island. When I started to work for Deltona in 1970, one of their proposed projects was to establish two artificial offshore reefs. One was to be placed three miles from the coast and the other was to be situated five miles from shore. Both reefs were completed a couple of years after I left and shortly afterwards fish began to collect on them.

I have no problems with artificial reefs if they are placed in the right locations. In the case of the Deltona reefs I initially didn't have any problems with the places they planned to establish them. However, when I moved to Florida I also had very little knowledge about the ecology of the Gulf of Mexico and its surroundings. It wasn't until several years after the Deltona reefs were in place that problems began to develop at the five-mile site. My discovery of this problem happened entirely by accident. Chuck Courtney, who still worked for Deltona, called me up and asked if I wanted to go snook fishing. He said that the fishing was really great on the five-mile reef. Being an avid fisherman I didn't hesitate to say yes and the following evening we headed out to the reef. As soon as the sun set the fish moved to the surface and began feeding. All around the boat you could hear the sound of snook gulping down pilchards. There must have been hundreds of them. As soon as we cast our lures into the school, the fish devoured them. To give you an idea of how aggressive they were, I actually had a lure pop out of one fish's mouth and within seconds had another fish strike the same lure. It was incredible! Ironically we didn't catch our limit that evening. Not because the fish stopped biting but because the big ones broke our lines. I estimated that we lost twelve lures in about two hours of fishing that night, and if we had stayed there another two hours we would have lost twice as many.

Eager to see how many snook were collecting over the reef, some of Deltona's scientists dove the area where we had fished and discovered snook stacked up like cordwood from the surface to a depth of thirty feet over an area of one-half mile. Most of them were large adults that had come to the reef to feed on the baitfish that had gathered there in the millions. Great, most would think, isn't that what is supposed to happen over an artificial reef? The answer is both yes and no. The reef was successful in creating an offshore environment that attracted many bottom dwelling and pelagic species of fish. But it wasn't far enough offshore to prevent snook from using it as a feeding ground. Hence, once the snook began to collect on the reef during the breeding season I believe two things came into play that put the species at risk. The first was that once so many snook began congregating in one area they became easy targets for unscrupulous fishermen. Most of the fishermen that fished the reef caught their limit and left, but there were a number that filled their boats with snook before heading back to shore. There were no cell phones back then, and those of us without a marine radio had to wait until we got back to shore to report the illegal activity to the marine patrol. I have no idea how many fishermen the marine patrol caught, but my guess is the majority got away with their crime.

The second problem generated by the reef was subtler, and one that will require some research to disprove. I believe the reef had a detrimental impact on the breeding activity of the snook that lived in the northern half of the Ten Thousand Islands. Before the reef was in place the snook would gather in the passes at the beginning of the rainy season to breed. Places like the snook hole south of Caxambas Pass was one of those locations. Once the snook discovered the five-mile reef, I believe they began to breed over the reef and it altered what happened to the juveniles. Juvenile snook are planktonic, which means that they have no control as to how they are transported by the ocean currents. Those snook that hatch near the shore are transported to areas along the coast where food is readily available, while those that hatch over the reef are swept out to sea into a less food rich environment. If the latter is happening at the five-mile reef, it could be one of the reasons we have experienced a steady decline in our local snook population.

Some fish stories are hard to believe. Dad and I had one of those experiences in Addison Bay near Marco Island. In order to cut down on fishing expenses Dad had decided the best way to keep our fish fresh would be to place them on a stringer and hang them off the back end of the boat. He insisted it would eliminate having to buy ice to keep the fish fresh. When I told him I would be happy to buy the ice he just pushed aside my suggestion and reminded me that his plan worked well when we fished on Long Island and Cape Cod and he saw no reason why it wouldn't work in Florida.

On the day the event took place, the tide was going out. That morning we had anchored up against an oyster bar and were catching a fair number of grey snappers and sheepshead. There were quite a few fish on the stringer so we decided to take a break and enjoy the scenery. It was a magnificent morning. There were lots of wading birds feeding along the edge of the creek as well as some spoonbills working the mudflats in a nearby shallow bay. Enjoying moments like this was part of the treat of fishing in the backwater of the Ten Thousand Islands. It was light years away from the city environment Dad and I had grown up in. It fact, it was such a beautiful and peaceful day that we were totally unaware of the scraping sounds coming from the back end of our boat. As the sounds grew louder Dad and I gave each other a puzzled look and began to hunt for the source of the noise. At first we thought the boat rubbing up against the oyster bar produced it, but when we checked over the side it was apparent that we were nowhere near the oysters. Next we checked to see if the boat was rubbing up against the mangroves, but that wasn't the case either. Now we were really perplexed. After listening to it a little while longer, Dad decided the noise was coming from underneath the boat. "Maybe we're hung up on a branch," he suggested as we both placed our ears closer to the bottom of the boat and listened. Maybe we were, I thought, so I had Dad pull up the anchor and we drifted a few feet away. Dad dropped the anchor and we stopped and listened for the scrapping sound again. When we couldn't hear anything we decided to forget about the noise and start fishing. As soon as we dropped our lines, Dad caught a large snapper and proceeded to attach it to our stringer. The only problem was he couldn't lift the stringer out of the water. Tugging at the line, he turned towards me with an exasperated look and said he thought the line was hung up on a tree limb. It was then that both of us noticed that the line was moving back and forth across the stern of the boat. If it were hung up, there was no way the string of fish would be doing that, so Dad began tugging on the line as hard as he could. At first nothing happened. Then it slowly rose to the surface. Much to our amazement, attached to the opposite end of our stringer was a huge goliath grouper. I can't tell you exactly how large that fish was, but if I were to guesstimate I would say it easily weighed more than two hundred pounds. The mystery of the scraping sound had been solved, but to our chagrin our entire catch now resided in the grouper's stomach. Dad was so upset he tried to pull our catch out of the animal's mouth but that was hopeless. The more Dad pulled on the line the more the grouper pulled in the opposite direction. The goliath grouper was not about to lose this battle so Dad finally cut the line and watched the fish descend into its hole. We only came home with one snapper for dinner that night, but I'm sure the grouper was very satisfied with the meal we provided.

You would think after that incident it would be the last time we would hang a string of fish off the back of the boat. Well, you'd be right. We never did hang one off the back end of a boat, but Dad still insisted on tying his catch to his waist when we were fishing in shallow water. I don't know how many times I told him I didn't think it was a good idea to have dead or injured fish dangling from his waist, that it was a good way to attract sharks, but he brushed aside my concerns and said that no shark would bother us in knee-deep water. He added that he was also getting too old to walk back to shore every time he caught a fish. He said his legs were worn out from all the walking and it was a lot easier just to attach the fish to his stringer.

For years, Dad fished this way and for years no sharks tried to eat his fish. After a while I decided that he was probably right about the sharks. Then it happened. It was a sunny day and we were wading off a sandbar south of Cape Romano. The whiting were biting so fast and furiously that we barely had one off the line before we hooked another. After an hour Dad had a least a dozen fish on his stringer so he yelled over to me that he was going to quit fishing for whiting and head over to the grass flats to try to catch spotted sea trout. As he turned to walk towards the sandbar he was surprised to find himself suddenly being pulled in the opposite direction. Darting in from the channel, a four-foot black tip shark had grabbed hold of his fish and was attempting to swim off with them. Dad turned and pulled on his stringer but the shark wouldn't let go. It twisted and thrashed about tearing at the string of whiting until almost nothing was left. Cursing and grumbling about all the fish he just lost I remember Dad waving at me to quit fishing and head back to the boat. When I got there I was glad so see that he hadn't gotten bitten and thought it better not to remind him of the times I had warned him about the stringer. Today, whenever I see fishermen wading in the water with a string of fish hanging from their sides or attached to a nearby pole I think about Dad's encounter and wonder if a shark is lurking nearby ready to grab an easy meal.

Dad and I had many incredible experiences in the Ten Thousand Islands, and there are still lots of wonderful discoveries to be made in this subtropical coastal forest, but I no longer journey into its deepest recesses. It is not a place to venture alone. I encourage those with an adventurous spirit to find someone to share the journey with them. Perhaps one day you'll find a crocodile sunning itself on the bank of a river or discover one of the fishing holes Dad and I left behind.

Molding a Vision

In 1974, The Collier County Conservancy, under the leadership of Bill Merrihue, explored the possibility of offering its own environmental education programs to the Collier County Public School system. The Conservancy was the county's first environmental organization. It was established in 1965 under the leadership of Charles Draper to halt the construction of a highway from East Naples to Marco Island, and as part of its efforts, the organization was able to raise enough money to purchase 1,600 acres of coastal wetlands that ultimately became known as Rookery Bay.

When the Conservancy presented their ideas to the school superintendent he listened politely and then told them that the Big Cypress Nature Center was already providing a similar program. Then the superintendent made a suggestion that would change the Nature Center's and my future forever. He proposed the Conservancy merge with us. He envisioned the union being extremely beneficial to both parties. He said that the Nature Center would get the additional monetary resources it needed for program expansion and the Conservancy would get its environmental education program.

In 1975, the Conservancy approached the Nature Center about a merger. In general, the Center's board liked the idea, but wanted a lot of specifics ironed out before committing themselves. In the final agreement signed by both parties in April of 1976, the Nature Center agreed to become the educational arm of The Collier County Conservancy. I would become the Director of Education for the Conservancy, and the Nature Center board would serve as an educational advisory body. In addition, the Collier County Conservancy agreed to provide health insurance for the Nature Center staff, assist the Center with future fund raising projects, and help the Center acquire more land so it could expand its existing facilities. The merger plans called for the gradual integration of the two organizations, but within six months we were both headed in directions that neither of us anticipated.

My initial idea of expanding the Nature Center involved the creation of a small museum on the existing property, but that idea was quickly abandoned when we discovered that the Center didn't own the land on which the access road was located and its owner wouldn't sell it to us. After realizing this, everyone agreed that we should look for a new piece of property on which to build our interpretive center. The search for land focused mainly on property close to Naples. Ultimately, we selected a piece on the south side of Jungle Larry's African Safari. The Conservancy liked this location because it was close to town and next to a lagoon that connected to the Gordon River.

Our plans were to build a modest facility when we started out, but as time went by the idea of constructing one building for the nature center was replaced with the idea of creating five separate buildings that would also house the Conservancy administrative offices joined by above ground walkways. The feeling was that a modular plan with above ground walkways would be more aesthetically pleasing and make it easier to obtain donations. Big contributors could now donate money to the module they liked and have it named after them.

To launch the fundraising effort, a series of dog-and-pony shows were set up at the old Nature Center. I presented a slide show to a group of carefully selected potential donors to explain the Nature Center's need for a new facility after which Bill Merrihue, the Conservancy's president, stepped forward and unveiled the organization's architectural plans. Bill was a smooth talking former General Electric executive whose friendly smile and firm handshake made contributors more than willing to open their wallets. Bill would always make sure that one of the people invited to the event would be ready to kick off the contributions with a sizable check. This tactic never failed to get others in the room to make similar donations, and before a full year had passed half of the three million dollars we needed to build the new center was in the bank.

At the same time the Conservancy was working on its plans to build a new nature center, the organization began a series of discussions with state and federal officials to turn Rookery Bay into a National Estuarine Research Reserve. It was a project that the Conservancy's research director Dr. Bernie Yokel and former Conservancy executive director Dr. Ted LaRoe spent a lot of time working on. The federal government at this time wanted to establish a series of National Estuarine Research Reserves throughout the United States where baseline research studies could be conducted on coastal wetlands. According to the government's plan, the National Oceanic and Atmospheric Administration (NOAA) would become the oversight agency for all the reserves, and in the case of Rookery Bay, the State of Florida would become the on-site manager with both the state and the Collier County Conservancy conducting research and educational activities within its borders. It was Bernie's hope that the Conservancy would support the operation of a marine lab within the Reserve and that he would be able to continue his baseline research projects. These talks both delighted me and left me a little awed at the magnitude of the responsibilities we would be assuming. Not only would I be responsible for operating our new, expanded in-town facility, but I also had to draw up plans for a second nature center in Rookery Bay and establish an education plan for the Reserve. I wasn't about to complain. This was the type of job opportunity most people dream about. Thus when the idea was presented to me I eagerly pulled out my pencil and began laying out the educational blueprints for two new facilities.

Meanwhile, the Nature Center's day-to-day operations were going well. Nancy Hunt, a graduate of Smith College joined our staff; Mildred MacClugage was brought on board to act as a receptionist; and Owen Waggoner joined the naturalists through the Career Education and Training Act (CETA). All of the new staff played important roles in helping the Center expand its base of operation. Nancy assisted with our operation Collier County Public School programs that now included all of the county's fourth- and seventh-grade students. Mildred's cheerful personality delighted visitors and frequently defused the angry outbursts of program registrants who failed to get their program registrations in on time. Owen was the brother of television star Lyle Waggoner, the lead actor in *Wonder Woman*. Since I didn't watch *Wonder Woman* it was nearly a month before I learned who he was, but the fourth grade teachers quickly discovered the relationship and it wasn't long before Owen was getting rave reviews for his classroom performances.

In addition to the Conservancy, two residents played an important role in the Center's future in the mid-1970s. The first was Emmy-award-winner Robert Anderson. Bob had recently settled in Golden Gate and wanted to embark upon a new career as a writer and wildlife photographer. After making an appointment to see me, we sat down together and he explained his future goals and asked if I would give him some assistance. In return, he offered to train the Center's naturalists and me to become wildlife photographers. The deal sounded great so I announced it to my staff. They were all eager to assist Bob, but only Dave Addison and I took him up on his offer to learn photography. During the time Bob worked with us our slide collection quadrupled, the quality of our adult education programs improved by several magnitudes, and both Dave and I became eager and above average photographers.

The other person who made a major impact on the Center was the director of Corkscrew Swamp Sanctuary, Jerry Cutlip. He and I had become friends shortly after I took the job at the Nature Center. Jerry was a very talented and creative individual who had a lot of dreams for National Audubon's Corkscrew Swamp Sanctuary. Like many things in life, however, timing is the most crucial component of success and some of Jerry's ideas were ahead of their time. Jerry wanted Corkscrew to become a model educational facility, but the home office in New York was not comfortable with some of his ideas. One of those involved creating an intern program. Jerry wanted to use students who were in their last year of college, or those that had just graduated from college, as naturalist assistants. He envisioned them helping run the gift shop, working as wildlife spotters, implementing education programs for school groups, and helping build and maintain the Sanctuary's boardwalk. Interns who were still in college would get housing and college credit. Those who had graduated from school would receive a stipend and living quarters. Jerry had experimented with the program in the early seventies and was pleased with the results, but a lack of monetary support caused him to back off the idea.

Jerry and I had a number of discussions over the years about establishing a similar program at the Nature Center, but up until the time of the merger I didn't have the resources to undertake such an initiative. In April of 1976, shortly after the Conservancy merger, I made a proposal to Jim Dupree, the Conservancy's vice president in charge of education, to hire an intern so we could expand our summer camp activities. After lengthy discussions about the pros and cons of the idea, Jim and the Collier County Conservancy board approved the idea provided I gave them a written report describing the results of the project together with a detailed account of its income and expenses. I had no problem with their request and within a week I began advertising for a person. Approximately two weeks before summer camp began I hired our first intern and started acquainting her with our programs. For her services we provided a weekly stipend, a place to live at the old Nature Center, and a promise of a letter of recommendation for future jobs if her performance proved satisfactory.

The whole scenario couldn't have turned out better. The intern's services generated considerably more operating funds than it cost us and we were able to get her a full-time job. From that day forward our intern program blossomed, and by the time I left the Conservancy we had built a dormitory to house interns and they were working in all facets of the Conservancy's operation.

After successfully running the intern program for several years, a summer visitor from England approached me and asked what I thought about incorporating interns from Great Britain into our program. This idea had a lot of merit and fit in with one of my ideas of offering internships to foreign students. So in 1981, my wife and I boarded a plane for England to do a presentation to a group of teachers from the University of London. After hearing what I had to say, the group was anxious to begin setting up a program. But first I had to get the okay from the Conservancy. When I got back to the states and presented the idea to the board they were initially lukewarm about the proposal. Some felt that I was going too far afield and that I should stick closer to home with intern recruitment. I understood where they were coming from and why, but I continued to press the issue, and by the mid 1980s they finally gave me the green light. Across the ocean, Dr. Colin Clubbe took over the project at the University of London and made arrangements for a one-year sabbatical in Florida where we planned to get together and work out the final details.

From 1978 through 1981, two projects consumed most of my time: one was the design and construction of the Conservancy Nature Center in Naples; the second was the construction of the Briggs Nature Center in the Research Reserve.

Designing and overseeing the construction of the nature centers proved a lot more challenging than I anticipated. In the beginning it meant reviewing architectural proposals and attending lots of meetings to discuss each plan. And once the architect was selected, it meant attending more meetings to modify the layouts as new issues cropped up. We all agreed that the Conservancy Nature Center buildings should be models of environmental engineering. Solar panels would be added to conserve energy, the buildings would be built on pilings to prevent any flooding during tropical storms, and only native plants would be used in landscaping.

No construction project, takes place without some glitches and we had a number of them. First of all, the solar panels on top of the education building produced too much hot water and had to be scaled back. In addition, the light sensors in the parking lot had to be modified so that birds couldn't land on them. It turned out the birds would defecate on the sensors causing them to stay on all day.

Another significant "glitch" involved two storage areas placed under the education building. Although originally planned to be above ground, the architect suggested putting them under the building to save money. By placing the storage areas at ground level, there was a good chance there would be flooding issues. To address my concerns, the architect had sump pumps installed. The solution had one serious drawback—it assumed that any flooding would occur from water moving inland from the Gulf of Mexico. Less than a year later a tropical storm whipped into Collier County during a spring tide and as a result of heavy rains and a high tide, the water from the lagoon poured over its bank flooding the storage areas and ruining thousands of dollars of valuable equipment. To address the problem, the architect recommended building a three-foot berm to prevent future flooding from the lagoon and had the sump pumps direct any overflow into a swale. Unfortunately, this also failed and the storage areas were finally removed from under the facility.

Meanwhile at Rookery Bay we had to select a site where we could construct the Briggs Nature Center. A couple of helicopter trips were made over the Reserve and a site chosen for the interpretive building. The plans were to place the Nature Center next to Shell Island Road and construct a boardwalk that would pass through upland scrub and coastal wetlands. The Briggs family provided the money for the Nature Center and a foundation grant was obtained to build the boardwalk. The major problem we had with the Briggs facility was a lack of fresh water. Several wells had to be dug before we found a lens from which we could draw freshwater and even this lens dried when we had an especially dry winter season.

After the initial phases of the construction projects were underway, the Conservancy expanded its capital and operating fundraising campaigns. There were more dog-and-pony shows at the old Nature Center, community organizations like Collier County Audubon and the Naples Shell Club were approached for money, and Bill Merrihue did a lot of one-on-one solicitation from members of the wealthy Port Royal community.

In early January of 1981, the staff and I began preparations for our move into our new Conservancy Nature Center headquarters that was officially scheduled to take place on April 8, 1981. Rick Bantz returned to Corkscrew Swamp Sanctuary to become their head naturalist and Owen Waggoner, who decided to pursue a job in banking, was replaced by Jim McMullen. Jim McMullen was the last employee we obtained through the CETA program. Jim had approached me several times about working at the original Nature Center, but even though I felt he would make a good addition to our staff, I didn't have the money to bring him on board. When Owen left us, I contacted the CETA office to see if we could hire Jim through their agency. After looking at Jim's background and qualifications they informed me that under CETA's new set of guidelines Jim was no longer a qualified candidate. Jim was very upset when he heard this and called the Veteran's Administration to complain about how the program was treating a decorated Vietnam veteran. After his call, CETA reversed its decision and allowed us to bring Jim on board as a naturalist trainee.

Jim was a man with a mission. As an employee he wanted to learn everything he could about the South Florida environment.

As an individual he was deeply concerned about the plight of the Florida panther. Throughout the twentieth century Florida's panther population had undergone a drastic decline in numbers and there were serious concerns that it was on the edge of extinction. Jim's quest for knowledge about Florida's panther population was relentless. Where had people seen them? What did they feed on? Where would he have the best chances of encountering one? Soon Jim was spending most of his free time in the Fakahatchee Strand and Big Cypress Swamp talking to people and searching for places where he might locate a panther.

I had answers to a few of his questions, but not as many as Jim wanted. I still remember the day he entered the Nature Center brimming with excitement. Guiding me towards the back of his station wagon, he asked if I could help him identify panther scat from a bunch of samples he'd collected in the Fakahatchee Strand and adjacent areas. I told him I would try but that I certainly was no expert in scatology. When he lifted up the rear door to his car I had to take several steps back to get a waft of fresh air. Individual piles of scat were laid out on newspaper and each pile had the locations where he'd collected them. After looking them over I identified a few that appeared like they might have come from a panther and suggested that he package them up and send them off to the Florida Game and Fresh Water Fish Commission for further analysis. I don't know how long the odor remained in his station wagon, but his wife Jane certainly deserved a lot of credit for supporting Jim during his mission.

Whenever a panther was found killed along the highway Jim was either the first to discover it or the first person people contacted. Frequently, his picture and that of the deceased animal would appear in the local newspaper with a statement about his concerns for the animal's future. Jim was very vocal about wanting the state and federal governments to do more to protect them. He wanted hunting banned in the Fakahatchee Strand, Big Cypress Preserve and adjacent wilderness areas as part of his efforts to insure their safety.

Newspaper and television reporters started to stop by the old Nature Center to ask Jim questions about his experiences with the Florida panther. Jim was a beguiling storyteller who had the unique gift of making the impossible seem plausible. Luck played a major role in his success, but I'm certain he also received a lot of help from a crafty leprechaun. In one instance a group of television reporters showed up at our doorstep to ask if he could take them to a place where he'd spotted a panther. Jim assured them that he could and when another reporter asked if they would see one, Jim's Irish eyes twinkled when he responded. "You just might." I cringed when I heard him give that flamboyant response. The odds were probably a million to one that they would encounter a panther. With a smile, I watched as the Pied Piper of the Fakahatchee led his entourage off to the swamp to do the interview. Little did I know, however, how powerful that leprechaun really was. That evening when Jim returned he was ecstatic. Apparently, just as the reporters got out of their vans to set up for the interview, a deer bolted out of the swamp behind Jim with a full-grown Florida panther in close pursuit. From that day on there was no doubt in the minds of the local populace that Jim was their leading expert on South Florida's panther.

Jim's search to find the Florida panther led him to write a book about his odyssey. *Cry of the Panther: A Quest for a Species* appeared in the bookstores after he left the Center. Pineapple Press published the first edition in hardback in 1984 and later McGraw Hill published the book in soft cover. Critics gave the book good reviews and the soft back edition appeared on *The New York Times* bestseller list. Jim used his fame as an author to help get the Florida panther listed as the state's mammal by the Florida Legislature, and he actively crusaded against the radio collar technique used to track panthers by the Florida Game and Fresh Water Fish Commission. It was his contention that the technique was flawed and there was a risk that collared animals could be injured when they tried to retrieve them. Some of his concerns were justified and at least one panther has been killed during the state's tracking program.

When April 8, 1981, arrived, everyone was ready for the grand opening of the Conservancy Nature Center. Temporary exhibits had been installed in one of the classrooms, the store was open for business, and all of the naturalists were on hand to give guided tours. Local politicians, school board members, school administrators, major contributors, Conservancy Board members, and Nature Center Advisory Council members were all present to participate in the gala event. The mayor and school superintendent made speeches about the Conservancy's new era in education and local dignitaries cut the ribbon in front of the entrance gazebo. It was truly a major achievement for the Conservancy president Bill Merrihue.

More forces for change, however, were underway. Despite Merrihue's success at raising funds for the new Center, some on the Conservancy Board felt Bill should step down as president. He was getting older and they wanted someone with broader administrative experience to take over. A number of names began circulating through the rumor mill, among them a former lawyer, Ned Putzell. In the meantime all I could do was work and await the outcome. I knew whoever was selected would mean changes for the Nature Center and for me. How I would deal with those changes was part of the challenge that lay ahead.

Island Hoppers

While our merger plans with the Conservancy were being completed I decided to proceed with a program to conduct natural history trips to the Bahamas and Caribbean. From my point of view South Florida was a natural jumping off point for this type of activity. Some of my board members, however, thought that these trips would detract from the Nature Center's primary mission of teaching people about the Southwest Florida environment. Conversely, I saw them as a good fundraising activity that would help us expand our environmental education programs. I also saw these trips as a method of beefing up our volunteer corps, expanding the Nature Center's membership, and broadening participants' understanding of other natural environments. In preparation, the staff and I went to the library to learn as much as we could about these exotic places. We spent numerous hours pouring through books learning about their flora and fauna. Then we made trips to the Florida Keys to get familiar with some of the plants that were native to these regions, and undertook snorkeling excursions to help us identify some of the different types of marine life we would encounter.

The next step was to decide which island to visit. After studying maps and reading the tourist literature, we concluded that our first natural history tour should be to Grand Cayman. In the seventies Grand Cayman was a wonderful place for a naturalist. It wasn't as built up as it is today and there were lots of unique natural habitats to explore. After Bernice and I finished our scouting trip we decided that the best place for a group to stay was the Tortuga Club. The hotel was situated on a pristine beach that was in close proximity to a fringing reef and its grounds provided a marvelous environment for our interpretive programs.

Back at the Nature Center we sent out a newsletter advertising our first natural history tour and waited to see what kind of response we would get. Only nine people signed up. That wasn't enough to make the trip a go so we offered it again in the fall when most of our members had returned to Florida for the winter. The second time around fourteen people signed up. We were still one person shy of making the trip a go so I approached my parents and asked them if they would be interested in joining us. Mom wasn't but Dad was excited about the idea. My parents didn't have enough money to pay for the trip so Bernice and I said we'd pay for Dad's expenses.

Weeks before the trip, Dad was constantly asking questions about what clothes he should bring, what type of snorkeling gear he should buy, and who he would be rooming with. I don't think I'd ever seen him so excited. On the other hand, Mom was nervous about Dad leaving her alone and reminded me more often than usual about watching over him to make sure nothing happened. Her heightened concern worried me and I began to wonder if her arthritis was making her feel less secure as she grew older.

Flight arrangements for our trip went according to plan; it was only after we landed on the island that things got dicey. As we exited the airport our group was greeted by a host of taxi crab drivers. All of them wanted to hustle us into their cabs and charge us an outrageous price to drive to the Tortuga Club. The extra cost for the cabs had not been included in our excursion fee, and when I tried to explain to them that we had vans from the hotel waiting to pick us up they started shouting that the hotels were trying to put them out of business.

The question was what to do next. Nothing I said persuaded the cab owners to change their minds. Looking around I suddenly spotted the hotel vans parked outside the airport entrance. From their reluctance to drive onto the airport grounds it was apparent they were not about to rescue us. It was also obvious that I needed to come up with a quick solution otherwise the Center's first natural history trip was going to be an economic disaster. Pulling my naturalist aside, I told him to gather up the group and move them and their luggage to the airport platform nearest the entrance while Dad and I slipped around back and talked to the van drivers. This scheme worked, but just barely. The van drivers reluctantly agreed to help, but only if we would distract the taxicab drivers. Jumping into the lead van, I guided them to where our people were waiting, and began negotiating with the taxicab people while my naturalist and the other van drivers hustled our participants into their vehicles. After they were loaded, I deftly slipped away from the cab drivers and got into a van. As we pulled away from the airport entrance it seemed like every taxicab driver on the island was pursuing us to the Tortuga Club. Shouting and waving their fists, they chased us down the island's main road and when we got to the Club they surrounded us and began yelling at the hotel manager. Eventually, the management came to some monetary agreement with the taxi cab drivers but I'm certain it was a lot less than the $50 per person they wanted to charge us.

After consuming well-spiked punch and eating a delicious evening meal the group settled into their rooms for a good night's sleep. Dad and I were scheduled to occupy a unit on the beach, but the club was overbooked for the first two nights so we wound up in the staff's quarters. The room was comfortable, and after a hot shower I hit the bed for what I hoped would be a quiet night's sleep. Unfortunately, about one in the morning my father rudely awakened me. "It's time to get going," he said as he waved a flashlight in my face. "We're supposed to be on the beach in twenty minutes." After shaking off the fog generated by several glasses of spiked punch, I finally realized what he was talking about. I had promised to do a night walk along the beach to look for marine critters.

"I cancelled that walk when everyone said they were too tired."

"Well I'm not too tired," he said, "and I would like to see what's out there." Was he serious I thought to myself? But after his continued prodding, I decided I'd never get any rest unless I took him down to the beach. So off we went, flashlights in hand, to explore the rocky shoreline.

Stumbling along the root-infested trail that led to the beach, I explained to Dad that this was the first time I'd done anything like this and I wasn't sure what we would find. I also remembered the promise I made to Mom about watching over Dad and cautioned him to take it easy as we climbed across the jagged lime rock shoreline. "Sure," Dad said, and before I knew it he was clamoring over rocks like a ten-year-old. When I finally caught up with him I told him he needed to slow down so we could see what was in the tide pools.

The first pool Dad and I came across was filled with four-tooth nerites that were actively feeding on microscopic algae. In another we found grazing bleeding tooth nerites and fuzzy chitons. At the edge of a rocky outcrop near the water's edge I told Dad to shine his light down to see if we could find anything else of interest. As soon as he did we spotted a green mantis shrimp. For a brief moment the creature seemed paralyzed by the light. Then, with a flick of its powerful tail, it disappeared into a small crevice below one of the rocks. Underneath a rocky outcrop, we discovered dozens of rock urchins. Their spines and translucent tube feet waved about as they slowly crawled away from us into the dark recesses of the iron shore. Perhaps our most amazing discovery was a foot-long octopus. Initially it was hiding underneath a ledge, but when our light uncovered a small swimming crab, the octopus emerged from its hiding place and pounced upon its unsuspecting victim.

It was three thirty in the morning when Dad and I returned to the room from our nocturnal explorations. By six thirty the tour group, including Dad, was up and ready to go. When he shook me awake and I trudged into the breakfast area at seven, I must admit I was not quite ready to jump into the day's agenda. Nevertheless, I greeted everyone with an enthusiastic "good morning" and led them on what would be the first of the Nature Center's many successful natural history adventures.

Almost everything on the Center's first tour went as planned except for one incident that makes me cringe whenever I think about it. On our third day, the Club planned a picnic to a remote beach. Before lunch I made arrangements for my naturalist to take half the group on a nature hike while I took the other half snorkeling over a nearby reef. The problem I faced with the snorkeling group was that I had to guide them through a bed of long-spined sea urchins before we could swim out to the reef. One by one, I carefully led each participant into deep water and was feeling pretty good about my efforts when the last person in the group stepped on my flipper. Unable to regain my balance, I found myself being thrust forward into a huge concentration of needle-like spines. I knew the landing was going to be ugly the minute I started to fall. The trick was trying to limit the amount of damage I was about to do to my body. Falling face down would have been a disaster so I decided to sacrifice my hands. Extending my arms straight out, I cringed as my hands slammed into the urchins. The pain was excruciating. I remember lying there in the shallow water trying to get over the shock when the person who stepped on my flipper bent over and asked me if I was all right. All right? Did I look all right? But as the leader of the group I simply groaned and asked him if he could lift me up. When I was finally able to stand up, my knees were shaking and it took every ounce of courage I could muster to look at my injured hands. When I did, I was appalled at the number of black spines that were stuck in them. How would I ever get rid of them? And how much pain would I have to endure? Hell, my hands hurt so much already I didn't want to think about it. Staggering back to the beach, I sat down on the sand and let one of the doctors we had on the trip look me over. The way he looked at me was all the diagnosis I needed. Before letting him remove the spines I asked my naturalist to lead my group out on the reef. Many small pieces of the urchin's splinter-like barbs remained embedded in my skin and without the proper instruments they would have to remain there until I got back to the Club. Not wanting to upset the day's activities any further, I led the second group on the nature hike and waited until after the picnic before heading back to finish the job. Before dinner, Dad used a small tweezers to remove more pieces of spine, but a number of them remained embedded in my flesh for several weeks before they working their way to the surface.

After the Center's first successful natural history tour, word spread rapidly and soon lots of people were asking about our next adventure. In November of 1976, the Nature Center staff decided to do another trip to the Cayman Islands. This time, instead of going to Grand Cayman we decided to go to Cayman Brac and Little Cayman. Our plan was to stay six days at Brac Reef Beach Resort on Cayman Brac and then spend a partial day at the Southern Cross Club on Little Cayman. The reason we chose Cayman Brac was because it had an impressive rocky landscape, interesting coral reefs, a number of unique species of migratory birds, a local population of green parrots, thousands of fruit bats, and several species of orchids. Conversely, Little Cayman was a low relief island made up of sand and coral rock. It promised to be a good fishing location, was surrounded by a coral reef, and had an indigenous species of lizard that predated the iguana. If our brief exploration of Little Cayman proved fruitful, it was my intention to add it to our list of future natural history tours.

When Dad heard that we were returning to the Caymans, he was among the first to sign up. This time he'd done some research and decided he wanted to catch a bonefish. He had read in a newspaper article that they were one of the world's best fighting fish, and all he talked about was what type of tackle he should bring and where I thought he could catch one. I told him I didn't know a lot about bone fishing, so I suggested he bring his spinning rod with twelve-pound test line and try his luck off one of the island's beaches. I said I'd heard bonefish liked to eat crabs and that when we got to the island I could help him look for some among the rocks. After thinking over what I'd said, he returned several days later and said he appreciated my offer but he'd decided to hire a guide. That sounded like a good idea but I let him know that a guide could be pretty expensive. "How much do you think one will cost?" he asked. I told him I didn't have a clue, but I'd be happy to have our travel agent check with the hotel.

About a week later, the agent informed me that there were a couple of local people on the island who served as bonefish guides and they usually charged around $100 for a half-day outing. When I told Dad the price he just shook his head and grumbled that he'd rather go off on his own to catch one. "Maybe you can get one of our participants to share the cost of a guide," I suggested, "then it wouldn't cost so much."

"Would you like to go with me?" When I told him I didn't think I'd have the time, he asked me if I'd contact some of the people on the trip and see if any of them wanted to go. I said that I'd try but thought it would be better if he approached someone during the trip.

The Brac Reef Beach Resort was an adequate base of operation for our natural history tour but it catered mostly to divers. As soon as we arrived Dad started asking more questions about bone fishing, and when the hotel couldn't answer them they said they'd make sure one of the local guides contacted him. When Dad returned to our room later in the day I asked him if he had had any success in getting in touch with a guide and he said, "No. Everyone is too busy with this dive group that just showed up. You should see the size of these guys," Dad grumbled. "We'll be lucky if there's any food left after they finish eating."

Dad wasn't joking about the divers being a hungry bunch. When we sat down to our buffet-style dinner about twenty of them entered the room and placed some hefty helpings of food on their plates. After that Dad announced that he wasn't going to be outdone by these burly intruders and as soon as the buffet was set up he was going to "muscle" his way to the front of the line to make sure he got his fair share. I think most of the divers were pretty amused by his antics because for the rest of the week, whenever Dad marched up to the buffet table, they would always step aside and let the five-foot-four "old fart" take all of the food he wanted.

On the third day of our tour, the hotel finally found a guide who could answer Dad's fishing questions. His name was Money. The hotel manager told Dad all he had to do was give Money a call. Dad thanked the manager and immediately went to the pay phone on the wall. Just as Dad was about to drop his money into the machine I entered the hotel lobby and asked him what was up. "I've got the phone number of a guide," he replied, "and I'm just about to give him a buzz."

"Why don't you use the phone at the hotel desk?" I asked.

"They said I had to use this one."

Shrugging my shoulders, I watched Dad place his coins into the machine and listen for an outside connection. As soon as the person at the other end picked up the receiver Dad shouted into the phone and asked if he was Money. His question was met with silence followed by a dial tone.

"What happened?" I asked.

"He hung up on me."

"Maybe you dialed the wrong number," I suggested.

Frustrated, Dad looked down at the number and said, "No." Reaching into his pocket, he picked out some more coins and dropped them into the machine and waited for the person to answer. After several rings, the person at the other end picked up the phone and Dad shouted, "Is that you, Money?" Once again, no response.

While this was happening the telephone at the front desk began to ring. Since there was no one on duty to answer that phone, Dad shouted to the person at the other end not to hang up because he had to answer the telephone at the front desk. Setting the receiver down, he raced over to the front desk, picked up the phone and asked who was calling. Surprise, surprise. The person on the front desk phone was Money and he was calling Dad to set up a fishing trip. "Money?" Dad replied in disbelief. "What are you doing on this line?" Realizing that someone else might be on the other line, Dad told Money to wait a minute while he raced over to the coin phone and apologized for the confusion. "But I'm Money," the person on the coin phone responded after Dad picked up the phone.

"You can't be Money," Dad replied. "You're on the other line."

Watching Dad run back and forth between the two telephones trying to figure out who the real Money was had me in stitches. It was like viewing the Bud Abbott and Lou Costello routine of who's on first and what's on second. Dad finally did figure out which Money was his fishing guide, but the glare he gave me after it was all over let me know he didn't appreciate my laughter.

It turned out Money didn't have a boat so he offered to walk Dad to some bone fishing spots along the beach. His price for a half-day outing was $100, which Dad complained was excessive. After a half hour of haggling, Dad finally got the price down to $75 and agreed to meet Money on the beach the following morning. During dinner Dad announced his intention to go bone fishing and lined up two other people to go with him. One was a perky gal of about sixty who was game for any new adventure and the other was a die-hard fisherman who had just undergone triple bypass surgery. I don't think any of them, including Dad, knew what they were getting themselves into, but at the break of dawn the sleepy trio met at the front desk and took off to meet Money with the hope of catching some bonefish.

That afternoon, after finishing a guided snorkeling trip, I met up with Dad and asked him how his fishing trip went. "All right," was his less than enthusiastic response.

"Did you catch a bonefish?" I asked.

"No, but I caught a jack."

"What about the others?" I inquired. As things turned out nobody caught a bonefish. After walking a couple of miles, the gal hooked up with one of the local residents and went off to party with a group of his friends; the fisherman who had had heart surgery gave up and plopped himself on a rock. When Dad asked him if he wanted to go back to the hotel he shook his head and said that he just wanted to sit down and recuperate. Later, when Money went back to check up on him he was still sitting on the same rock so he called the hotel for someone to pick him up.

I felt sorry that things didn't work out, so I promised Dad I'd check into some other places where he could go bone fishing when we got back to Florida. Dad was agreeable and that evening he was back to being his ornery self as he muscled his way to the front of the chow line to make up for the breakfast he had missed.

The next day our entire group flew to Little Cayman. The plan was to do a tour of the island, have lunch at the Southern Cross Club and divide the group up in the afternoon. Half would go snorkeling with me and the other half would go on an interpretive walk to look at the island's plant and animal life. The planes we used were the small four-seat variety so it took several trips to get all of us to the island. As we flew over the Southern Cross Club the first thing we realized was that there was no paved runway and if we expected to land safely we'd have to buzz the grassy field in order to get rid of the goats. Down went the plane and off ran the goats. Unfortunately, no one told the goats that they should stay away, so when the planes circled around to make their landing the goats reappeared. Once again the plane zoomed across the landing strip and once again the goats reappeared after running into the bushes. It took several more passes before the pilots finally convinced the goats not to come back. By then most of our participants were pretty shaken up by our aerial maneuvers, but not Dad. He told me he thought the aerial acrobatics were pretty cool.

Once on the ground, the locals apologized about the goats and told us they normally had them tethered when they knew a plane was about to land. It was hard for us to believe they didn't know we were coming, but we graciously accepted their apology and boarded their open truck to begin our island tour. The road we traveled on was a combination of lime rock and sand with a plethora of deep potholes that tested the resilience of our participants' aging backs. Nevertheless, we were able to observe several species of unusual birds and a quite a few iguanas. Most of the large lizards were resting underneath the bushes trying to find

234 Journey to the Edge of Eden

some relief from the intense heat, but one individual managed to display itself prominently beneath the island's only road sign which read "Caution, Iguana Crossing."

By the time we returned to the Southern Cross Club everyone was anxious to crawl out of the truck and straighten up their complaining backs. During lunch more than a few cold beers were gulped down before we headed out for our afternoon activities. Dad was in the hiking group and when I returned from snorkeling he was very anxious to tell me about the bonefish and tarpon that lived in a nearby lagoon. Of course it was too late for him to do any fishing, but I knew from his enthusiastic demeanor that he would have loved to have had his fishing pole along so he could have caught a few.

Dad never did make it back to Little Cayman. A year later, when we went to the Florida Keys to collect aquarium specimens for the Nature Center, I tried to make arrangements for him to go bone fishing but the guide got sick. By now I was wondering if Dad would ever get a chance to catch one. However, he was determined to make it happen and when we planned our next trip to the Bahamas he was once again one of the first ones to sign up.

Dad's last trip outside the country was to Stella Maris Resort on Long Island in the Bahamas. My wife and I love this place. The hotel sits atop a hill overlooking the Atlantic, the living accommodations are great, and the hospitality was always outstanding. As part of your weeklong visit to the resort they always held a cave party, offered regular trips to local beaches and provided a bar hopping tour to island pubs so you could get acquainted with some of the locals.

From a natural history standpoint, Long Island has a lot of great things going for it. The island has an interesting upland community made up of stunted subtropical hardwoods, wet lowland areas with an abundance of epiphytic air plants and orchids, some rocky shoreline with tide pools, coastal mangrove forests, and lots of coral reefs and shallow water marine habitats.

Dad convinced Mom to join him on this trip. He thought she would really enjoy participating in some of the activities as well as spending some time with people they volunteered with at the Nature Center. Needless to say, Dad's primary goal was to catch a bonefish and as soon as we set foot on the island he pulled me aside and asked me to contact the club's management to set up a fishing trip.

Setting up Dad's fishing trip was a piece of cake. Shortly after we arrived and had our welcome drink the managers arranged a bone fishing outing for him. Dad was ecstatic when he heard the news, but Mom wasn't too pleased. This was a special trip for her, and Dad's fishing trip reminded her of the morning he had left her to go fishing on their "honeymoon." Thankfully, Dad was able to smooth things over with her and the next day I found the two of them happily engaged in a conversation with some of their friends.

It was on the fourth day of our tour that a very remarkable series of events took place. After a visit to one of the local beaches in the morning, I scheduled an afternoon hike to look for air plants and orchids. The resort provided a truck to take us to a spot that I had previously scouted out and promised me they would return two hours later to pick us up. After spending the latter part of the afternoon looking for plants, we gathered along the road to await our transportation back, but there was no vehicle in sight. Being late is not uncommon in the Bahamas so we sat along the roadside joking about being on Bahamian time. After another forty-five minutes passed I began to get concerned that maybe the truck had broken down. We had taken extra water with us so most of the people were hydrated, but the intense heat of the late afternoon sun was beginning to wear on some of them, and I started to wonder if I shouldn't hike back to the hotel to see what had happened. At this point a car pulled up and said that the truck would be with us shortly. The driver told me that the hotel staff had been called away to make an emergency pickup at the airport and that the managers appreciated our patience. Ten minutes later our truck arrived and we bounced off to the hotel to make preparations for the evening cave party.

The cave was within walking distance of the inn, but in order to get to it you had to negotiate a narrow lime rock path with some uneven steps. This generally wasn't a problem because the hotel placed a series of lights along the trail so you could see where you were going. Rock tables and seats were scattered about the cave and during dinner a large serving table was set up at the back end of the room.

My wife and I always found the cave party to be a lot of fun and I was certain that our group would find it equally enjoyable. As a special service, the hotel also baked a birthday cake for any member of your group if you let them know a couple of days ahead of time. Since two of our participants were celebrating a birthday, I asked the mangers if they could bake two cakes and serve them during the party. As always, they were delighted to do so and offered to present them just after dinner.

There was an especially large crowd this night and it was quite evident that the management had gone to a lot of extra effort to make this party a gala affair. Festive decorations had been placed about the cave and a special meal had been prepared. At first I thought how nice it was for the club to do all this for us and then I realized, there was no way the hotel staff would go through all this extra effort just for our group.

Everyone in our party, including Mom and Dad, was thrilled with the food, and when the entertainment began I got up to talk to the managers about the birthday cakes. As I approached, they were having a animated discussion with one of their guests about the possibility of continuing the evening's festivities in the dining room. They said they would be able to accommodate him, at which time they introduced me to Elliot who told me he was also celebrating his birthday and wanted to know if our group would like to join him. "I'm sure they would," I said after we shook hands. It wasn't until I began walking back to the table that I began to think about how much Elliot reminded me of someone. When I sat down next to the Canadian gal who was a member of our group, she asked what was up. After I told her that the gentleman at the rear of the cave had just invited us to celebrate his birthday in the dining room, she looked up and her jaw dropped in disbelief. "It can't be," she stammered.

"It can't be what?" I asked.

"Him. I can't believe it's him."

"And who is he?" I asked.

"It's Trudeau. It's our Prime Minister. I hate that man. He's responsible for the slaughter of thousands of seal pups."

Now everything made sense. The late pickup with the truck, the large crowd, the special meal, the decorations in the cave; they were all part of a celebration they were holding for the Prime

Minister. Before I could turn around to continue my conversation, the Canadian gal disappeared into the crowd in hot pursuit of her nation's leader. I learned later that she never did catch up with him, which, under the circumstances, was probably just as well. Meanwhile our two birthday boys enjoyed their cakes and decided to take the Prime Minister up on his invitation to join him in the dining room.

Mom and Dad were among those who left for the party, but I missed out on the festivities. About half way up the hill I encountered one of our group who was in a state of panic. It appeared that her roommate had too much to drink and had wandered off the trail. She said she had looked everywhere for her and was concerned that something awful had happened.

One of the worst things a group leader can hear is that something bad has happened to one of the participants. As soon as I realized the severity of the situation I contacted my naturalist and we started looking for the woman with our flashlights. It was extremely dark that night and the woods surrounding the trail were filled with solution holes. It was easy to see how someone who was unsteady on their feet might fall and get injured. Moving slowly over the lime rock terrain, we called out her name hoping she would hear us. At least a half an hour passed with no response. Then the naturalist heard a faint cry for help from the top of a ridge. Sidestepping the solution holes, we pushed our way into a clearing and discovered that she'd fallen into a lime rock crevice. To everyone's relief she wasn't severely injured, but she did have quite a few scrapes and bruises on her arms and legs. It took us a while to get her safely back to her room. By then I was too exhausted to attend Trudeau's party, so I walked back to my room and collapsed hoping that the following day's activities would not be as stressful.

The next morning I met up with Dad in front of the hotel to make certain he and the fishing guide connected with one another. The guide turned out to be a Bahamian who had lived on the island for nearly fifty years and knew a lot about the local waters. Before they took off, the guide promised Dad that he'd catch a bonefish. I couldn't help but smile and think that this would be the day that Dad would finally hook the "big one."

I spent the rest of the morning snorkeling with the group at Poseidon Point. In my opinion, this was one of the best snorkeling spots in the Bahamas. It possessed huge patches of staghorn and elkhorn corals and had one of the healthiest tropical fish populations I'd ever seen. During our snorkel, dense schools of blue tangs glided among the reef's coral boulders, French and grey angelfish darted among the coral crevasses, and jewel-like blue chromis suspended themselves above finger-like coral columns. Along the rocky shore we also found a large lobster hotel whose residents waved their antennae at us as we peered into their hiding place. The group spent over two hours exploring this reef, and when time came for us to leave most of them told me that they wanted to come back and visit it again on their free day. I had to agree; the reef definitely was worth a second look, so on the last day we spent several more hours enveloped in this kaleidoscopic world of color and motion. For all of those who participated, it remained one of the more memorable experiences of our natural history outing.

Today, this fairyland reef, with its magnificent coral forest, no longer exists. When I took a group from the Conservancy to snorkel there in 1998 almost every inch of coral was dead. Most of the reef's staghorn and elkhorn corals were broken and scattered across the ocean floor. The few pieces of coral that remained standing were bleached and covered with thick layers of algae. No longer were there large schools of tropical fish darting in and out of the coral formations. The purple and green sea fans that swayed to and fro with wind driven waves had disappeared, and gone too were the yellow and orange fan worms that added dabs of color to the coral boulders. Resort owners claimed that an increase in water temperature had brought about its demise. I'm glad that Dad got to see the reef when it was vibrant and alive. I'm also certain that he would have shared a tear with me when I returned to my room that night and thought about what a beautiful living thing was no longer part of our world.

On an upbeat side, I'm happy to report that Dad finally did catch his bonefish. It didn't happen the way he anticipated. The first day he went out his reel broke and his fish got away. Feeling bad about what had happened, the guide offered to take him out again and this time Dad landed a whopper. I still recall the excitement in his eyes when he came to dinner that night and described the battle he had with that fish.

As far as the natural history tours were concerned, they were as big a success as I hoped they would be. Besides generating income, they increased our membership and volunteer corps and resulted in some very substantial contributions. One donor paid for the construction of our wild animal hospital and another left us with a hefty $1,000,000 endowment for our education program. The reason these trips were so successful, in my opinion, was the personal touch we offered our participants. During dinner, they got a chance to sit with the Nature Center staff and listen to our vision of the Center's future and the role we wanted to play in protecting Southwest Florida's environment. To me, these special moments were a way we could share the dream together.

Turtle Revelations

About a year after we moved into our new facility, the Conservancy Board replaced Bill Merrihue as President and appointed former lawyer Edwin "Ned" Putzell Jr. to the position. Ned took over in April 1982, while Bill was made Senior Vice President for Gifts and Endowments. As things turned out Ned found it took a lot more time to run the Conservancy than he initially anticipated and four years later he hired Toivo Tammerk to take over as chief executive officer. Toivo had been the director of the Naples Airport and knew Ned when he served on the airport board. During Toivo's term I was given the additional task of taking over the Conservancy's sea turtle program. It would be the last major Conservancy project that I would oversee.

Beginning in May, huge female loggerhead turtles crawl onto the beaches of Southwest Florida to lay their eggs. My father and I had watched them dig their nests and lay their eggs on several occasions. It was always a wondrous sight. Compelled by maternal instincts to perpetuate their species, these massive reptiles lumber onto Southwest Florida's beaches at night to seek out suitable nesting sites. Nothing deters the female from her goal once egg laying begins, not the hundreds of mosquitoes that suck blood from around her eyes nor the watchful raccoons that lay in wait for an easy meal. With her mission accomplished she returns to the Gulf. No further thought is given to her developing embryos. She has done her best to perpetuate the species. Raccoons and other wild animals might come to devour her eggs and waves from tropical storms might drown her embryos, but these are factors beyond her control. Those turtles that hatch face all kinds of danger. Ghost crabs and other animals feast on them as they struggle to reach the Gulf, while snook and dolphin swallow them whole until their distended stomachs are filled with their wiggling masses. Only one in a thousand of the newly hatched turtles survives to become an adult, and those that do will undertake a long and perilous journey before returning to the place where they were born. Driven by the same instincts that guided their parents, they eventually crawl up on to the same beach to produce another generation of offspring

My job was to oversee a team of people who would patrol the beaches on Key Island just south of Naples from late April through August looking for nesting loggerheads. Once a nesting turtle was discovered we would insert a metal tag into its flipper and mark its location. The tags were inserted so we could keep track of the turtle during its egg laying activity as well as determine how often it came to nest on Key Island or other places along Florida's coast.

A lot of work went into preparing for the nesting season. Since running the education department was a full-time job, I got the Conservancy to let me hire a field supervisor, Ron Meszich. After Ron was hired, interns had to be employed, ATVs and other equipment purchased, living accommodations set up for the staff, work schedules prepared, and weekly meetings planned to determine what problems needed to be addressed.

There was nothing glamorous about monitoring sea turtle nesting activity. All of the work was done at night on a barrier island infested with sand flies and mosquitoes. We got to the island by boat and once there set up our base of operation in a house donated by one of the Conservancy's members. Every half hour a patrol was sent out to check for nesting turtles. Sleep was a rare commodity, especially if it was an active nesting season. Tagging a turtle meant waiting for just the right moment to insert the metal clip plus you had to record the size and condition of the animal as well as its nesting location. All of this took place while hordes of mosquitoes and sand flies sucked blood from every exposed part of your body and sweat poured out of your pores. Your eyelids, ears, nose, and hands felt like they were on fire, and on extremely bad nights you inhaled copious numbers of these insects. While inserting the metal tag you also had to be mindful of fire ants. If the turtle was laying her eggs in the vicinity of an ant colony, there was a good chance angry hordes would crawl under your clothing and bite the hell out of you.

Weather was another factor we had to deal with. June through mid October were hot months with daily thunderstorms. And there was always the threat of tropical storms and hurricanes. Care had to be taken not to send out a patrol during a lightning storm. On several occasions while we were monitoring turtles, bolts of lightning struck so close we were sure someone in our group had been fried. Tropical storms and hurricanes were even a bigger problem. Once the storm warning went up we suspended our operation and pulled everyone off the island. This meant securing our living quarters and heading out into choppy seas to get back to the mainland before storm force winds enveloped us. Despite all these hazards we did gather some valuable data on nesting loggerheads.

One of the first things we discovered was that predation on loggerhead eggs was very high on Key Island. Raccoons were the primary culprits, in part because people fed them during the winter and their population levels grew beyond the island's natural carrying capacity. Ron and I agreed that something needed to be done to overcome this problem. We thought about initiating a public relations campaign encouraging people not to feed the raccoons but decided against this course of action when we realized that by the time the summer rainy season arrived most of the people responsible for feeding them had left. The simplest solution seemed to be placing a wire cage over the top of the nests so the raccoons couldn't get at the eggs. But this didn't work because we didn't have a satisfactory way to anchor the cages and the raccoons simply found a way to dig underneath them.

The following year we decided to build a chain link enclosure. We planned to transport all the loggerhead eggs laid along the beach into a secure cage where they'd be protected from predators. This turned out to be more labor intensive than we expected because the eggs had to be extracted from the nest, driven to the enclosure and placed in the new nest in relatively the same position as they'd been in the original.

However, the most serious problem with our plan didn't show up until after the turtles hatched. We had made sure the mesh in the chain link fence was wide enough to let the newly hatched turtles through, but what we hadn't counted on was that the enclosure would act as a magnet for predators. Subsequently, once the raccoons and other predators discovered the turtles crawling out of the enclosure all they had to do was collect outside the fence and wait for the food to come to them. To some extent we were able to cut down on the predation by chasing away the raccoons and other predators. But once the turtles were in the ocean they were on their own and we had no way of getting rid of the predatory fish and marine mammals that waited for them.

During my third year overseeing the program the chief executive officer instructed me to publish a research report on our project. Doing sea turtle monitoring and conservation was one thing, but conducting a publishable scientific investigation was something else. When I asked how much money would be available to carry out this study he said, "None." Now there was a challenge I hadn't anticipated.

Back in my office I sat down with Ron and had a long discussion about what kind of research we could do with no additional funding. Ultimately, we decided to do a two-pronged study on the impact exotic Australian pines had on the nesting activities of loggerheads. These trees had established themselves along most of Florida's beaches where they were constantly being uprooted and their twisted root systems ensnaring nesting loggerheads as they tried to reach suitable nesting sites. So for the first part of our study we decided to quantify the impact these uprooted trees were having on the turtles.

The second part of our research project involved determining how much Australian pines impacted the incubation temperature of sea turtle nests. Australian pines grow very tall, and on the west coast of Florida these trees provide refreshing shade to beach goers during the hot summer rainy season. However, refreshing shade for a beach enthusiast could mean unnatural incubation temperatures for sea turtles. Hence the question: Was the shade from these trees sufficient enough to cool the egg chamber and change the sex ratio of the developing turtles?

No equipment was needed for the first half of our study, but we did need funds to monitor the nest temperatures. I was able to get money for the temperature recording devices from private donors who were as anxious as we were to find out the results of our study. After a year of intensive field research and careful analysis of our data, the two-pronged investigation revealed that Australian pines were definitely having a detrimental impact on the nesting activities of loggerheads. Because of overturned trees turtles were finding fewer suitable nesting sites and some turtles were getting caught up in the roots and dying. We also found that loggerhead turtle nests that had been in the shade of Australian pines had much cooler incubation chambers than we imagined. This resulted in longer incubation periods and suggested that the nests were producing mostly male turtles.

I never completed all of the work I would like to have done on this project, but Ron reported our findings at a sea turtle conference in the Florida Keys. One intriguing question that I carried away from this program was that if the Australian pines could cool the nest temperatures to a level that could influence a turtle's sex, how much would the shadow cast by a large condominium impact them?

Fish Tales from the Edge of Eden

During the times when Dad and I weren't collecting and studying the marine environment at Tigertail, exploring the Ten Thousand Islands or hiking and fossil collecting at different sites along the Florida peninsula, we spent a lot of time fishing off Tigertail's beach.

Every fishing day began at five thirty in the morning. I would get up, have breakfast, pack my fishing gear, and head over to my parents' mobile home. By six forty-five, Dad and I would be driving down the "Trail" towards Marco discussing the best places to fish and what type of tackle to use. By seven forty-five, I would park my car near the access point to Tigertail and we'd head towards Big Marco Pass.

In the early years the majority of the people we met along the beach in the morning were fishermen. As Marco became more developed, more shell collectors and birders showed up. Many of these people would stop to talk to us as we headed up the beach. Some were interested in what kind of fish we hoped to catch while others were looking for information. I remember one day when a young woman approached us and asked if there was some place she could swim where there weren't all those things in the water. When Dad asked her what those "things" were, she grimaced and said, "those little fish."

Dad lifted his hat and scratched his bald spot while he gave her questions some thought. "I can't think of any," he responded, "but I can assure you that they are harmless."

"It's not that I think that the fish will hurt me," she replied, "it's just that I can't stand them pecking at me."

Dad gave her a quizzical look. "Pecking at you?"

"Yes," she said, "they keep pecking at the hairs on my leg and it gives me the creeps." When Dad looked down at her legs he immediately knew what her problem was. She was one of those women who didn't shave her legs and she had a healthy growth of hair. Trying to be as diplomatic as possible, Dad explained to her that the hairs on her legs were collecting plankton and other debris from the water. As a result, the small fish found her food-filled body hair an ideal place to look for something to eat.

At first she thought Dad was joking, but when she saw he meant what he said she looked at me and curled up her nose, "That's disgusting," she said. "I never heard of such a thing. Maybe if they cleaned up the water these fish wouldn't hang around. I'm going to get in touch with someone in the county and see if they can do something about this." We never found out if she ever contacted anybody in the county, but we were sure if she did they were quite amused by her request.

On several occasions we met nude bathers on the beach. Dad always had a problem with them. He told me he didn't think that it was appropriate for anyone to display their naked bodies on a public beach. One day when we were headed back from one of our fishing trips Dad suddenly stomped off in the opposite direction without telling me where he was going. Realizing that he was no longer with me, I turned around to find out where he'd disappeared. To my chagrin I saw he was making a beeline towards a nude bather. Knowing Dad, I knew there would be trouble so I scurried back to get him just as he planted himself in front of the unsuspecting sun worshiper. When the man realized Dad was staring down at him he opened his eyes and squinted at my father. "Does it burn?" my father asked.

"Does what burn?" the man inquired.

"That," Dad grinned and pointed to his penis. At this point the man became quite defensive and told my father it was none of his damn business. "I'm just trying to be helpful," Dad said. "If it got sunburned, you'd be in a lot of pain and you might not be able to use it anymore. And what if you got skin cancer. God, I hate to think about what it would be like to have it removed." At this point the man became so flustered he didn't know what to say and I tugged at Dad's shirt and suggested we leave. "Well I think he should cover it up, don't you?" Dad said as he reluctantly turned to follow me. "It could have a serious impact on his sex life." The last we saw of the sunbather he was beating a hasty retreat into the bushes to put on some clothes.

In the early years we fished the southeast end of Big Marco Pass. Our routine involved wading out to the edge of the channel, driving two long pieces of PVC pipe into the bottom, and attaching our bait buckets to the plastic poles. When we were finished setting up we cast our lines out along the edge of the channel and let the bait drift down the sandy ridge with the tide. In order to attract the fish we would periodically jerk our lines. We found this to be the most effective way to scare away the smaller fish and get the larger ones to bite. On good days we'd catch a dozen or more fish. The majority were sheepshead, whiting and spotted seatrout with an occasional snook and redfish.

It's interesting how your body adjusts to the warm South Florida temperatures. Initially Dad and I would fish in the Gulf wearing just a bathing suit when the water temperature was a little over 60° F. But after a couple of years, we couldn't tolerate standing in waist deep water when the water temperature was below 70° F. To overcome the chill, Dad and I started wearing sweatshirts during the dry winter season, and on very cold days we didn't venture into the Gulf at all. Not being able to walk out to the edge of the channel on cold days, meant that we were depriving ourselves of the best fishing. So Dad decided to do something to improve our winter catch. After talking to a fellow at the local dive shop, he purchased a three-quarter-length, yellow and blue wet suit and suggested that I do the same. Being a lot younger than he, I refused to follow up on his idea, figuring I could tough it out when the weather was bad. This turned out to be a mistake. I can still see Dad standing in the frigid water with his bright yellow and blue wet suit waving to me to come out to the edge of the channel. He was catching one fish after the other as I was shivering on the beach hoping he would quit fishing so I could go home and get warm.

During our third year fishing Big Marco Pass, a tugboat ran aground on the sandy shoals along the east side of the channel. It happened during a strong cold front, and the company that owned the vessel announced it was going to pull the boat off of the sandbar when the seas subsided. However, the ship mysteriously caught fire a couple of weeks after it ran aground and all that was left was a charred hull and a portion of the main cabin. A rumor circulating at the time suggested that the company deliberately set fire to the ship so it could collect the insurance, but nothing of that nature was ever proven. During the months that followed, the waves battered what was left of the vessel and the entire structure eventually sank to the bottom of the channel.

What was bad for the company was great for the people who fished Big Marco Pass. Within a year, the ship's hull became encrusted with all kinds of marine life, and a mini nearshore reef was established. On days when the water was clear Dad and I would wade out to the edge of the channel at low tide and watch hundreds of fish swim around the sunken structure. It soon became an obsession with us to find a way to catch them. If we threw the line too close to the wreck the fish would grab the bait and dart into a crevice where they'd cut our line on encrusted pieces of the hull. In order to avoid this, we had to cast our lines well in front of the wreck when the tide was going out and a good distance in back when the tide was coming in. This worked for the small fish like sheepshead and grey snapper but was not as successful with large species like redfish and snook. Even when our drags were tightened, the bigger fish would dart towards the tugboat and cut us off. Eventually, we started using heavier line that helped us pull the fish away from the structure.

As more and more large fish collected over the wreck, we encountered more feeding frenzies. This happened mostly at the end of the rainy season when the ship's hull was blanketed by massive numbers of small baitfish. We witnessed our first feeding outburst in October about three years after the boat sank. A huge school of redfish collected near the structure and started feeding on pilchards. The water above the wreck quickly turned into a boiling cauldron of activity and every time we cast our line towards the boat a big red would grab our bait and race across the flats. During this feeding activity, line screeched off our reels so fast we weren't sure we'd be able to stop it. Most of the time we were able to turn the fish towards the beach, but in a few instances the fish were so big they cut us off before we got them under control. We caught a total of forty redfish that day. We released thirty-six and took the remaining four home to eat. Years later we often talked about that fishing trip. Dad said that it was one of the best ones he'd ever had. I had to agree. Both of my arms and shoulders ached for a couple of days after that outing, but it was a good kind of hurt, one that helped preserve fond memories and instilled a desire to go back and try again.

After spending the first couple of years walking to Big Marco Pass, Dad and I started to look for a way we could drive to and from our fishing spot. When we explored the region behind Tigertail's coastal dune we discovered a road on the backside that some people used to get to the pass. Dad thought it would be neat if we could use it but it wasn't an option since neither one of us had a vehicle that could traverse the rugged terrain. They say walking is healthy for you, but walking to and from the pass with all of our fishing gear became quite a challenge even with the cart and backpack Dad rigged up. It was especially bad during the rainy season when we were trying to dodge thunderstorms. Consequently, Dad and I started looking for a used car to drive along the back road. Most of the cars that I looked at were out of my price range. Then one day Dad called me up and said that one of his neighbors had an old car for sale. He said it was a second-hand Mercury that lacked air conditioning, but had a lever on the dashboard that raised and lowered the rear window. Except for the fact that it didn't have four-wheel drive, the car sounded ideal for our purposes so I asked Dad to find out how much it would cost. He got back to me the same day and said its owner would sell it to us for $300 cash. After a brief discussion with Bernice, I drove over to the mobile home park with money in hand and the next day we were a two-car family.

Even though the vehicle had no air conditioning, I grew to love that car. And of course one of the first things my father and I did was find out if we could drive it along the back road to Big Marco Pass. Most of the road's surface turned out to be lime rock, but there were several stretches of soft sand and a small tidal creek with shelly bottom that we had to traverse in order to reach our destination. After looking it over Dad was convinced that we'd have no problems, but I had some serious reservations especially about the stretches of soft sand and the creek. One of the sandy stretches was about twenty feet wide and I could see us getting stuck during the dry season. Finally, I agreed to try to drive the car to the pass but only after I threw some planks and an extra jack into the trunk.

For several years we drove back and forth to Big Marco Pass and I'm glad to say we only got stuck twice. The biggest problem we had was the creek. Although the bottom of the creek was solid, a foot-and-a-half of water collected in it during high tide. This meant the underside of the car got a good soaking. Dad didn't think the saltwater was such a big deal and said there was a coating on the underside of the car that would protect it from rusting out. I wasn't convinced of that and I was certain that the car manufacturer didn't expect their patrons to drive through a saltwater creek, so I insisted we wash down the underside of the vehicle with freshwater after every outing. Eventually, despite all the hosing we did, the bottom of the car did start to rust, and Dad and I soon had to straddle holes in the floor when we drove down the highway. The only good thing I can remember about those holes was they gave a good view of road kills as we sped over them.

One afternoon my favorite car met an untimely end when the mother of one of the children in our Nature Center classes plowed into it in the parking lot at about twenty miles an hour. It is still difficult to image how she accomplished this feat, but I distinctly remember the loud collision from inside my office. When I arrived at the scene of the "accident" I encountered an extremely distraught mother who began profusely apologizing for what she had done. It was apparent after looking at the results of this collision that my poor Mercury would no longer be crossing the creek to get to Big Marco Pass. After reporting the incident to the police, I called for a tow truck and had them bring the car to the local junkyard. To my amazement the junkyard owner paid me $300 for the Mercury. After years of abuse the net cost of that car turned out to be zero. I never made a better automobile purchase and I don't think I will again.

For about six years after the tugboat sank, reef fishing was outstanding at Big Marco Pass. But winter storms slowly tore apart what remained of the boat and the constant deposition of sand from Hideaway Beach, situated at the north end of Marco Island, buried what was left.

As fishing at the Pass became less productive, Dad and I started to look for other places along Tigertail to fish. One of the sites that looked good was a lagoon that was beginning to form at the north end of the beach. The lagoon was similar to the area Dad and I were studying at the south end but was separated from it by a large shallow, sandy ridge. Several times Dad and I tried to catch fish in the lagoon but the results were always the same—nothing. Then one day we encountered two guys fishing along its south rim where the water dropped off to six feet. To our amazement these two fellows were catching one fish after another. After watching them awhile we became curious as to why they were so successful and we weren't. Our first thought was that they had found a place where the fish congregated on the incoming tide to feed on small baitfish. So the next time we went to the lagoon we waded over to the exact spot where they'd been fishing and tried our luck. Our total catch after standing two hours in the water was zero. There obviously had to be some other secret to their success and Dad was determined to find out what it was.

Several weeks later the fisherman showed up again. This time Dad wandered over to where they were fishing and asked how things were going. "Not too bad," one of them replied and pointed to a string of fish attached to a PVC pipe. Not wanting to appear too pushy, I watched from a distance until Dad waved me over.

"Look at that catch," Dad said as I waded up alongside them. "That's pretty darn good." When I saw the string of fish that was dangling from the PVC pipe I shook my head in agreement. On it were several large speckled trout, a nice size snook and a decent Gulf flounder. "They said they catch them with pinfish," Dad noted.

"Do you buy the bait?" I asked.

"Yeah," one of them replied, "we purchase them from the Marco Island Marina for about thirty-five cents each." As we continued our conversation we noticed that they had no sinkers on their lines and they were hooking the pinfish through the mouth and letting it swim along the bottom. We had never used this technique before, so after we wished them luck we headed back to the beach to discuss how we would fish the lagoon the next time we came out.

"I'm not paying thirty-five cents for a pinfish," Dad grumbled as we sat on the stump of an Australian pine and watched the fisherman haul in another trout.

"We could bring the seine," I suggested, "I'm sure we could get all the bait we need in a couple of drags." Dad liked that idea and suggested we bring an extra PVC pipe to hold our bait buckets.

By the following weekend we were ready to fish the lagoon. Since I no longer had the old Mercury, we packed everything into our newly purchased johnboat and launched it from the Isles of Capri north of Big Marco Pass. Our plan involved crossing the Pass, anchoring the boat near the north end of the lagoon and setting up our PVC holders on the east side of the sandy ridge.

This proved to be one of the best fishing days we ever had at Tigertail. After seining up our bait and setting our poles into their holders the fish began scoffing up our bait and dragging our lines all over the lagoon. In total that day, we hooked several large snook, a half dozen large sea trout, four hefty redfish, and a large gulf flounder.

The best fishing in the lagoon always took place in the fall on an incoming tide. As Dad grew older he usually got tired after seining so I brought along a chair so he could sit and watch the poles from the beach. As soon as one of the poles began to bend one or both of us would race out and set the hook. One day one of our poles almost got launched into the Gulf before Dad reached it. The next thing I knew Dad was being pulled towards Big Marco Pass as he tried to turn the fish back towards the lagoon. The battle seemed to last forever. Every time Dad thought he had the fish under control it would make another run towards the pass. Initially I thought he'd hooked a large black-tip shark, but when it didn't leap out of the water and continued to make dramatic runs away from the beach I became convinced it was a large redfish. Dad was nearly exhausted by the time I netted the fish, but I'll never forget how proud he was when we held it up for some of the local beachcombers to look at. Quite a few of them had stopped to watch the fight and were just as curious as we were to see what kind of fish Dad had caught. That redfish weighed over twelve pounds and when we got back to the mobile home park Dad made sure everyone got a chance to see it.

Getting to and from the lagoon with our johnboat was risky and it got even trickier when Dad's hemorrhoids started to act up. He no longer wanted to sit on the boat's metal seats and insisted I place a lawn chair in the center of the boat so he'd be more comfortable. I didn't like the idea and told him so. I tried to explain that the chair wasn't very stable and that if we ran into rough weather there was a good chance he'd get tossed overboard.

But no amount of reasoning worked, so I reluctantly agreed to let him sit in the chair when we motored back and forth to the lagoon. During the summer rainy season this worked fine, but when the seasonal residents returned to Marco, and the amount of boat traffic in the channel increased dramatically, getting to and from Tigertail got hairy. One day, halfway across the channel, we encountered a large cabin cruiser racing out of the pass. The wake it generated was substantial and all I could think about as it approached was trying to avoid getting swamped. The thought of my father being in any kind of trouble never entered my mind, and it wasn't until I looked over to warn him about the next round of approaching waves that I realized he'd disappeared. As the boat bounced up and down I frantically scanned the surrounding water hoping to see him. He was nowhere in sight. Then I got this sinking feeling in the pit of my stomach. Suppose my father had drowned. How was I going to explain that to my mother? I was supposed to take care of him. Frantic shouts followed, but there was no response. Then I spotted what I thought was a yellow float near the mouth of the pass. Could it be? I turned the bow of the boat around and headed towards the entrance of the channel as fast as I could. When I got closer I immediately recognized Dad's ridiculous yellow and blue wet suit. Thank God I'd found him. Eagerly reaching over the side, I grabbed him by his arm and asked him if he was all right. Staring up at me with a disgruntled look he said, "Of course I'm all right. What the hell took you so long?" Now there was a fine thank you I thought to myself. I was so relieved to see that he was safe that I completely ignored his caustic response. Dad was alive and acting like his cranky self. The next thing I knew he grabbed the back end of the johnboat and we started to sink.

"Don't do that," I shouted, "you'll swamp us." Initially he looked at me like I was crazy, but finally he grasped the severity of the situation and moved to the side of the boat. With my father clinging to the side I slowly made our way to the lagoon where he staggered ashore and plopped himself on the beach.

After what had happened I thought it best we call it quits and go back home, but Dad would have none of that. He said if Mom saw him come back early looking the way he did she'd know something was up and he didn't want to deal with that. So we stayed out until one p.m. and even brought some fish home. As for Mom, she never did find out about that calamity and I'm thankful that she didn't.

That incident marked the end of fishing with the johnboat. About a week later Dad found someone in the mobile home park who was selling a used fifteen-foot McKee Craft and we bought it for several hundred dollars. The boat needed some repairs and the engine had to be serviced, but it certainly proved to be a lot safer to maneuver across Big Marco Pass.

During the following rainy season I had my own frightening encounter at Tigertail. The lagoon at the northern end of beach was beginning to fill in with sand and the fishing had started to decline. We were fishing on an outgoing tide and by noon we had caught only one small redfish. At Dad's suggestion we put our gear into the McKee Craft and dragged the boat over the shallow bar to see if the fishing on the Gulf side was any better. When we got to a spot that Dad thought looked good, I dropped the anchor and was jolted by a sharp pain in my right leg. At first I thought I had dropped the anchor on my foot so I grouched about the stupid move I'd just made. It wasn't until I tried to lift my foot that I realized something was terribly wrong. All of a sudden my leg flew off the bottom and something began shaking it from side to side. The pain was excruciating and the blood rising to the surface scared the hell out of me. The first thing that entered my mind was that a shark had grabbed my leg. Terrified by the thought that my leg was about to be torn off, I grabbed the side of the McKee Craft and screamed for Dad's help. Unfortunately, my father was looking the other way when all this was taking place and his hearing wasn't very good. It took another loud scream to gain his attention and when he turned around he wanted to know what all the fuss was about. "A shark's got my leg," I yelled, "help me get into the boat." From the look of disbelief on his face I knew he thought I was crazy. But when he saw all the blood in the water he grabbed my arms and started to pull me on board. All of a sudden I felt whatever grabbed me let go and I scrambled into the McKee Craft. The pain was almost unbearable and I was too frightened to look down to see what had happened to my leg.

Dad brought me back to my senses. Bending over to look at my injury he grumbled, "Your leg looks fine to me." Was he kidding? The pain shooting through my body was so intense I was certain my foot was gone. To my astonishment Dad was right. My foot was still there but it was sitting in a pool of blood.

Realizing that I was not about to die, Dad wanted to know what all the commotion was about. I was still in too much pain to appreciate his cavalier attitude so I ignored his remarks and proceeded to take off my sneaker and sock. To my surprise my sock was missing and the blood collecting on the bottom of the boat was coming from a hole on the side of my foot. When I examined the jagged edges of the wound I knew exactly what had happened. I had dropped the anchor on top of a large stingray and the animal had responded by whipping its tail around driving its spine through my sneaker and sock into the side of my foot. When I lifted my foot, the stingray attempted to swim off, but it couldn't because its spine was still embedded in my foot and shoe. Flapping its wings in a frantic effort to escape, the stingray's spine started to tear at my flesh creating excruciating pain and copious amounts of blood. Locked together and unable to get free, I lost control of my leg until Dad grabbed hold of me. Perhaps the most bizarre thing that happened was that the stingray was not able to free itself of my sock. It remained attached to the animal's spine and was dragged away through the hole in my sneaker.

There is no doubt in my mind that stingray wounds are among the most painful injuries anyone can experience. To give you some idea just how bad they can be I'll relate the comments passed along to me by a kayaker I encountered in Rookery Bay. This gentleman was out paddling around in one of the shallow bays when he decided to stop and do some fishing. Shortly after he got out of his kayak a stingray drove its spine into the calf of his leg. He said he had been shot three times in Vietnam and none of those bullet wounds were anywhere near as excruciating as the wound he received from the stingray. He said it took nearly a month to get over the injury and he still had nightmares about the encounter.

The reason a stingray wound is so painful is because there is a mass of tissue at the base of the spine that produces a powerful protein toxin. When the spine penetrates your skin, pressure is placed against the tissue and the toxin is released into your flesh. To facilitate the flow of toxin there is a groove in the center of the spine that helps the venom pour into the wound. There is no anti-venom to treat the wound and there is no pill you can take to eliminate the pain. There is only one thing you can do and that is soak the injury in hot water and Epsom Salt. This works because the protein venom is destroyed by heat.

The problem I faced was twofold: stop the flow of blood and eliminate the pain. Fortunately, I was able to stop the bleeding with a pressure bandage, but the only thing I could do to diminish the pain was to keep the sneaker off and expose my foot to the heat of the sun. Needless to say, we quit fishing. Dad pulled our gear together and I drove the boat back to the Isles of Capri. It took all of my willpower to concentrate on getting back to the marina and on the way in Dad kept asking if the pain was getting any better. It wasn't, of course, but I didn't want to let Dad know that so I told him I'd be fine.

As soon as we got to the dock I staggered into the tackle shop and asked if there was anyone there who could back my trailer up so we could pull our boat out of the water. Unfortunately, none of the men in the shop could operate my truck's standard transmission.

"Do you want me to get someone to help you out?" the sympathetic shop owner asked.

"No," I groaned, "I'll see if my father can do it."

It had been years since Dad had backed up the trailer, but he said he'd see if he could handle it. When he got it halfway to the ramp it was obvious he wasn't going to be able to guide it into the water, so I got into the driver's seat and gritted my teeth. I'll never know how I accomplished the task. Every time I hit the clutch, pain shot up my leg and blood seeped through the bandage onto the floor.

Somehow Dad and I managed to get the boat onto the trailer. Now all I needed to do was drive home. But before I did, I stepped onto the seawall at the marina and got rid of my lunch. The thirty-minute drive home seemed to last forever and there were times when I didn't think I was going to make it. As we pulled up to my parents' mobile home I asked Mom to call Bernice and let her know what happened. I also asked her to tell Bernice to prepare a tub full of hot water and Epsom Salt. It took another half hour to get home, but I was never so glad to see a tub full of hot water in my entire life. As soon as I put my foot in the tub it was like somebody had flipped a switch. The pain generated by the toxin instantaneously disappeared. I soaked myself in that tub for nearly three hours, and when we ran out of hot water Bernice boiled water to add to the tub.

People often ask me when do you know it's time to stop soaking your injury in hot water. The answer is simple—when you remove the injured part of your body from the water and it no longer hurts.

After neutralizing the toxin I went to the doctor and got the wound cleaned out and bandaged. It took another four weeks before I was able to walk around without a limp. And I'm pleased to say, unlike some people who have been wounded by stingrays, I've had no serious after effects.

I always did and always will have a great respect for stingrays. I still wear shoes when I'm wading in the water, and I always shuffle my feet when I know I'm in a place where I suspect stingrays might be feeding. It's not their intention to harm you, but they have a very potent weapon on their tails and they will use it to defend themselves. As far as the recent fad in which tourists are invited to wade or snorkel around in the water and feed stingrays, I recommend you don't do it. All you have to do is make one mistake and you could wind up with an injury you'll regret for some time, if not for the rest of your life.

I no longer fish at Tigertail, but the adventures Dad and I had there remain an important part of me. I still wander down the beach and watch the fisherman at Big Marco Pass. During these outings I always get a lot of joy watching a father and son standing at the edge of the channel trying to catch the big ones, and at times I get the urge to join them.

Slip Sliding Away

As the years passed Dad and I did less and less fishing and hiking through the swamps. In part it was because Mom wasn't feeling well and he wanted to stay home to take care of her. But it was also because his body couldn't withstand the rigors of our explorations as well as it used to. I remember one day we were walking around the mobile home park reminiscing when he suddenly stopped, shook his head, and gave me one of those wistful looks. "You know there are days when I wake up and think I'm forty and then I look in the mirror and I realize I'm an old man." Now that I've reached those twilight years I know what he meant. It's a real drag growing old. Life's journey is bittersweet, and I continued to hope that a few more adventures still awaited Dad and me.

During this time in his life Dad spent more time volunteering at the Conservancy and helping Mom out around the house. He also spent a lot of time using his limited artistic talents to create pieces of art from things we had collected on the beach. Sometimes when I stopped by the mobile home he would throw his arm around me and insist on showing me his latest masterpiece. Most were weird looking little animals with button-size eyes. Others were self-professed artistic creations that he'd carved out of driftwood. As I fondled these miniature sculptures and praised Dad for their uniqueness, I reflected on my own life and wondered if this was the way I'd spend my final days.

Neither of my parents were big on owning pets. Other than the dog and cat we had when I was young, Mom's only other pet was a canary. She said she bought it because she liked listening to it sing. Later in life she bought a budgerigar to help keep her company. In the morning my parents would let the bird out of its cage to eat with them and they even trained it to pull a toy cart across the kitchen table. Of course the bird's toilet habits weren't the best and it would often defecate on the table. In their younger years they would never have tolerated such unsanitary eating conditions, but as they grew older their ability to see diminished and I suspect an occasional speck of bird dropping was consumed during mealtime.

During the day the bird was king of the roost, flitting from one room to another screeching at my parents or nibbling on the furniture. It was this routine that eventually got Dad into trouble. One day while Mom was cleaning the bird's cage she yelled out to Dad that the bird was heading in his direction. Unfortunately, Dad's hearing was bad and he never heard Mom's warning. The next thing Dad knew the bird was attempting to land on his shoulder as he walked out the door. Slam went the door and off came the bird's head. Mom heard the bird's final screech and immediately ran to the door to see what had happened. When Dad turned around she started screaming at him.

"Look what you've done. If you'd gotten a hearing aid like I asked, this would never have happened."

Dad was equally devastated and promised Mom he'd fix things. In a hapless gesture of remorse, he picked up the bird's head and body and brought it to the Conservancy. I knew something bad was up when my secretary Margie came into the office and told me my father was waiting outside and wanted to speak to me. Usually Dad didn't visit the office unless he called ahead of time, so I told Margie to send him in. When he entered, tears were streaming down his face as he unfolded the cloth to show me the bird.

"Your mom will never let me back in the house and she'll never speak to me again unless you do something." I'd never seen him so distraught. Here was a man who could withstand the pain of a catfish spine in his stomach, sobbing like a child. Standing up, I threw my arms around him and told him I thought I might have a solution.

Several days earlier someone had dropped off a cockatiel at our Wild Animal Rehabilitation Center, and since we didn't take care of non-native species we were looking for someone to take care of it. That morning Sarah Denham, our rehab supervisor, informed me that she thought she might have found someone, so I immediately called her to see if they'd picked it up. Fortunately, there was no one at home when she phoned, so I told her not to give the bird away, that I'd found just the right home for it. Dad was both relieved and thrilled with my news, but his plight wasn't over. He would still have to convince Mom that the cockatiel was a suitable substitute for the bird he'd just beheaded. I wasn't around when he attempted to do this, but he obviously succeeded because he called me up several days later and told me Mom had forgiven him and that they were having lots of fun with their new pet. Mom named the bird Topsy and when I went to visit them the following weekend it was already joining them for breakfast. It would be the last pet they would own and I still remember it flitting around the trailer screeching at my parents whenever it felt ignored.

In the early 1980s, the motor on the McKee Craft died and we decided to buy a new boat. After looking at several different models we agreed that a fifteen-foot Boston Whaler was just the boat for us. Before I purchased it, however, I had Dad sit in it to see if it was comfortable enough for him. After a close inspection of the boat's hull and trying out all the seats, Dad announced it was perfect. As a surprise I had the shop apply the name *OH HENRY!* on the hull. Dad was tickled pink to see his name on the vessel, and when we launched it on its maiden voyage he told everyone he met at the boat ramp that our boat was named after him.

Mom's health took a turn for the worse after we purchased the *OH HENRY!* She was in a lot of pain and she often complained about not being able to eat as well as she once did. I think Mom suspected she was dying but was reluctant to go to the doctor. When the pain got so bad she couldn't tolerate it anymore she decided to go to her primary care physician and have some tests done to find out what was wrong. The test results were devastating to the entire family. Mom had pancreatic cancer and it had spread to other organs. I remember Dad asking the doctor how long she had to live. Three to six months was the grim prognosis. When I met him outside her hospital room he was crying. "She always said that I would die before she did," he sobbed. "I guess things don't necessarily work out the way you think they will."

Dad remained a loving caregiver for the remaining six weeks of Mom's life. During these trying times my wife would cover for him so he could go fishing in the *OH HENRY!* One day while we were out fishing my father looked over at me and said, "You know I used to think when I was young that I'd live forever, but now I know that's not going to happen. I was certain that someone would come along and invent a miracle drug that would stop me from aging. It was all wishful thinking and when I realized this, I started to think about how much I'm really going to miss this world. There'll be no more fishing trips to the grass flats. I won't be able to watch the birds come home to roost and there'll be no more hikes into the swamp. The world is really a beautiful place and I took it for granted. I should have been more concerned about how man was treating our planet. We're slowly destroying our Garden of Eden. I don't think man was cast out of the garden, he simply forgot he was part of it. You're doing the right thing by teaching kids about protecting our world. Maybe they can do something to save it. I know it's too late for me to do anything."

Mom died several days after that fishing trip. The family gathered around her on a cold November day to say goodbye. I remember Dad bending over to kiss her on the cheek just after she had taken her last breath. The tears rolled down his face as he gently stroked her hair. "I'll miss you a lot," he said and then stood up and left the room.

Mom wanted to be cremated, so when Dad and I arrived at the funeral home the director asked us if we wanted to place her ashes in a special urn. Dad thought about this then shook his head. "No," he responded, "she always told me to keep things simple. She said dead people could care less about what kind of fancy urn or coffin they're buried in."

Dad placed the cardboard box containing Mom's ashes on his bedroom dresser. After several weeks I noticed it still sitting there and I asked if there was a special place he wanted to distribute her remains. He told me he'd thought about that a lot and hadn't decided. He thought the best place would be on Cape Cod. She loved that place, but he didn't think he could let go of her just yet. It was the last we talked about Mom's ashes and on the day he died we found them on the table next to his bed.

After Mom passed away I would take Dad out fishing in the *OH HENRY!* and frequently invite him over to dinner. The rest of the time Dad stayed at the trailer where he puttered around with household chores. Several times during the week Bernice would stop by during lunch to see how he was doing and make sure he was eating properly. It was during this time in his life that he started writing letters to people. Mom used to be the letter writer in the family, but before she died she made Dad promise that he would stay in touch with everyone. Because of his limited education, letter writing was not easy for him. When I visited him one afternoon I found him bent over the kitchen table writing a letter to my sister. There was an open, large print dictionary next to him and he was flipping the pages back and forth attempting to look up a word. As I approached he turned and said, "I have to give Mom a lot of credit. Writing letters is lot harder than I thought. The hardest part seems to be finding the words in the dictionary." When I asked him what word he wanted to spell he said, "pleasure." Reaching over, I thumbed through the pages and pointed to the word with my finger. Since I was in no rush to leave, I asked if there were any other words he needed help finding. He said he didn't think so, but when he finished he wanted to talk about writing a book.

His desire to write a book came as a surprise. I didn't see him being able to take on a project of this magnitude so I sat down on the sofa and waited for him to finish his letter. "I've done a lot of interesting things in my life," he said when he put his pencil down, "and I thought the rest of the family might be interested in learning about them." I had to admit I was, so I asked him if he thought he was up to the challenge.

"Why not?" he asked. "In fact I've already begun to write it. Would you like to read it?"

"Yeah, sure," I said as he walked into the bedroom and returned with a yellow legal pad on which he had written down some of his early experiences. As I sat and read through the first few pages I was amazed at the number of secrets my family had.

"Some of these stories are really interesting," I told Dad. "Do you mind if I take this home for Bernice to read?"

He beamed. "Go right ahead."

When I returned home that afternoon and told Bernice about Dad's new project she offered to type up what he had written. Dad was extremely pleased that she was willing to do this, and for the next several months he immersed himself in writing his memoir. It was a project he never finished, but it was one that gave me some valuable insights into his life and a feeling of pride.

When Mom was alive she discouraged Dad from doing a lot of things. One of them was purchasing a hairpiece. Dad had lost most of his hair by the time he was thirty and had tried to convince Mom to let him buy one, but she thought it was a frivolous waste of money that she wouldn't like anyway. Now that Mom was no longer here he wondered if Bernice and I would take him to a place where he could buy one.

A toupee wasn't very expensive, but on Dad's limited income we wanted to make sure it was something he really wanted to do so we sat down with him and discussed the matter further. That dialogue didn't last too long. He told us in no uncertain terms he was not about to give up on getting one so Bernice took him to a local shop in Naples. Different styles were tried on, and after several rejections, a decision was made. Surprisingly, Dad's toupee looked quite good on him and I complimented him on his selection when he returned home. With his new hairpiece Dad had a full head of wavy grey hair that would look remarkably similar to mine when I grew older.

One of the problems Dad had was keeping his hairpiece on straight. This was partly because of Topsy. During the day Dad would fall asleep in his recliner and the bird would start pulling on his toupee. When the bird was finished playing on the toupee, its hairs would stand straight up and the entire hairpiece would be pulled to one side of his head.

Rearranging the toupee wasn't the only threat Topsy presented to Dad's hairpiece. The bird also chewed holes in it and left behind its droppings. I don't remember how long it took Dad to realize how much damage Topsy was doing, but one day he showed up at our house and announced that he had been sold a defective toupee. Pointing to the large hole in the center of the hairpiece he wanted to know if Bernice would take him back to the shop so he could get a new one. After looking at Dad's toupee, it was quite obvious what had happened. But even after we explained it to him he still wanted Bernice to take him back to the shop. So off they went to see if he could exchange it. When they got to the store Dad showed the shop owner his "defective" toupee and demanded that he give him a new one. I don't know what the owner thought when he examined the hairpiece but he was very gracious about the whole situation and gave Dad a new toupee without any questions. Bernice was a bit surprised at the owner's generosity, but Dad was elated. Now that he had a new toupee he informed us he was ready to attend his granddaughter's wedding. This announcement came as a bit of surprise, but we were glad he wanted to go. After talking it over, we decided Bernice would go with him, and plans were made for Dad's trip to New Jersey and Pennsylvania.

Weeks before the event Dad talked continuously about how exciting it was going to be to see old friends and surprise everyone with his new hairpiece. "Do you think they'll recognize me?" he asked one day as he adjusted his toupee.

"They might not," I said and smiled.

Bernice and I were also looking forward to Dad getting reacquainted with everyone. However, it turned out Dad had a serious medical problem he'd been keeping a secret—an enlarged prostate. When I realized the magnitude of his problem I suggested he go to a doctor immediately. He told me he wasn't about to do that, and when I told him he could have some serious issues during the trip, he just shrugged his shoulders and said, "The doctor's already given me some pills and told me they should take care of things."

After I learned about Dad's prostate I told Bernice she might have some difficulties with him during the trip. In hindsight, Bernice and I should have insisted he see his doctor again, but Dad was so determined to see his old friends and watch his granddaughter get married it would have been almost impossible to prevent him from going.

As expected, Dad's issues with his prostate plagued him throughout the trip, and ultimately Bernice had to bring him home early to have surgery. Nevertheless, his little adventure did provide him with some magical moments. He managed to have a brief reunion with the people that raised him, and he became one of the main attractions at my niece's wedding when people failed to recognize him in his new toupee.

By the time Dad approached his eightieth birthday the number of fishing trips he went on had dwindled to one a month. He complained it took him too long to recover from our outings. It was the third week in October in 1987 that we went on our last trip together. It was a warm, calm morning with clear skies. Dad was a little slower than usual getting his gear together, so I patiently waited for him to sort through his equipment and put it into our boat. Glancing up to watch him from the rear view mirror, I noticed he was having some trouble with his tackle box so I stuck my head out the window and asked him if he needed a hand. When I did, he grumbled something about the box's lock being broken and then proceeded to the passenger's side of the car where he complained some more about the high step he had to take to get into my 4-Runner.

As we drove to Marco that morning I remember looking over at my father and thinking how frail he looked. He wasn't the same man who had taken me fishing as a youngster on Long Island and Cape Cod, had helped me explore the grass flats at Tigertail, and had spent long hours fishing the wreck at Big Marco Pass. The prostate operation and a number of other insidious ailments that came with age were taking their toll.

The tide was high at Caxambas as we eased the boat into the water. Just off shore a large school of jacks was feeding at the surface while dozens of terns hovered overhead. These were signs that got even a novice fisherman excited. Heading slowly towards the pass, the humid morning air was saturated with the sweet smell of death. It came from the oily flesh of the fish the jacks were feeding on. I'd smelled it before when I went blue fishing in New Jersey. As soon as the "blues" started their feeding frenzy the spray from the oil slick would seep into our nostrils. Dad used to call it the "perfume of fishing fever."

By the time we reached the offshore channel, the dolphins had joined the jacks in pursuit of fish. The dolphins leaped out of the water and twisted their bodies in midair before plummeting back into the Gulf. Impressed with their acrobatics, I leaned over and asked Dad if he wanted to watch them a little while longer. When he nodded yes I shut down the motor and let the boat quietly drift towards the pod. For nearly a half hour the dolphins continued their antics before diving underneath the boat and disappearing. Whether they left because they had enough to eat or because the fish had moved elsewhere we would never know for sure. A tight cluster of dorsal fins was the last glimpse we had of them as they dipped below the surface and headed out into the Gulf.

With the show over I looked at Dad and asked him where he wanted to go fishing. "Why not try the worm reef in Gullivan Bay. We've fished there before and it's been an great place to catch redfish on an outgoing tide."

As we headed south through the "snook hole" we saw all kinds of fish feeding along the mangroves. And when we arrived at the north end of Gullivan Bay hoards of birds were diving over the grass flats. Even the entrance to the worm reef was alive with baitfish.

Although we referred to it as a "worm reef" the reef was really made up of thousands of worm-like shells. These mollusks establish themselves in calm water and cement themselves into huge rock-like slabs that are identified on the Ten Thousand Island navigational charts as reefs. All kinds of creatures live in association with these worm shells. Juvenile stone crabs and snapping shrimp hide among the living "rocks" as well as several species of marine worms and mollusks. This was the smorgasbord of food we anticipated the redfish and sheepshead would come to feed upon.

Dad learned that the best way to catch fish off the reef during an outgoing tide was to use a weighted popping cork with two hooks attached to a short leader. I don't know whether this was something he read in a magazine or a technique that someone in the mobile home park had told him about. Wherever he learned the technique, it worked. Once anchored, we cast our lines towards the reef and let the popping cork drift along its edge. If we were lucky, the popping sound produced by the cork would lure the fish into believing that a feeding frenzy had begun and encourage them to attack our bait. After a couple hours we had caught several large sheepshead and snapper but none of the big redfish we were hoping for. Thinking that the redfish might have moved to the western side of the reef, we pulled up the anchor and repositioned ourselves but still failed to have any success.

Now, with the tide halfway out, we had a decision to make: stay where we were and hope that the large redfish would show up or move to a new location. I wanted to stay put, but Dad suggested we move to an area just north of Blind Pass. We finally agreed that Blind Pass offered the best chance to catch big fish.

The trip from the reef to the site at the north end of Blind Pass took us about a half hour, but as soon as we got there and cast our lines out, the fish began to bite. Within a short period of time I had caught two five-pound redfish and Dad had landed a three-pounder.

It was just about noon when I heard Dad yell he'd hooked a big one. When I looked over he was desperately holding on to his pole as the line raced off of his reel. I'm not sure how he did it, but he turned the fish towards the boat before the line snapped off the spool. For the first time in his life Dad didn't seem pleased that he'd just hooked a whale of fish. Each time the fish made its run away from the boat he grimaced in pain and his breathing became labored. When I asked him if he wanted some help he mumbled something about being all right then lifted the tip of his pole up to show me he had the animal under control. I wasn't sure who was going to win the battle. Age may have taken its toll on Dad's body but he was not about to give up. Every time he got the fish close enough to the boat for me to net it, the fish would make another offshore run and Dad would brace himself against the side of the boat. This scenario went on for what seemed like an eternity. Then the fish finally surfaced near the stern. It was enormous, even bigger than the redfish Dad had caught off Tigertail, and I wasn't sure I could use our net to bring him into the boat. Realizing I'd need the gaff, I looked around to see where it was and discovered I'd left it home. After the exhausting struggle Dad had just undergone I had no choice but to try to net the fish. Thrusting the net into the water, I snared the front end of the animal and tried to hoist it into the boat. This was not a cool move. The handle of the net began to bend under the weight of the fish. Determined not to lose the redfish, I grabbed its tail to relieve some of the pressure on the net and lifted it over the side. Thank God the fish was too worn out to fight back or I'd never have landed it.

When I looked over at Dad he was too exhausted to say anything so I reached down and removed the hook from the fish's mouth. It was a beautiful creature. Its large golden scales shimmered in the afternoon sun as it gasped for air from a world that offered no relief. When I turned towards Dad and told him I didn't think the fish would fit in our cooler he put his arm on my shoulder and gasped, "Let him go."

"Let him go? Are you sure that's what you want me to do?" I asked. Still sucking air into his lungs through parted lips, he nodded yes and motioned for me to pick him up.

While Dad watched, I hoisted the fish over the railing and deposited him back into the Gulf. At this point the animal was so overcome with fatigue it lay on the surface gasping for air. "It looks like the two of us are pretty winded," Dad said as he watched the fish try to revive itself. "Maybe we should try to give it a hand."

When I grabbed the fish by its tail and placed my other hand underneath its belly the fish offered no resistance, so I gently pulled the animal back and forth through the water to see if I could resuscitate it. It took a while, but the fish finally began to breathe on its own. Dad seemed happy that the fish had managed to survive its ordeal, and after watching it swim off into the murky water he looked over at me and said he didn't think he'd ever be able to bring in another fish like that. I could see what he meant. As I went towards the bow of the boat to pull up the anchor his hands were shaking and he was having difficulty breathing.

As Dad's final days approached he spent most of his weekends at our house. Clothes were packed, Topsy was relegated to his cage, and his tan Volvo was brought to a screeching halt at our front door.

Bernice and I were always glad to see that Dad had survived his latest trip to our house. When I think about Dad's driving skills later in life I believe even Mario Andretti would have been impressed with his bravado. No obstacle could prevent Dad from reaching his destination. If a car was blocking the highway, that was no problem, he simply drove his car up on to the sidewalk and scooted around this minor inconvenience. Pedestrians, of course, frequently incurred his wrath. They were always in the middle of the road where they shouldn't be. "No wonder so many of you wind up as flattened fauna," Dad would grumble as he honked his horn. Bicyclists were also a menace. According to Dad they were an unpredictable breed and a "pain in the ass" to all tax-paying citizens who owned an automobile. If Dad had had his way he would have banned all cyclists from the roadway and shipped their bicycles to China.

After having achieved the miraculous task of getting to our house Dad would find a suitable place for Topsy and begin to look for something to do. Poking his head into different places he would ultimately come up with some suggestions regarding home improvements that Bernice and I knew he wasn't physically capable of handling. Bushes needed to be cut down. If only we had a sharper axe, he could take care of that. Where was our shovel? He needed to dig some holes in our backyard to bury a couple of dead animals he'd discovered. And then there was the grass. It was definitely too long. If only the mower blade were sharper, he could cut it for us.

"No," "no," and "no," were our answers to those suggestions. "How about helping us take out the garbage or clean the dishes?" From the scowl on his face it was obvious he wasn't pleased with those ideas.

Whenever we were away from the house there was no telling what mischief Dad would get into. Being forewarned not to try to do something that would require a lot of exertion Dad would give us an agreeable nod and then go out and do what he wanted. Upon arriving back home we would often discover a partially mowed lawn or some other bit of property maintenance that we wished he'd never undertaken. More lectures about not doing this type of thing were met with a disgusted wave of the hand.

It was during one of those times when Bernice and I were away from the house that Dad decided to take an axe and chop off the tops of the cypress knees that were protruding above ground. He had complained that they were a nuisance to mow around. I told him they were nothing he should worry about, that they were part of the root system of the cypress trees and that any attempt to cut them off might harm the tree. My lecture was not very persuasive because when I returned home I found Dad sitting on the stump of a tree totally exhausted. There was no need to ask what he'd been up to. Lying on the ground next to him was a sharpened axe and the chopped off tops of several cypress knees. From the look on his face and the fact that he had difficulty breathing I suspected he'd had a heart attack. Dad insisted he was okay and refused to let me take him to the hospital. When I suggested we stop by the doctor's office instead, he scoffed at me and insisted all he needed was some time to rest.

Dad was never the same after that. When we finally got him to the doctor the next day he told us Dad's heart was beginning to fail. At night Dad had difficulty breathing and he would crawl out of his bed onto the floor. He said that there was more air closer to the ground and it was a lot easier for him to breathe. He also blamed his inability to breathe on the disappearance of the ozone layer. Without the ozone layer to protect us he said we would all die. He insisted that our planet was being attacked by "red devils" that were sucking up all of the planet's oxygen.

During Dad's final days he made very few trips out of the house. However, at his insistence we did take one last trip to the beach. The weather was almost perfect on the day we chose to go. There was a gentle breeze out of the east and large numbers of terns were diving into the Gulf's milky-green water. For Dad it was a nostalgic moment. He knew he would never see the ocean again, so he began to reminisce about some of the fishing adventures we'd shared.

"Do you remember the big redfish I caught off Tigertail," he asked, "and what about the time that goliath grouper swallowed our entire catch?" When he finished reminiscing I watched a tear form in the corner of his eye. Too embarrassed to let him know that I had seen it, I looked over at the diving terns and asked if he thought the trout would be biting. I don't think he ever answered that question. Shaking his head, he reached over and took hold my arm.

"It's such a marvelous world," he reminded me again as we turned to leave. "I'm going to miss it. It'll be up to you to teach people some of things we learned from our adventures."

I tried not to show any feelings of remorse as we walked slowly back to the car. With each step Dad complained bitterly about the red devils and how I needed to do something about them. "Soon there won't be any air left for anyone to breathe," he gasped and tried to exhale through pursed lips.

Before Dad got into the car I promised him I would take care of the red devils. I'm not sure he believed me, but for the moment my answer seemed to satisfy him. Several days later he went to the hospital. His breathing problem had gotten a lot worse and the doctors wanted to examine him more closely. After some preliminary tests, a heart specialist was called in for a consult.

Many anxious moments passed before we got a chance to speak to him. When we did, the prognosis wasn't good. He told us that Dad was very ill and that he wanted to insert a catheter into my father's heart to see if there was some way he could prolong his life. He said that the procedure was risky, but if he didn't do it my father would certainly die within days.

There was no alternative. I gave my permission, and Bernice and I waited at the hospital to hear the outcome. Several hours passed before we saw the doctor in the waiting room. The procedure had been a success but the prognosis remained bad. Dad had a severely damaged and inoperable heart valve.

When Bernice and I went to visit Dad in the intensive care unit that night, we were visibly shaken by what we saw. Dad's hands were strapped to the side of the bed and at least a half-a-dozen tubes and wires were hooked up to different parts of his body. Over his head there was a series of monitors recording his irregular heartbeat and other vital signs. When I asked the nurse why his hands were strapped down she said they had to do it to prevent him from pulling the tubes out of his arm.

I was certain that this was not the way Dad wanted to die, but I didn't know what else I could do. The whole scenario was heart wrenching, and when I took hold of his hand it took all the strength I could muster not to break down and cry. Leaning over, I whispered in his ear that I had heard that the fishing was pretty good where he was going. He never responded, but when he squeezed my hand I knew he'd heard me.

That evening Dad's heart stopped twice and each time they revived him. I didn't know why they did that. I had shown the hospital his explicit request not to resuscitate, but someone had ignored those orders and decided to revive him anyway. The doctor was equally annoyed with what the night staff had done and this time he made it quite clear to them what father's wishes were.

Dad died at one a.m. on April 18, 1988. When the hospital staff reached me slightly after one they asked if I wanted to see him one more time before the funeral-home people came to pick him up. I told them I didn't, that I would rather remember him the way he was when he was alive—fishing at Tigertail or laughing over the snake he'd just snagged with his fishing lure. I was grateful that Dad got to see Halley's comet shortly before died. We shared that experience in Rookery Bay. He said it wasn't as bright as he remembered it, but that was true of a lot of things, as he got older.

It took several months to clear up Dad's affairs. Among the hardest things to do after someone you love passes away is to clear out their home. I'd visited people's houses with University of Florida and Conservancy staff to pick up donations after they'd passed on and always found it very depressing. Every home I'd gone into was cluttered with personal treasures the deceased had collected throughout their lives. Entering these places was like stepping on sacred ground and it always filled me with a deep sense of remorse.

When Bernice and I entered my parents' trailer to clear out their things, that same feeling came over me. Scattered about the porch were several of Dad's fishing poles and reels in various states of disrepair. In the shed were a couple of tackle boxes filled with fishing lures that Dad had stopped using years ago, and stacked on the shelves were dozens of jars filled with assorted nuts and bolts. Distributed about the house were numerous examples of Dad's shell creations. Photo albums filled with hundreds of family pictures were stored in the closet. Mom's favorite dishes lay stacked in the kitchen cupboard, all of them apparently unused since she'd passed away. It was amazing how many times you could visit a person's home and not realize how much stuff they'd accumulated.

It took too many visits to clear out the trailer. And each time I went it took all the courage I could muster to complete the job. Removing things from my parents' mobile home was like erasing their existence. And in the end, I knew the only thing left would be the memories.

Dad's journey had almost come to an end. The funeral home had placed his ashes in a cardboard box and it took me more than a year to decide where to distribute them. Initially, I thought about spreading them over the grass flats at Tigertail, but later I decided he might like it better if I placed them in the open waters of Gullivan Bay just south of Cape Romano.

Bernice and I took Dad on his final journey in the *OH HENRY!* It was on a warm, calm day in May. The clouds had started to form in the east and the water was crystal clear over the sandy shoals. Near the surface, schools of baitfish were trying to avoid the ravenous jaws of hungry jacks and the piercing bills of diving terns. The birds' excited cries attracted my attention and for a brief moment I thought about the cycle of life and what a crazy journey it could be.

Using Dad's favorite filet knife, I cut open the box and cast his ashes over the side. For a short while they remained suspended on the surface then slowly sank towards the bottom. Stardust, I thought to myself, that's what the descending ashes reminded me of as they sparkled in the sunlight. Dad had finally become part of the watery world he loved so much.

Epilogue

In 1988, shortly after Dad's death, I left the Collier County Conservancy. I resigned with regret. I'd been told I was no longer going to oversee the education division and that I had been assigned the job of grant writer. For me, environmental education was the most important component of our operation and not being a part of it would have left a great void in my life.

Bernice and I still live in Naples, Florida. During the intervening years I helped set up the Marjorie Stoneman Douglas Biscayne Nature Center in Miami, served on the board and as president of the Bailey-Matthews Shell Museum on Sanibel Island, taught environmental science and oceanography at Edison State College, wrote a young adult novel called *The Gift*, and co-authored two books on native wildflowers of Southwest Florida. I currently lead fossil collecting trips and wildflower walks for the Conservancy and other groups. To date, I have described thirty-one new species of fossil mollusks. All of the specimens have come from Chipola Formation sites in the Florida Panhandle. I still spend a lot of time exploring the Fakahatchee and the Big Cypress, and I still fish in the Ten Thousand Islands but now in the *OH HENRY! II*. Tigertail will always remain one of my favorite places to visit.

After years of thinking about where we should distribute Mom's ashes I had my sister discreetly scatter them in one of the botanical gardens Mom loved to visit. I'm sure Dad would have been pleased with the decision since it was a place he often reminisced about in his final years.

As far as the other people I've shared life's journey with, many have passed on but a few still are involved with conservation efforts in Florida and other places. I have no idea what has happened to George Spinner. Bud Kirk lived to a ripe old age and had many wonderful stories to tell about his life in Florida when someone stopped by to listen. Kappi Kirk remained in her Goodland home until the day she died at the age of ninety. Chuck Courtney went back to school to get his Master's degree. He stayed with Deltona until they closed their lab on Marco Island. Bernie Yokel had a very successful career at Florida Audubon and became board president of the Trout Lake Nature Center near Mt. Dora, Florida. We still see one another on occasion and reminisce about our times at the Conservancy. Bill Merrihue passed away at ninety and is now touted as one of the founding fathers of the organization, and the street entering the Conservancy has been named after him. Ned Putzell has also passed on. He served as the Mayor of Naples for four years.

Jim McMullen remains dedicated to protecting the Florida panther. He still lives in Golden Gate, Florida, and spends time trekking through the Big Cypress Swamp and Fakahatchee Strand now with the added goal of finding Bigfoot. When I've discussed the creature with local residents, nearly all of them shake their heads and laugh. According to the Florida Game and Fresh Water Fish Commission, no such animal exists in the Big Cypress Swamp and they have no intention of doing any research on it until they have some solid evidence. Jim, however, is still firmly convinced that the creature lives in the Big Cypress and says that he intends to collect hair and skin samples left behind by the animal so that scientists can look at its DNA.

Dave Addison still works for the Conservancy but exclusively on the sea turtle project. Ron Meszich is a biologist with the Florida Fish and Wildlife Conservation Commission, and our Wild Animal Rehabilitation Supervisor, Sara Denham, is the Wildlife Resource Center Manager of the McHenry County Conservation District in Illinois.

After I left the Conservancy, Dr. Colin Clubbe came to Florida on sabbatical, and together with one of my education specialists Georgia Jeppesen, completed final arrangements for our international intern program. As I anticipated, the program turned out to be a big success and during its operation more than thirty interns from Great Britain participated in the program. Some of these students returned to England to work as naturalists, and one (Joe Cox) remained in Collier County where he has completed the development of the county's first children's museum. Today, the international intern program no longer exists primarily because of the documentation and paperwork needed to bring students into the country after 9/11. Georgia is now a Branch Chief in the division of Educational Outreach for the U.S. Fish and Wildlife Department.

In 1990 the Conservancy lost its public school funding. This ended the countywide environmental fieldtrip programs it ran for all third-, fourth-, and seventh-grade public school children. But the Conservancy still conducts environmental education classes for some public and private school children as well as summer camps.

In 2000, the Collier County Conservancy changed its name to The Conservancy of Southwest Florida. The volunteer program begun at the Big Cypress Nature Center has been enlarged, and the Conservancy now has almost five hundred people assisting them with various projects. The intern program I started in 1976 at the Big Cypress Nature Center has been greatly expanded. At last count, twenty-one interns work for the Conservancy each year. The Wild Animal Rehabilitation Program, started at the original Big Nature Center in 1973 as part of the Junior Audubon Program, has become one of the major operating divisions of the Conservancy. It has its own animal hospital and it is under the supervision of paid staff. In 2012 it hired a full-time veterinarian and the hospital doubled in size. The Conservancy no longer has staff-led natural history trips to the Bahamas, Caribbean, Central and South America, although they periodically have had tours to more far-flung places. The Briggs Nature Center is no longer in operation; the Florida Fish and Wildlife Department currently occupies this facility. However, there is still a boardwalk behind the building that the public can use to explore the scrub and wetland communities in Rookery Bay.

I'm glad I was able to play a role in protecting South Florida's natural environment and I am equally glad that Dad got to share some of this experience with me. I'm also proud that I had the privilege of working for the Big Cypress Nature Center and The Conservancy of Southwest Florida. There is still a lot of work to be done to protect South Florida's ecosystem. From both Dad's and my point of view, the Everglades-Big Cypress-Ten Thousand Island complex forms a subtropical Eden that comes as close to paradise as anyone can find on this planet.

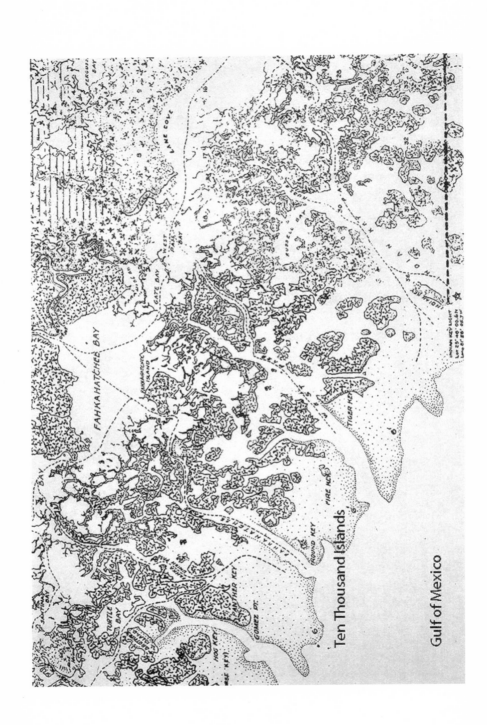

Ten Thousand Islands

Gulf of Mexico